ELIA KAZAN

INTERVIEWS

CONVERSATIONS WITH FILMMAKERS SERIES
PETER BRUNETTE, GENERAL EDITOR

Photofest

ELIA
KAZAN

INTERVIEWS

EDITED BY WILLIAM BAER

UNIVERSITY PRESS OF MISSISSIPPI / JACKSON

www.upress.state.ms.us

Copyright © 2000 by University Press of Mississippi
All rights reserved
Manufactured in the United States of America

08   07   06   05   04   03   02   01   00   4   3   2   1

∞

Library of Congress Cataloging-in-Publication Data

Kazan, Elia.
    Elia Kazan : interviews / edited by William Baer.
        p.   cm. — (Conversations with filmmakers series)
    Filmography: p.
    Includes index.
    ISBN 1-57806-223-3 (cloth : alk. paper). — ISBN 1-57806-224-1
(paper : alk. paper)
    1. Kazan, Elia Interviews.   2. Motion picture producers and
directors Interviews.   I. Baer, William.   II. Title.   III. Series.
PN1998.3.K39A5   2000
791.43'0233'092—dc21   99-38772
                                                              CIP

British Library Cataloging-in-Publication Data available

CONTENTS

INTRODUCTION

ELIA KAZAN IS ONE of the most important artistic figures that
America has produced in the twentieth century, and he's also one of the
most controversial. In the late 1940s, Kazan revolutionized American theater by his innovative direction of Tennessee Williams's *A Streetcar Named
Desire* and Arthur Miller's *Death of a Salesman*. At the same time, Kazan's
early feature films like *Gentleman's Agreement* and *Pinky* were challenging
American audiences to consider previously avoided social problems like
anti-Semitism and racial prejudice, and these early films laid the founda-
tion for Kazan's later, classic films like *On the Waterfront* with Marlon
Brando and *East of Eden* with James Dean. Later, beginning with *America,
America* in 1961, Kazan would undertake a new career as a best-selling novelist, and in 1988 he wrote an important and revealing autobiography
entitled *A Life*. But, of course, everything that Elia Kazan has done since
1952 has been affected by his decision to give "friendly" testimony at the
HUAC (House Committee on Un-American Activities) hearings, a decision
that still ignited controversy in 1999 when the Academy of Arts and
Sciences finally awarded Kazan its Lifetime Achievement Award at the
Academy Awards ceremony in March.

Given his unique life, achievements, and controversies, it's not surprising
that Kazan's various interviews, collected in this book, make fascinating
reading. This is further accentuated by Kazan's remarkable honesty—an
honesty that's blunt, never pretentious, and sometimes brutal and vulgar.
Never satisfied with any of his many accomplishments, Kazan is always
striving after something new and better, and he never blames anyone but

himself when things haven't worked out the way he wanted. His 1962 remarks to *Show Business Illustrated* are typical: "If there's anything wrong with *Splendor in the Grass,* you don't blame anybody else—you blame me. I chose the script—I cast it like I wanted to, and I chose the story because I saw something in it. Failure or success, it's my own."

Kazan's first national success was as a New York theatrical director, so it may be surprising for readers to learn that Kazan's first love was always the cinema. His first artistic heroes were the Soviet filmmakers Eisenstein and Dovzhenko, and long before his Broadway success, he worked as assistant director on *People of the Cumberland* (1937), a short, socially-conscious, documentary film about Tennessee strip-mining. In one of his earliest interviews, Kazan tells Frederic Morton of *Esquire* in 1957, "I want to do more movies than ever. In the theater the director just serves the author. But a movie director can create. The camera is such a beautiful instrument. It paints with motion." Nearly twenty years later in his 1976 American Film Institute interview, Kazan clearly hadn't lost his enthusiasm for film, exclaiming, "I think it's the most wonderful art in the world."

Elia Kazan (Elia Kazanjoglou) was born an Anatolian Greek in Istanbul in 1909, and he emigrated from Turkey to the United States with his parents when he was four years old. This fundamental fact of Kazan's unique origin has indelibly marked his entire life, and, as the interviews consistently reveal, it's responsible for the two primary and related themes that run through all his work: personal alienation and an outrage over social injustice. As Kazan told Brian Case in 1988, "I'm tougher than most people, I think. I was an outsider kid, and I had to be tough to survive. Jimmy Baldwin said I was a nigger so I accepted that as a compliment." Whatever one's position on Kazan's testimony before HUAC in 1952, it's impossible to deny the conclusion of Budd Schulberg, author of the screenplays for *On the Waterfront* and *A Face in the Crowd,* that Kazan never lost his "identification with the oppressed that brought him to the Communist Party during the depths of the Depression."

Given his long apprenticeship with the Group Theater in New York City and his eventual triumphs on Broadway, it's not surprising that Kazan's films are justly famous for the power and intensity of his actors' performances. He was the crucial figure in launching the film careers of Marlon Brando, James Dean, Julie Harris, Eva Marie Saint, Warren Beatty, Lee Remick, and many others. Performers in Kazan's films were nominated for an amazing twenty-one Academy Awards, and nine of them received Oscars. Most famous for his use of "method" actors, especially Brando and Dean, Kazan admitted to Brian Case in 1988, "I did whatever was necessary to get a good performance *including* so-called Method acting. I made them run around the set, I scolded them, I inspired jealousy in their girlfriends. You know the boxer Tami Mauriello? I hit him in the face to get a reaction on *Waterfront!* The director *is a desperate beast!*" Yet, Kazan, as is often the case, is too hard on himself. It's very clear that his actors loved working with him and considered it a special privilege, and Kazan, in his interview at the A.F.I. in 1976, admitted that "the people I choose to work with are creative people who are sensitive, who want to be good, who have some aspiration in them. You don't deal with actors as dolls. You deal with them as people who are poets to a certain degree."

Another obvious aspect of Kazan's filmmaking that was formed in the New York theater was his close collaboration with many other highly-talented artists, especially writers. On Broadway, he worked with Arthur Miller, Tennessee Williams, and William Inge; in film, he worked with Williams (*A Streetcar Named Desire* and *Baby Doll*), Inge (*Splendor in the Grass*), Budd Schulberg (*On the Waterfront* and *A Face in the Crowd*), John Steinbeck (*Viva Zapata!*), and Harold Pinter (*The Last Tycoon*). He also tried to produce Miller's waterfront screenplay, *The Hook,* in 1951, but the project was never completed. As with the numerous actors he introduced to the American public, Kazan was also an instrumental figure in the careers of many of the best writers of his time, and, as the interviews show, he always treated them and their work with the utmost respect.

Given Kazan's natural impulse for social drama, his films are often justly praised for their cinematic "realism." Like the Italian Neo-Realists, Kazan preferred shooting on location, enjoyed working with unknown actors, and strove to depict social reality with both accuracy and vivid intensity. Yet despite the high passions and occasional violence that his stories generally required, Kazan is equally well known for the powerful and unforgettable lyric moments that give balance to his best films. Kazan clearly treasures these "muted" poetic interludes that give his films such emotional and visual depth, and he worked very hard to achieve them. As he remarked to Charles Silver and Mary Corliss in 1977, "If you look at *On the Waterfront,* what scenes do people remember most from it? What's good about the picture is the tenderness in the middle of the violence."

Most interviewers are naturally eager to ask Kazan about his social themes, his relationship with actors, his collaborations with writers, and his filmic styles. They're also unable to resist raising the controversy surrounding his HUAC testimony in 1952. Surprisingly, they find that Kazan is not only willing to discuss his actions and their repercussions, but that he still remains firmly convinced he made the right decision to give the names of former Stalinist comrades. As he told Michel Ciment in 1976, "There was no doubt that there was a vast organization which was making fools of all the liberals in Hollywood, and taking their money, that there was a police state among the Left element in Hollywood and Broadway.... I would rather do what I did than crawl in front of a ritualistic Left and lie the way those other comrades did, and betray my own soul. I didn't betray it. I made a difficult decision." The fact that the Communist Party had treated Kazan brutally in New York City (putting him on trial for not seizing control of the Group Theatre from Harold Clurman), the fact that the names he mentioned at the hearings were already known to the committee, the fact that there were "white" lists before there were blacklists, and the fact that Stalinists were seizing power in several key Hollywood unions, makes no difference to Kazan's legion of detractors and never will. But Kazan remains defiant, telling *U.S. News and World Report* in 1988, "I wouldn't do anything differently.... New York intellectuals who had not been in the Communist Party, who only had been to a meeting or two, had no goddamn business making judgments of the actions of people who had been in the party, as I had. How can you say anything unless you've been there?" As liberal historian Arthur Schlesinger, Jr., pointed out in *The New York Times* during the 1999 Academy Award controversy, if Kazan had given the names of fascists, he would have been considered a hero.

Regardless of one's point of view on the political issues, the artistic stature of Kazan and the scope of his achievement is undeniable. In his *Directors at Work* interview in 1970, Kazan claimed that "the purpose of art is to make man confront his humanity." He admitted that this goal is "a very complex thing, and a very difficult thing," but, as Kazan's long career illustrates, he constantly rose to the challenge of his own aspirations. Elia Kazan was a legendary director on Broadway who also became one of the major filmmakers of his time. He was a pioneer and visionary who greatly affected the history of both stage and cinema. His direction of *Death of a Salesman* and *A Streetcar Named Desire* was a high point of world theater in the current century, and his film masterpiece, *On the Waterfront,* is one of the greatest films in the history of international cinema.

As with the other books in the Conversations with Filmmakers series, the following interviews have been presented chronologically, reproduced in their entirety, and only slightly edited. Given that the interviews cover a span of nearly forty years, there's naturally some repetition of subject matter, but Kazan consistently enlivens his thoughtful responses with new information and forceful examples which will fascinate and intrigue those generally interested in his films as well as the scholarly reader.

Concerning the brief "Chronology" of Elia Kazan's life and work which follows this introduction, I've listed all of his feature films along with many other significant highlights from his crowded career. But no attempt has been made to comprehensively list all of Kazan's various projects and achievements: his numerous acting performances in theatrical productions and Hollywood films, the wide variety of plays he directed in New York, all of his published novels, his countless awards, and all the Oscars and other special recognitions won by his feature films.

I would like to sincerely thank a number of people who have generously helped me with this project: Arthur Miller, Budd Schulberg, Eileen Shanahan, Kathleen O'Hara, Stephen Greiner, Mike Carson, Jeanine Kappenman, Joyce Harrington, Kisha Tracy, Kathryn Bartelt, Mary Corliss and Terry Geesken, Peter Brunette, Anne Stascavage, Elizabeth Young, Seetha Srinivasan, and, of course, Elia Kazan.

CHRONOLOGY

1909 Born Elia Kazanjoglou in Constantinople (now Istanbul), Turkey, on September 7, 1909, to Greek parents, George and Athena Kazanjoglou.

1913 Family moves to New York City.

1930 Graduates *cum laude* in English from Williams College.

1932 Leaves Yale Drama School after two years in the graduate program.

1933 Joins the Group Theatre in New York City, initiating a eight-year association with Harold Clurman and Lee Strasberg, working as an actor, stage manager, and director.

1934 Joins a Communist Party cell in New York City, but remains a member of the Communist Party for less than two years.

1935 Performs as an actor in *Waiting for Lefty.*

1937 Performs as an actor in *Golden Boy.* Assistant director on the short documentary film *People of the Cumberland.*

1942 New York theatrical direction of *The Skin of our Teeth* by Thornton Wilder, starring Tallulah Bankhead and Montgomery Clift.

1945 *A Tree Grows in Brooklyn,* Kazan's first feature film, starring Dorothy McGuire and James Dunn, wins Academy Award for Best Supporting Actor.

1947   New York theatrical direction of *All My Sons*, written by Arthur Miller, starring Ed Begley and Arthur Kennedy. Wins Tony Award for Direction. *Sea of Grass*, starring Spencer Tracy and Katherine Hepburn, and *Boomerang!*, starring Dana Andrews and Jane Wyatt. New York theatrical direction of *A Streetcar Named Desire*, written by Tennessee Williams, starring Marlon Brando and Jessica Tandy. *Gentleman's Agreement*, starring Gregory Peck, wins Academy Awards for Best Picture, Best Director, and Best Supporting Actress.

1948   Co-founds the Actors Studio in New York City with Cheryl Crawford.

1949   New York theatrical direction of *Death of a Salesman*, written by Arthur Miller, starring Lee J. Cobb. Wins Tony Award for Direction. *Pinky*, starring Jeanne Crain and Ethel Waters.

1950   *Panic in the Streets*, starring Richard Widmark, wins the International Prize at the Venice Film Festival.

1951   *A Streetcar Named Desire*, starring Marlon Brando and Vivien Leigh, wins the Special Jury Prize at the Venice Film Festival, an Oscar nomination for Best Director, and Academy Awards for Best Actress, Best Supporting Actor, and Best Supporting Actress.

1952   Gives testimony before the House Committee on Un-American Activities (HUAC). *Viva Zapata!*, starring Marlon Brando, Jean Peters, and Anthony Quinn, wins an Academy Award for Best Supporting Actor.

1953   New York theatrical direction of *Tea and Sympathy*, written by Robert Anderson, starring Deborah Kerr. *Man on a Tightrope*, starring Fredric March.

1954   *On the Waterfront*, starring Marlon Brando and Eva Marie Saint, wins Academy Awards for Best Picture, Best Director, Best Actor, and Best Supporting Actress.

1955   New York theatrical direction of *Cat on a Hot Tin Roof*, written by Tennessee Williams, starring Barbara Bel Geddes. Nominated for Tony Award for Direction (1956). *East of Eden*, starring Julie Harris and James Dean, receives an Oscar nomination for Best Director and wins the Academy Award for Best Supporting Actress.

1956   *Baby Doll,* starring Carroll Baker and Eli Wallach.

1957   *A Face in the Crowd,* starring Andy Griffith and Patricia Neal.

1958   New York theatrical direction of *J.B.,* written by Archibald MacLeish, starring Christopher Plummer. Wins Tony Award for Direction (1959).

1959   New York theatrical direction of *Sweet Bird of Youth,* written by Tennessee Williams, starring Paul Newman and Geraldine Page. Nominated for Tony Award for Direction (1960).

1960   *Wild River,* starring Montgomery Clift and Lee Remick.

1961   *Splendor in the Grass,* starring Natalie Wood and Warren Beatty. Publishes his first novel, *America, America,* which becomes a best-seller.

1962   Becomes the director of the newly-created Lincoln Center Repertory Company in New York City.

1963   *America, America,* starring Stathis Giallelis, receives Oscar nominations for Best Picture, Best Director, and Best Screenplay (written by Kazan).

1969   *The Arrangement,* starring Kirk Douglas and Faye Dunaway.

1971   *The Visitors,* starring Patrick McVey.

1976   *The Last Tycoon,* starring Robert De Niro.

1987   Receives the D. W. Griffith Award for lifetime achievement from the Directors Guild of America.

1988   Publishes his autobiography, *Elia Kazan: A Life.*

1999   Receives a special Lifetime Achievement Award from the Academy of Motion Picture Arts and Sciences.

FILMOGRAPHY

1937
PEOPLE OF THE CUMBERLAND
Frontier Films
Producer/Director: Ralph Steiner
Assistant Director: **Elia Kazan**
Cinematography: Ralph Steiner
16mm, B&W
20 minutes

1945
A TREE GROWS IN BROOKLYN
20th Century Fox
Producer: Louis D. Lighton
Director: **Elia Kazan**
Assistant Directors: Saul Wurtzel, Nicholas Ray
Screenplay: Tess Slesinger and Frank Davis, based on the novel by Betty
Smith
Cinematography: Leon Shamroy
Editing: Dorothy Spencer
Art Director: Lyle Wheeler
Set Decorators: Thomas Little and Frank E. Hughes
Special Effects: Fred Sersen
Music: Alfred Newman
Orchestrations: Edward B. Powell

Costumes: Bonnie Cashin
Sound: Bernard Freericks
Cast: Dorothy McGuire (Katie Noland), Joan Blondell (Aunt Sissy), James
Dunn (Johnny Nolan), Lloyd Nolan (McShane), Peggy Ann Garner (Francie
Nolan), Ted Donaldson (Neeley Nolan), James Gleason (McGarrity), Ruth
Nelson (Miss McDonough), John Alexander (Steve Edwards), B. S. Pully
(Christmas Tree Vendor), Ferike Boros (Mrs. Rommely), J. Farrell
MacDonald (Carney), Adeline DeWalt Reynolds (Mrs. Waters), George
Melford (Mr. Spencer), Mae Marsh and Edna Jackson (Tynmore Sisters),
Vincent Graeff (Henny Gaddis), Susan Lester (Flossie Gaddis), Johnny
Berkes (Mr. Crackenbox), Lillian Bronson (Librarian), Alec Craig (Werner),
Charles Halton (Mr. Barker), Al Bridge (Cheap Charlie), Joseph J. Green
(Hassler), Virginia Brissac (Miss Tilford), Harry Harvey, Jr. (Herschel), Art
Smith (Ice Man), Norman Field and George Meader (Principals of School),
Erskine Sanford (Undertaker), Martha Wentworth (Mother), Francis Pierlot
(Priest), Al Eben (Union Representative), Peter Cusanelli (Barber), Robert
Anderson (Augie), Harry Seymour (Floor Walker), Edith Hallor.
35mm, B&W
128 minutes

1947
SEA OF GRASS
MGM
Producer: Pandro S. Berman
Director: **Elia Kazan**
2nd Unit Director: James C. Havens
Assistant Director: Sid Sidman
Screenplay: Marguerite Roberts and Vincent Lawrence, based on the novel
by Conrad Richter
Cinematography: Harry Stradling
Editor: Robert J. Kern
Art Directors: Cedric Gibbons and Paul Groesse
Set Decorators: Edwin B. Willis and Mildred Griffiths
Special Effects: A. Arnold Gillespie and Warren Newcombe
Music: Herbert Stothart
Costumes: Walter Plunkett and Irene Valles
Sound: Douglas Shearer

Cast: Spencer Tracy (Jim Brewton), Katherine Hepburn (Lutie Cameron), Melvyn Douglas (Brice Chamberlain), Robert Walker (Brock Brewton), Phyllis Thaxter (Sarah Bess), Edgar Buchanan (Jeff), Harry Carey (Doc Reid), Ruth Nelson (Selena Hall), William "Bill" Phillips (Banty), Robert Armstrong (Floyd McCurtain), James Bell (Sam Hall), Robert Barrat (Judge White), Charles Trowbridge (Cameron), Russell Hicks (Major Harney), Trevor Bardette (Andy), Morris Ankrum (Crane), Nora Cecil (Nurse), Pat Henry (Brock as a baby), Duncan Richardson (Brock at 3), James Hawkins (Brock at 5), Norman Ollestead (Brock at 8), Carol Nugent, William Challee, Paul Langton
35mm, B&W
131 minutes

1947
BOOMERANG!
20th Century Fox
Executive Producer: Darryl F. Zanuck
Producer: Louis de Rochemont
Director: **Elia Kazan**
Assistant Director: Tom Dudley
Screenplay: Richard Murphy, based on a *Reader's Digest* article, "The Perfect Case," by Anthony Abbott [Fulton Oursler]
Cinematography: Norbert Brodine
Editor: Harmon Jones
Art Directors: Richard Day and Chester Gore
Set Decorators: Thomas Little and Phil D'Esco
Special Effects: Fred Sersen
Music: David Buttolph
Musical Director: Alfred Newman
Orchestrations: Edward B. Powell
Costumes: Kay Nelson
Wardrobe Director: Charles Le Maire
Sound: W. D. Flick and Roger Heman
Cast: Dana Andrews (Henry L. Harvey), Jane Wyatt (Mrs. Harvey), Lee J. Cobb (Chief Robinson), Cara Williams (Irene Nelson), Arthur Kennedy (John Waldron), Sam Levene (Woods), Taylor Holmes (Wade), Robert Keith (McCreery), Ed Begley (Harris), Leona Roberts (Mrs. Crossman), Philip

Coolidge (Crossman), Lester Lonergan (Cary), Lewis Leverett (Whitney), Richard Garrick (Mr. Rogers), Karl Malden (Lieutenant White), Ben Lackland (James), Helen Carew (Annie), Barry Kelly (Sergeant Dugan), Wyrley Birch (Father Lambert), Johnny Stearns (Reverend Gardiner), Guy Thomajan (Cartucci), Lucia Seger (Mrs. Lukash), Dudley Sadler (Dr. Rainsford), Walter Greaza (Major Swayze), Helen Hatch (Miss Manion), Joe Kazan (Mr. Lukash), Ida McGuire (Miss Roberts), George Petrie (O'Shea), John Carmody (Callahan), Clay Clement (Judge Tate), E. J. Ballantine (McDonald), William Challee (Stone), Edgar Stehli (Coroner), Jimmy Dobson (Bill), Lawrence Paquin (Sheriff), Anthony Ross (Warren), Bert Freed (Herron), Royal Beal (Johnson), Bernard Hoffman (Tom), Fred Stewart (Graham), Lee Roberts (Criminal), Pauline Myers (Girl), Jacob Sandler (Barman), Herbert Rather (Investigator), Anna Minot (Secretary), Brian Keith (Demonstrator), Mayor Charles E. Moore and the people of Stamford
35mm, B&W
88 minutes

1947
GENTLEMAN'S AGREEMENT
20th Century Fox
Producer: Darryl F. Zanuck
Director: **Elia Kazan**
Assistant Director: Saul Wurtzel
Screenplay: Moss Hart, based on the novel by Laura Z. Hobson
Cinematography: Arthur Miller
Editor: Harmon Jones
Art Directors: Lyle Wheeler and Mark-Lee Kirk
Set Decorators: Thomas Little and Paul S. Fox
Special Effects: Fred Sersen
Music: Alfred Newman
Orchestrations: Edward B. Powell
Costumes: Kay Nelson
Wardrobe Director: Charles Le Maire
Sound: Alfred Bruzlin and Roger Heman
Cast: Gregory Peck (Phil Green), Dorothy McGuire (Kathy), John Garfield (Dave Goldman), Celeste Holm (Anne), Anne Revere (Mrs. Green), June

Havoc (Miss Wales), Albert Dekker (John Minify), Jane Wyatt (Jane), Dean
Stockwell (Tommy Green), Nicholas Joy (Dr. Craigie), Sam Jaffe (Professor
Lieberman), Harold Vermilyea (Jordan), Ransom M. Sherman (Bill Payson),
Roy Roberts (Mr. Calkins), Kathleen Lockhart (Mrs. Minify), Curt Conway
(Bert McAnny), John Newland (Bill), Robert Warwick (Weisman), Louis
Lorimer (Miss Miller), Howard Negley (Tingler), Victor Kilian (Olsen),
Frank Wilcox (Harry), Marlyn Monk (Receptionist), Wilton Graff (Maitre
D), Morgan Farley (Clerk), Robert Karnes and Gene Nelson (Ex-GIs),
Marion Marshall (Guest), Mauritz Hugo (Columnist), Jesse White (Elevator
Starter), Olive Deering, Jane Green, Virginia Gregg, Helen Gerald
35mm, B&W
118 minutes

1949
PINKY
20th Century Fox
Producer: Darryl F. Zanuck
Production Manager: Joseph Behm
Director: **Elia Kazan**
Assistant Director: Wingate Smith
Screenplay: Philip Dunne and Dudley Nichols, based on the novel *Quality*
by Cid Ricketts Sumner
Screenplay Supervisor: Rose Steinberg
Cinematography: Joe MacDonald
Camera Operator: Til Gabbani
Editor: Harmon Jones
Art Directors: Lyle Wheeler and J. Russell Spencer
Set Decorators: Thomas Little and Walter M. Scott
Special Effects: Fred Sersen
Music: Alfred Newman
Orchestrations: Edward B. Powell
Wardrobe Director: Charles Le Maire
Sound: Eugene Grossman and Roger Heman
Cast: Jeanne Crane (Pinky), Ethel Barrymore (Miss Em), Ethel Waters (Aunt
Dicey), William Lundigan (Dr. Thomas Adams), Basil Ruysdael (Judge Walker),
Kenny Washington (Dr. Canady), Nina Mae McKinney (Rozelia), Griff Barnett
(Dr. Joe), Frederick O'Neal (Jake Walters), Evelyn Varden (Melba Wooley),

Raymond Greenleaf (Judge Shoreham), Dan Riss (Stanley), Arthur Hunnicutt (Police Chief), William Hansen (Mr. Goolby), Everett Glass (Mr. Wooley), Bert Conway (Loafer), Harry Tenbrook (Townsman), Robert Osterloh (Police Officer), Jean Inness (Saleslady), Shelby Bacon (Boy), René Beard (Teejore), Tonya Overstreet and Juanita Moore (Nurses), Hernert Heywood, Paul Brinegar
35mm, B&W
102 minutes

1950
PANIC IN THE STREETS
20th Century Fox
Producer: Sol C. Siegel
Production Manager: Joseph Behm
Director: **Elia Kazan**
Assistant Director: Forrest E. Johnston
Screenplay: Richard Murphy, based on a story by Edna and Edward Anhalt
Adaptation: Daniel Fuchs
Screenplay Supervisor: Stanley Scheuer
Cinematography: Joe MacDonald
Camera Operator: Til Gabbani
Editor: Harmon Jones
Art Directors: Lyle Wheeler and Maurice Ransford
Set Decorators: Thomas Little and Fred J. Rode
Special Effects: Fred Sersen
Music: Alfred Newman
Orchestrations: Edward B. Powell and Herbert Spencer
Costumes: Travilla
Wardrobe Director: Charles Le Maire
Sound: W. D. Flick and Roger Heman
Cast: Richard Widmark (Dr. Clinton Reed), Paul Douglas (Police Captain Warren), Barbara Bel Geddes (Nancy Reed), Walter Jack Palance (Blackie), Zero Mostel (Raymond Fitch), Dan Riss (Neff), Alexis Minotis (John Mefaris), Guy Thomajan (Poldi), Tommy Cook (Vince), Edward Kennedy (Jordan), H. T. Tsiang (Cook), Lewis Charles (Kochak), Ray Muller (Dubin), Tommy Rettig (Tom Reed), Lenka Peterson (Jeanette), Pat Walshe (Pat), Paul Hostetler (Dr. Gafney), George Ehmig (Kleber), John Schilleci (Lee), Waldo Pitkin (Ben), Leo Zinser (Sergeant Phelps), Beverly C. Brown (Dr.

Mackey), William A. Dean (Cortelyou), H. Waller Fowler, Jr. (Major Murray), Red Moad (Wynant), Val Winter (Commissioner Quinn), Wilson Bourg, Jr. (Charlie), Irving Vidacovich (Johnston), Mary Liswood (Mrs. Fitch), Aline Stevens (Rita), Ruth Moore Matthews (Mrs. Dubin), Stanley J. Reyes (Redfield), Darwin Greenfield (Violet), Emile Meyer (Beauclyde), Herman Cottman (Scott), Al Theriot (Al), Juan Villasana (Hotel Proprietor), Robert Dorsen (Coast Guard Lieutenant), Harry Marmet (Anson), Arthur Tong (Lascar Boy), Tiger Joe Marsh (Bosun)
35 mm, B&W
96 minutes

1951
A STREETCAR NAMED DESIRE
Group Productions
Producer: Charles K. Feldman
Production Manager: Norman Cook
Director: **Elia Kazan**
Assistant Director: Don Page
Screenplay: Tennessee Williams, based on his own play
Adaptation: Oscar Saul
Cinematography: Harry Stradling
Editor: David Weisbart
Art Director: Richard Day
Set Decorator: George James Hopkins
Music: Alex North
Musical Director: Ray Heindorf
Costumes: Lucinda Ballard
Sound: C. A. Riggs
Cast: Vivien Leigh (Blanche DuBois), Marlon Brando (Stanley Kowalski), Kim Hunter (Stella Kowalski), Karl Malden (Mitch), Rudy Bond (Steve), Nick Dennis (Pablo), Peg Hillias (Eunice), Wright King (A Collector), Richard Garrick (Doctor), Ann Dere (The Matron), Edna Thomas (Mexican Woman), Mickey Kuhn (Sailor), Chester Jones (Street Vendor), Marietta Canty (Negro Woman), Maxie Thrower (Passer-by), Lyle Latell (Policeman), Mel Archer (Foreman), Charles Wagenheim (Passer-by)
35mm, B&W
122 minutes

1952
VIVA ZAPATA!
20th Century Fox
Producer: Darryl F. Zanuck
Director: **Elia Kazan**
Screenplay: John Steinbeck
Cinematography: Joe MacDonald
Editor: Barbara McLean
Art Directors: Lyle Wheeler and Leland Fuller
Set Decorators: Thomas Little and Claude Carpenter
Special Effects: Fred Sersen
Music: Alex North
Musical Director: Alfred Newman
Orchestrations: Maurice de Packh
Costumes: Travilla
Wardrobe Director: Charles Le Maire
Sound: W. D. Flick and Roger Heman
Cast: Marlon Brando (Emiliano Zapata), Jean Peters (Josefa), Anthony Quinn (Eufemio), Joseph Wiseman (Fernando), Arnold Moss (Don Nacio), Alan Reed (Pancho Villa), Margo (Soldadera), Harold Gordon (Madero), Lou Gilbert (Pablo), Mildred Dunnock (Señora Espejo), Frank Silvera (Huerta), Nina Varela (Aunt), Florenz Ames (Señor Espejo), Bernie Gozier (Zapatista), Frank De Kova (Colonel Guajardo), Joseph Granby (General Fuentes), Pedro Regas (Innocente), Richard Garrick (Old General), Fay Roope (Diaz), Harry Kingston (Don Garcia), Ross Bagdasarian (Officer), Leonard George (Husband), Will Kuluva (Lazaro), Fernanda Elizcu (Fuentes' Wife), Abner Biberman (Captain), Philip Van Zandt (Commanding Officer), Lisa Fusaro (Garcia's Wife), Belle Mitchell (Nacio's Wife), Henry Silva (Hernandez), Ric Roman (Overseer), George J. Lewis (Rurale), Salvador Baguez and Peter Mamakos (Soldiers), Henry Corden (Senior Officer), Nestor Paiva (New General), Robert Filmer (Captain Of Rurales), Julia Montoya (Wife), Danny Nunez
35mm, B&W
113 minutes

1953
MAN ON A TIGHTROPE
20th Century Fox

Producer: Robert L. Jacks
Associate Producer: Gerd Oswald
Director: **Elia Kazan**
Assistant Director: Hans Tost
Screenplay: Robert Sherwood, based on the story "International Incident" by Neil Paterson
Cinematography: Georg Krause
Editor: Dorothy Spencer
Art Directors: Hans H. Kuhnert and Theo Zwirsky
Musical Director: Franz Waxman
Orchestrations: Earle Hagen
Songs: Bert Reisfeld
Costumes: Ursula Maes
Wardrobe Director: Charles Le Maire
Sound: Martin Mueller, Karl Becker, Roger Heman
Cast: Fredric March (Karel Cernik), Terry Moore (Tereza Cernik), Gloria Grahame (Zama Cernik), Cameron Mitchell (Joe Vosdek), Adolphe Menjou (Fesker), Robert Beatty (Baravik), Alex D'Arcy (Rudolph), Richard Boone (Krofta), Pat Henning (Konradin), Paul Hartman (Jaromir), John Dehner (The Chief), Dorothea Wieck (Duchess), Philip Kenneally (The Sergeant), Edelweiss Malchin (Vina Konradin), William Costello (Captain), Margaret Slezak (Mrs. Jaromir), Hansi (Kalka, the midget), The Brumbach Circus (The Cernik Circus), Gert Froebe (Plainclothes Policeman), Peter Beauvais (SNB Captain), Robert Charlebois (SNB Lieutenant), Rolf Naukhoff (Police Agent)
35mm, B&W
105 minutes

1954
ON THE WATERFRONT
Horizon
Producer: Sam Spiegel
Assistant to Producer: Sam Rheiner
Director: **Elia Kazan**
Assistant Director: Charles H. Maguire
Screenplay: Budd Schulberg, based on articles by Malcolm Johnson
Cinematography: Boris Kaufman
Editor: Gene Milford

Art Director: Richard Day
Music: Leonard Bernstein
Costumes: Anna Hill Johnstone
Sound: James Shields
Cast: Marlon Brando (Terry Malloy), Eva Marie Saint (Edie Doyle), Karl Malden (Father Barry), Lee J. Cobb (Johnny Friendly), Rod Steiger (Charley Malloy), Pat Henning ("Kayo" Dugan), Leif Erickson (Glover), James Westerfield (Big Mac), John Heldabrand (Mutt), Rudy Bond (Moose), John Hamilton ("Pop" Doyle), Barry Macollum (J.P.), Don Blackman (Luke), Arthur Keegan (Jimmy), Mike O'Dowd (Specs), Martin Balsam (Gillette), Tony Galento (Truck), Tami Mauriello (Tillio), Fred Gwynne (Slim), Abe Simon (Barney), Joyce Lear (Bad Girl), Thomas Hanley (Tommy), Anne Hegira (Mrs. Collins), Nehemiah Persoff (Driver), Pat Hingle (Waiter), Rebecca Sands (Police Stenographer), Tiger Joe Marsh, Pete King and Neil Hines (Policemen), Vince Barbi, Lilian Herlein, Donnell O'Brien, Clifton James, Michael Vincente Gazzo
35mm, B&W
108 minutes

1955
EAST OF EDEN
Warner Bros.
Producer: **Elia Kazan**
Director: **Elia Kazan**
Assistant Directors: Don Page and Horace Hough
Screenplay: Paul Osborn, based on the novel by John Steinbeck
Dialogue Director: Guy Thomajan
Cinematography: Ted McCord (CinemaScope)
Color Process: Warnercolor
Editor: Owen Marks
Art Directors: James Basevi and Malcolm Bert
Set Decorator: George James Hopkins
Music/Musical Director: Leonard Rosenman
Costumes: Anna Hill Johnstone
Sound: Stanley Jones
Cast: Julie Harris (Abra), James Dean (Cal Trask), Raymond Massey (Adam Trask), Richard Davalos (Aron Trask), Burl Ives (Sam, the Sheriff), Jo Van

Fleet (Kate), Albert Dekker (Will Hamilton), Lois Smith (Ann), Timothy
Carey (Joe), Mario Siletti (Piscora), Lonny Chapman (Roy), Nick Dennis
(Rantani), Harold Gordon (Mr. Albrecht), Jonathan Haze (Piscora's son),
Barbara Baxley (Nurse), Bette Treadville (Madame), Tex Mooney
(Bartender), Harry Cording (Bouncer), Loretta Rush (Card Dealer), Bill
Phillips (Coalman), Jack Carr, Roger Creed, Effie Laird, Wheaton
Chambers, Ed Clark, Al Ferguson, Franklyn Farnum, and Rose Plummer
(Carnival People), John George (Photographer), Earle Hodgins (Shooting
Gallery Attendant), C. Ramsay Hill (English Officer), Edward McNally
(Soldier), Jack Henderson, Ruth Gillis, Joe Greene, Mabel and June Smaney
35mm, Color
115 minutes

1956
BABY DOLL
Newtown Productions
Producer: **Elia Kazan**
Production Manager: Forrest E. Johnston
Director: **Elia Kazan**
Assistant Director: Charles H. Maguire
Screenplay: Tennessee Williams, based on his one-act plays *27 Wagons Full
of Cotton* and *The Unsatisfactory Supper* or *The Long Stay Cut Short*
Cinematography: Boris Kaufman
Editor: Gene Milford
Art Director: Richard Sylbert
Associate Art Director: Paul Sylbert
Music: Kenyon Hopkins
Costumes: Anna Hill Johnstone
Wardrobe: Flo Transfiled
Speech Consultant: Marguerite Lamkin
Sound: Edward J. Johnstone
Cast: Carroll Baker (Baby Doll Meighan), Karl Malden (Archie Lee
Meighan), Eli Wallach (Silva Vacarro), Mildred Dunnock (Aunt Rose),
Lonny Chapman (Rock), Eades Hogue (Town Marshal), Noah Williamson
(Deputy), Jimmy Wiliams (Mayor), John Stuart Dudley (Doctor),
Madeleine Sherwood (Nurse), Will Lester (Sheriff), Rip Torn (Brick), and
the people of Benoit, Mississippi

35mm, B&W
114 minutes

1957
A FACE IN THE CROWD
Newtown Productions
Producer: **Elia Kazan**
Production Manager: George Justin
Director: **Elia Kazan**
Assistant Director: Charles H. Maguire
Screenplay: Budd Schulberg, based on his short story "Your Arkansas Traveller" from his book *Some Faces in the Crowd*
Cinematography: Harry Stradling
Associate Cinematographer: Gayne Rescher
Camera Operators: Saul Midwall and James Fitzsimons
Editor: Gene Milford
Art Directors: Richard Sylbert and Paul Sylbert
Music: Tom Glazer
Costumes: Anna Hill Johnstone
Wardrobe: Flo Transfield
Sound Editor: Don Olson
Sound: Ernest Zatorsky
Technical Advisors: Charles Irving and Toby Bruce
Cast: Andy Griffith (Lonesome Rhodes), Patricia Neal (Marcia Jeffries), Anthony Franciosa (Joey Kieley), Walter Matthau (Mel Miller), Lee Remick (Betty Lou Fleckum), Percy Waram (Colonel Hollister), Rod Brasfield (Beanie), Charles Irving (Mr. Luffler), Howard Smith (J. B. Jeffries), Paul McGrath (Macey), Kay Medford (1st Mrs. Rhodes), Alexander Kirkland (Jim Collier), Marshall Neilan (Senator Fuller), Big Jeff Bess (Sheriff Hesmer), Henry Sharp (Abe Steiner), Willie Feibel and Larry Casazza (Printers), P. Jay Sidney (Llewellyn), Eva Vaughan (Mrs. Cooley), Burl Ives (Himself), Bennet Cerf, Betty Furness, Faye Emerson, Virginia Graham, Sam Levenson, and Mike Wallace (Extras in bar sequence), Logan Ramsey (TV Director), Earl Wilson, Walter Winchell, Vera Walton, John Stuart Dudley, Fred Stewart, Rip Torn, Granny Sense, Harold Jinks, Diana Sands, Charles Nelson Reilly, Sandy Wirth
35mm, B&W
126 minutes

1960
WILD RIVER
20th Century Fox
Producer: **Elia Kazan**
Director: **Elia Kazan**
Assistant Director: Charles Maguire
Screenplay: Paul Osborn, based on the novels *Mud on the Stars* by William
Bradford Huie and *Dunbar's Cove* by Borden Deal
Cinematography: Ellsworth Fredericks (CinemaScope)
Color Process: De Luxe Color
Color Consultant: Leonard Doss
Editor: William Reynolds
Art Directors: Lyle R. Wheeler and Herman A. Blumenthal
Set Decorators: Walter M. Scott and Joseph Kish
Music: Kenyon Hopkins
Costumes: Anna Hill Johnstone
Sound: Eugene Grossman and Richard Vorisek
Cast: Montgomery Clift (Chuck Glover), Lee Remick (Carol Garth), Jo Van
Fleet (Ella Garth), Albert Salmi (Hank Bailey), Jay C. Flippen (Hamilton
Garth), James Westerfield (Cal Garth), Barbara Loden (Betty Jackson),
Frank Overton (Walter Clark), Malcolm Atterbury (Sy Moore), Robert Earl
Jones (Ben), Bruce Dern (Jack Roper), James Steakley (Mayor), Hardwick
Stewart (Marshal Hogue), Big Jeff Bess (Joe John), Judy Harris (Barbara-
Ann), Jim Menard (Jim Junior), Patricia Perry (Mattie), John Dudley
(Todd), Alfred E. Smith (Thompson), Mark Menson (Winters), Pat Hingle
(Narrator)
35mm, Color
109 minutes

1961
SPLENDOR IN THE GRASS
Newtown Productions/NBI
Producer: **Elia Kazan**
Associate Producers: William Inge and Charles H. Maguire
Director: **Elia Kazan**
Assistant Directors: Don Kranze, Ulu Grosbard (New York scenes)
Screenplay: William Inge
Screenplay Supervisor: Marguerite James

Cinematography: Boris Kaufman
Color Process: Technicolor
Editor: Gene Milford
Production Designer: Richard Sylbert
Set Decorator: Gene Callahan
Music/Musical Director: David Amram
Costumes: Ann Hill Johnstone
Wardrobe: Florence Transfield and George Newman
Choreography: George Trapps
Sound: Edward Johnstone
Cast: Natalie Wood (Wilma Dean Loomis), Warren Beatty (Bud Stamper), Pat Hingle (Ace Stamper), Audrey Christie (Mrs. Loomis), Barbara Loden (Ginny Stamper), Zohra Lampert (Angelina), Fred Stewart (Del Loomis), Joanna Roos (Mrs. Stamper), Jan Norris (Juanita Howard), Gary Lockwood (Toots), Sandy Dennis (Kay), Crystal Field (Hazel), Marla Adams (June), Lynn Loring (Carolyn), John McGovern (Doc Smiley), Martine Bartlett (Miss Metcalf), Sean Garrison (Glenn), William Inge (Reverend Whiteman), Charles Robinson (Johnny Masterson), Phyllis Diller (Texas Guinan), Buster Bailey (Old Man at the Country Club), Jake La Motta (Waiter), Billy Graham and Charlie Norkus (Young men at party), Lou Antonio (Roustabout), Adelaide Klein (Italian Mother), Phoebe Mackay (Maid), Mark Slade, Marjorie J. Nichols, Richard Abbot, Particia Ripley
35mm, Color
124 minutes

1963
AMERICA, AMERICA
Warner Bros.
Producer: **Elia Kazan**
Associate Producer: Charles H. Maguire
Production Assistant: Burt Harris
Director: **Elia Kazan**
Screenplay: **Elia Kazan**, based on his own novel and his unpublished story "Hamal."
Screenplay Supervisor: Marie Kenney
Cinematography: Haskell Wexler

Camera Operator: Harlowe Stengel
Optical Effects: Film Opticals, Inc.
Editor: Dede Allen
Production Designer: Gene Callahan
Music: Manos Hadjidakis
Lyrics: Nikos Gatsos
Costumes: Anna Hill Johnstone
Sound Editor: Edward Beyer
Sound: L. Robbins and Richard Vorisek
Cast: Stathis Giallelis (Stavros Topouzuglou), Frank Wolff (Vartan
Damadian), Harry Davis (Isaac Topouzoglou), Elena Karam (Vasso
Topouzuglou), Estelle Hemsley (Grandmother Topouzuglou), Gregory
Rozakis (Hohanness Gardashian), Lou Antonio (Abdul), Salem Ludwig
(Odysseus Topouzuglou), John Marley (Garabet), Johanna Frank (Vartuhi),
Linda Marsh (Thomna Simnikoglou), Paul Mann (Aleko Sinnikoglou),
Robert H. Harris (Aratoon Kebabian), Katherine Balfour (Sophia Kebabian),
Dimitris Nicolaides, Leonard George, Gina Trikonis, George Stefans, Peter
Dawson, Xander Chello, Carl Low
35mm, Color
168 minutes

1969
THE ARRANGEMENT
Athena Enterprises
Producer: **Elia Kazan**
Associate Producer: Charles H. Maguire
Director: **Elia Kazan**
Assistant Director: Burtt Harris
Screenplay: **Elia Kazan**. Based on his own novel
Cinematography: Robert Surtees (Panavision)
Color Process: Technicolor
Editor: Stefan Arnsten
Production Designer: Gene Callahan
Art Director: Malcolm Bert
Set Decorator: Audrey Blasdel
Music: David Amram
Costumes: Theodora Van Runkle

Sound Editor: Larry Jost
Sound: Richard Vorisek
Cast: Kirk Douglas (Eddie Anderson/Evangelos), Faye Dunaway (Gwen),
Deborah Kerr (Florence Anderson), Richard Boone (Sam Anderson), Hume
Cronyn (Arthur), Michael Higgins (Michael), John Randolph Jones
(Charles), Carol Rossen (Gloria), Anne Hegira (Thomna), William Hansen
(Dr. Weeks), Charles Drake (Finnegan), Harold Gould (Dr. Liebman), E.J.
André (Uncle Joe), Michael Murphy (Father Draddy), Philip Bourneuf
(Judge Morris), Diane Hull (Ellen), Barry Sullivan (Chet Collier), Ann
Doran (Nurse Costello), Chet Stratton (Charlie), Paul Newlan (Banker),
Steve Bond (Eddie at 12), Jim Halferty (Eddie at 18), Joseph Rogan/Joseph
Cherry (Gwen's baby), Clint Kimbrough (Ben), Kirk Livesey, Bert Conway,
John Lawrence, Elmer J. McGovern, Barry Russo, Dee Carroll, Richard
Morrill, Betty Bresler, Virginia Peters, Pat Paterson, Dorothy Konrad,
Maureen McCormick
125 minutes

1972
THE VISITORS
Chris Kazan — Nick Proferes Productions
Producers: Chris Kazan and Nick Proferes
Director: **Elia Kazan**
Screenplay: Chris Kazan
Cinematography: Nick Proferes
Lighting: Michael Mannes
Assisted by: William Mamches
Editor: Nick Proferes
Music: Bach's Suite No. 16 for lute, played by William Matthews (guitar)
Sound Editor: Nina Schulman
Assistant Sound Editor: Marilyn Frauenglass
Sound: Dale Whitman
Cast: Patrick McVey (Harry Wayne), Patricia Joyce (Martha Wayne), James
Woods (Bill Schmidt), Chico Martinez (Tony Rodriguez), Steve Railsback
(Mike Nickerson)
Super 16mm, Color
90 minutes

1976
THE LAST TYCOON
Paramount
Producer: Sam Spiegel
Director: **Elia Kazan**
Screenplay: Harold Pinter, based on the novel by F. Scott Fitzgerald
Cinematography: Victor Kemper
Editing: Richard Marks
Production Designer: Gene Callahan
Art Director: Jack Collins
Set Decorators: Bill Smith and Jerry Wunderlich
Music: Maurice Jarre
Costumes: Anna Hill Johnstone
Cast: Robert De Niro (Monroe Stahr), Tony Curtis (Rodriquez), Robert
Mitchum (Pat Brady), Jeanne Moreau (Didi), Jack Nicholson (Brimmer),
Donald Pleasence (Boxley), Ingrid Boulting (Kathleen Moore), Ray Milland
(Fleishacker). Dana Andrews (Red Ridingwood), Theresa Russell (Cecilia
Brady), Peter Strauss (Wylie), Tige Andrews (Popolos), Morgan Farley
(Marcus), John Carradine (Guard), Jeff Corey (Doctor), Diane Shalet
(Stahr's Secretary), Seymour Cassel (Seal Trainer), Anjelica Huston (Edna),
Bonnie Bartlett and Sharon Masters (Brady's Secretaries), Eric Christmas
(Norman), Leslie Curtis (Mrs. Rodriquez), Lloyd Kino (Butler), Brendan
Burns (Assistant Editor), Carrie Miller (Lady in restaurant), Peggy Feury
(Hairdresser), Betsy Jones-Moreland (Writer), Patricia Singer (Girl on
beach)
35mm, Color
125 minutes

ELIA KAZAN

INTERVIEWS

Man of the Theater

LEWIS GILLENSON / 1951

FOR A MAN WHO was once told that he would never make a living in the theatre, director Elia Kazan has done tolerably well. In 1931 the Group Theatre, which he was then serving as an apprentice, suggested that he'd do better in some other field. Twelve years later, in 1943, he made them eat their words: he directed five Broadway hits, among them a Pulitzer Prize winner—a feat comparable to hitting five home runs in a game, one with the bases loaded.

Kazan's appraisal of that year as "pure fluke—accidents, accidents, accidents," is disproved by what has happened since. On Broadway, from 1943 to 1949, Kazan directed seven shows. Five were hits; two of them, *Death of a Salesman* and *A Streetcar Named Desire*, won Pulitzer Prizes; while assorted plaudits were bestowed upon *All My Sons* and *Deep Are the Roots*.

Kazan, whose first ambition was to be a movie director, started directing pictures in 1944, confessing at the time that "any script girl knows more about it than I do." Three years later he won an Academy Award for *Gentleman's Agreement*. The Oscar, however, failed to convince him that he knew enough about the camera, and two years ago he took a sabbatical from the stage to direct two films—*Viva Zapata,* not yet released, and *A Streetcar Named Desire* (both starring protégé Marlon Brando). While *Streetcar* sent the critics searching for new ways to say "tremendous" and "overpowering," Kazan calmly started preparations for a new Broadway production.

From *Harper's Bazaar*, November 1951.

A fellow with a searching interest in principle, Kazan describes his philosophic *modus operandi* in a pithy line. "You've gotta keep fighting. You've gotta risk your life every six months if you want to keep living."

This faith in calculated risk characterizes Kazan's creative personality. Producers try to convince him that a big-name star can make a picture a sure success. Kazan ignores the well-intentioned advice, instead hires relatively unknown Broadway actors chosen solely for their talents. In *Zapata* and *Streetcar* he used only one contract player in each film; the other actors were recruited from Broadway, many from the Actors' Studio, a Kazan sponsored dramatic school in New York.

Few of his productions have been considered "safe"—Broadway jargon for a script loaded with the yaks, schmalz and tears that are supposed to lure the out-of-town buyers to the $4.80 seats. The plots in some, like *Death of a Salesman,* twist like a maze in a psychologist's laboratory. The generally less than popular problem of miscegenation was threaded through *Deep Are the Roots*; even in the few musicals he has done, Kazan avoided conventional musical comedy characterization and presented real people who behaved according to his idea of reality, an attitude far from consistent with Shubert Alley box office theory. His success created a pleasing paradox—the intelligentsia applauding while a corps of ticket brokers grew rich.

Yet those who capitalize the "A" in art, even when it appears in the middle of a sentence, find Kazan a difficult orphan to adopt. For example, they are pained at his affection for what they consider the low caste world of cinema. They, in turn, give him a pain.

In the movies, as on the stage, Kazan has insisted on his prerogatives of choosing script and cast. In the short time Kazan has directed pictures he has won popular and critical acclaim with such unorthodox film themes as anti-Semitism (*Gentleman's Agreement*) and Negro-prejudice (*Pinky*) while employing nonprofessionals to act in their on-location habitats instead of casting office extras in a plaster-of-Paris set.

In *Boomerang* he roped off the main streets of Stamford, Connecticut, borrowed local police, storekeepers, his aged uncle Avraam and made a picture that helped activate a trend to liberate Hollywood directors from the Southern California clime.

One shooting day in Connecticut it rained, and the cameramen, unfamiliar with such celestial disturbances, began collapsing their equipment.

Against advice that the murky skies would ruin the scene, Kazan ordered it shot.

"You can't tell me the audiences will lose the illusion because the rain is real. Let's go!"

For a film told in documentary style, the lighting was perfect. The cobblestones glistened authentically and the actors huddled under their collars like anyone being drenched by real rain.

In *Panic in the Streets,* the story of a pneumonic plague carrier on the loose in New Orleans, Kazan skidded his cameras around the city with the fluidity of a Notre Dame quarterback maneuvering his backfield. They filmed the chase through real warehouses, rat-infested wharves and the ancient back alleys of the city. Nobody had a more exciting time than the kinetic director—unless it was a bevy of ladies Kazan recruited as extras from one of the town's popular disorderly houses. A taxi driver who had doubled as an informal booking agent for the establishment came upon them before the cameras.

"M'gawd," he exploded, "who'da expected it. The whole house's gone legit!"

The earthiness which marks Kazan's work comes with a naturalness that is understandable when viewed against his origins and upbringing. He was born in Constantinople forty-three years ago and until he arrived in this country at the age of four, spoke nothing but Greek. The son of a rug merchant, he was raised in New Rochelle where he was treated by his playmates rather diffidently as that "quiet foreigner." When he grew sixty-five inches high, nature quit. A black luxuriant tangle of hair, a melancholy nose, swarthy skin, a somewhat underslung posterior and burning eyes heightened his exotic pedigree and intensified his shyness. As a result, Kazan is probably the only successful actor-director in recent history who never starred in the high school play and therefore never had the chore of unlearning the lessons of the high school coach.

Nor was this histrionic virginity sullied during his college days. Williams College, sometimes referred to as the place "where the ivy has ivy," couldn't have been a more inappropriate choice for one with Kazan's modest means and upbringing. However, a scholarship and a job waiting on tables in the fraternity houses he was never asked to join helped him depart from Williams with honors and a studied indifference to alumni affairs.

During his last college year he had begun thinking seriously and secretly of becoming a movie director. For those who express surprise that the greatest dramatic director of the age should have preferred pictures to a stage career, Kazan has a simple answer. Like everyone else he went to the movies, but until he left college he rarely attended a Broadway play. Kazan divulged his secret to his Williams roommate and friend Alan Baxter, now a well-known actor. Partly through Baxter's persuasion, in great part to avoid the rug business, Kazan entered the Yale Graduate School of Dramatic Art in 1931.

This decision met with anything but enthusiasm in the Old World atmosphere of the Kazan household. The elder Kazan had a respect for college—as the one way to become a doctor, lawyer or engineer. Actors to Papa Kazan were people who looked like John Barrymore or Gary Cooper, certainly not like his boy Elia. People who looked like his son would do better to go into the rug business. It was with extreme misgivings and a shaky hand that he signed the first tuition check.

Baxter remembers that among the most painful sights he ever had to witness was the shy, fidgety Kazan forcing stage presence upon himself in Alexander Dean's acting class.

Backstage, it was another story. He had strong, willing hands, and a facility with tools that inspired Baxter to tag him "Gadget," a sobriquet shortened by time to "Gadge."

He flew backdrops, hammered, painted, tripping around the stage like a ballet dancer stuffed with tools. In the library he pored over the classics, developed the love for Chekhov he still possesses and the vague urge that he might become a playwright. He met and fell in love with another student with the same ambition, Mollie Day Thatcher, late of Vassar, Phi Beta Kappa and the campus Daisy Chain. They married a year later and came to New York's newly formed Group Theatre, where Kazan and Baxter got jobs as apprentices.

The turbulent Group in those days shook with ambition. To its members it gave ideals, wonderful plays, inspired productions and not quite enough money to eat. It did, however, enunciate a philosophy of theatrical integrity, a belief in the Stanislavsky method and a respect for public taste that no other theatre group before or since has even approached. Kazan downed these principles like a thirsty barfly, following behind Harold Clurman, the learned director, absorbing his disquisitions, scrawling what he could into notebooks which even at that stage were assuming heroic

proportions. Today they represent his private five-foot shelf—memora-
bilia, memos to himself, reflections on life and the jottings of a man who
hates to see time disappear unused.

The Group was somewhat less enamored of him. He was taken aside one
day by Cheryl Crawford, one of the directors, and sadly informed that the
Group savants could see no future for him anywhere in the theatre. The
rug business was gently suggested as a possibly more secure future.

"It hurt like hell," Kazan explains, "and I resented them for their opinions. Also, I had to respect them for giving it to me straight. But since they
weren't paying me anyhow, I just refused to get out."

To pay the Group for its enforced indulgence of him, he pasted clip-
pings, repaired scenery, painted and typed. His father, who at this stage
was even more devoutly convinced of the folly of acting, grudgingly paid
him ten dollars weekly for value received—five half days shifting rugs in
the showroom. Mollie had been hired as a reader for the Group and, by
depression standards, they lived reasonably well on both incomes.

"In any event," she says, "there never was one of those 'if-this-doesn't-
work-out-I-go-back-to-Pop's-business' episodes. Gadge had found a home
in the theatre and wasn't moving out."

In the summer of 1933 the Group put on a musical review at Green
Mansions, a hotel in New York's Adirondack Mountains, under the direc-
torship of its good friend Phil Loeb, the Theatre Guild director. Loeb was
given a company and with it verbal notations as to the talents and limitations of each member. At the tail end was Kazan's name.

"Not for acting," explained Harold Clurman; "he's for stage managing."

Loeb, however, struck by what he recalls as the most bombastic energy
and driving ambition he had ever encountered in anyone, tried him in a
skit, opposite Alan Baxter.

Until this time Kazan had entertained few thoughts of earning his living as an actor. But the plays of Group authors like Clifford Odets included
parts ideally tailored to Kazan's lithe personality. Boris Aronson, the set
designer, recalls that in those days "Gadget darted around like a man with
a time bomb in his belly. You never stayed near him that you weren't
aware something was about to happen."

In *Waiting for Lefty,* Kazan played the explosive cab driver who charged
down the aisle onto the stage spitting his muscular lines with a passion
few conventional dramatic schools of the day would have recommended.

The realistic impact of the performance so impressed Walter Winchell that he flashed the "inside dope" that Kazan had recently been hustled off a hack especially for the show.

The illusion that this, as well as the other parts Kazan played so vigorously in *Night Music, Golden Boy* and *Paradise Lost,* represented the instinctive outpouring of a roughneck couldn't have been less accurate. Kazan prepared his performances as cerebrally as a draftsman blueprinting construction plans. An actor working with him in *Night Music* one day picked up his script. The back pages were divided into three big sections under the headings "mood," "identification," "golden box" (meaning experience). He carefully broke down the components of each scene, what it meant to him, how he could attune himself to the nuances of Odets' character. With his exacting mind and probing curiosity he created the personality he was to play, then clawed his way into it. His performances won rave notices; one critic called him "one of the most exciting actors in America."

His work impressed one of those Hollywood scouts who are ever on the alert to replenish the supply of expendable movie gangsters. His subsequent portrait of Googie the gangster in the film *City for Conquest* convinced a Hollywood mogul that his studio had at last found the most colossal gangster of the century. He offered Kazan a four-figure weekly contract and a new name—Cézanne. When Kazan protested that Cézanne was a great French painter, the undaunted producer answered confidently, "A couple of good performances from you and they'll forget the other guy."

The four figures and the horrific vision of becoming a permanent gangster named Cézanne catapulted the turbulent Kazan back to New York. The Group, after a half dozen shaky crises and false finishes, had come to life again, and in 1939 Kazan realized an old ambition—he was given Robert Ardrey's *Thunder Rock* to direct. It was labeled an artistic success, but laid an egg at the box office. His venture a year later, Irwin Shaw's *Quiet City,* fared even worse; in the week it stayed open, few critics were inclined to favor it even with the faint phrase "artistic success."

Kazan is aggressively proud of his flops as being no less expressive of his true capacities than his hits. He bitterly protests the box-score cult established around writers and directors.

"If a painter doesn't like his canvas he rips it up. You can't erase an imperfect play production. Why the hell should you try? What's perfect that lives?"

The Group finally breathed its last in 1941, and that year Kazan got himself an assignment to direct *Café Crown.* His staging of that play led Michael Myerberg and Thornton Wilder, producer and author of *Skin of Our Teeth,* to hire him as director of their play. By any standards, this was a lollapalooza to stage. Concocted of dinosaurs, earthquakes, bathing beauties and manholes into which the principals dropped at odd moments, it was a bagatelle for Kazan's methodical, precise mind. The dazzling package also included its tempestuous star, Tallulah Bankhead. It became patently clear soon after chunks of Albert Johnson's scenery began flying between star and director that something had to give. There were no "dahlings" as Tallulah laid it on the line: either that ―― johnny-come-lately got out or she would.

"You've got a pile of dough in the show. Mike, I'd better get out," offered Kazan less calmly than these words read.

Myerberg, a punter in matters theatrical, played a long shot, forcing star and director to make the best of it. Metaphorically speaking, the scenery kept flying until opening night when Bankhead gave a glittering performance. Backstage after the show, the elder Kazan, now at peace with the theatre, accepted congratulations for his son. Sensing the chance for a sweet needle, Gadge ushered his father into the center of La Bankhead's group of gushing admirers.

"Well, young lady," said Papa, giving her a knowing nudge in the ribs, "my boy made you a success, hah!"

In what will probably remain the only situation of its kind before and since, Tallulah was struck dumb.

A calmer man today, Kazan evaluates those bellicose sessions with compressed humility.

"Maybe I shouldn't have swung so hard. But everybody's got one big fight in him. It either makes or breaks you. Failure destroys. After slugging that one out, I knew I could tackle anyone."

Since the Bankhead bout, Kazan has never been troubled with star temperament. An adherent to the gospel that nothing can take the place of intelligence, talent and feeling, he casts his shows without regard for "name" players.

"Too many of them keep seeing their past performances in their private mirrors. That's no way to build new character."

Kazan's every step in the theatre has been dedicated to bringing dramatic art to a level of pure reason. His mind cuts quickly through complexities. The handfuls of dust blown off the palm to obscure a murky idea seldom blind him. His opinions on anything from a Brooklyn Dodger second sacker to a Tennessee Williams second act shoot out of him in crisp terse phrases, often brocaded with a selection of men's room expletives that could easily curl the paper on the walls.

Cross-legged on a desk in the barnlike top floor study of his Manhattan brownstone, his discussions with a playwright on script changes sound like anything but a model of academic review: "Goddam character annoys the hell outta me. He's not on the level. Let's fix him so he fits into the story. Right now he's walking on stilts."

The terseness should not be construed as the case of the director rough-housing the playwright. Authors like Arthur Miller, Tennessee Williams and S. N. Behrman have paid public tribute to the sharpness of Kazan's insight and to his contribution in making prerehearsal patching and mending painless and purposeful.

During the cast meetings that follow, everyone sits in bull sessions around Kazan—talking out the play, agreeing on meanings, interpretations and purposes. Not a line goes into rehearsal until Kazan is convinced everyone is zeroed in with the playwright.

Once actual rehearsal begins he's a fountain of warm enthusiasm. He climbs on the back of a chair or glides around the stage with a springy, catlike swiftness. He speaks softly, raising his voice in enthusiasm, seldom in anger. Casts respect him to the point of adoration for the way he will quietly work out an obstreperous scene with an actor. He encourages actors to work out their own ideas, and a bovine performer can make him show signs of approaching illness.

A producer describing the spirit that infuses a Kazen production, with its ostensibly spontaneous integration of script, set and, above all, acting, said:

"There's nothing cute about him. He operates on the theory that everyone feels it in the belly—audience as well as actor. If he doesn't understand a line, an idea or a movement, then the audience shouldn't be expected to either."

Though actors have a healthy regard for Kazan's own acting talents, they never get a performance from him while he's directing. Personal movements, gestures, mannerisms he believes should come out of the actor's own feeling for the character he is to portray. Kazan's own senses are closely attuned to that character. Synthetic posturing—a telltale sign that an actor's grip over the character is slipping—he is cat-quick to catch. At such moments Kazan will take the actor aside and search with him for the emotional cues to get him back on the track. Sincere actors love him for it. They respond to him as to a chemical stimulant. "Gadge stretches you," explains John Garfield. "First thing you know, you're doing things you never dreamed possible."

Kazan, however, does not excel in *all* the qualities that can make a director great. Unlike George Kaufman or Garson Kanin, he is not equipped to pound out the necessary rewrite of a scene should the author fail.

Harold Clurman's facility for spinning lacework patterns of subtlety are not generally associated with Kazan's more eruptive staging.

The brilliant Josh Logan infuses comedies and musicals with joyousness unparalleled in the modern theatre. Kazan, who must associate himself with a sense of reality in any script, isn't comfortable with straight comedy and has never tackled it. It also troubles him slightly that he hasn't been able to handle musical plays with any great success. He was offered *Oklahoma* and confesses wryly that "I couldn't see a ghost of a chance for it." *Love Life,* his most recent musical effort, impressed some critics with its adult atmosphere; others called it "gloomy," indicating that for a musical perhaps too much mind and not enough froth was injected into its direction.

The success of Kazan's finished product must rest upon a combination of happy accidents and acquired assets that make him what he is. To begin with, there are twenty long years of stagecraft—achieved in what appears like an almost conscious sense of progression, from student to stagehand to stage manager to actor to director. Those who prefer to call it "genius," Kazan shrugs away with stubborn candor: "I learned my trade by working with every facet of it. Everything a guy does in the theatre today is governed to a great degree by what he learned yesterday. You're not born to get good notices. You earn them."

He feels just as strongly about the training required to direct movies. Because he devoted all of 1950–1951 to films, columnists began hinting that Kazan preferred the movies and that *Death of a Salesman* represented his stage swan song.

"Must I make doctrinaire choices?" he asks in protest. "I'll work wherever I find a good script. Truth is, I spent eighteen years in the theatre and finally got to know something about it. First time I ever directed a picture was in 1943. The movie industry is twice as complicated as the theatre. I stuck close to Hollywood these last two years to learn something about making pictures. That's all."

His methods of learning are as uncluttered as his personality. He buttonholes cameramen, directors, electricians, cutters, sound men, anyone in fact who knows what he doesn't, and pumps them for facts. The pertinent answers wind up in the ubiquitous notebook.

"It's a different business from the stage," he explains with the intensity of a man reporting a falling bomb. "You're the director and you sit there. All around you a hundred people are waiting, actors, cameramen and that nervous guy who watches the budget. Every minute that's unused costs piles of money. Everybody waits for you to do something. And sometimes you just don't know what the hell to do."

Kazan's last picture, *A Streetcar Named Desire,* reveals that at last the Oscar-winning director (*Gentleman's Agreement*) knew very much what he was doing. The frank treatment of the script's psycho-sexual problems reaches heights of sustained emotion rarely witnessed in modern films.

Because he's one of the few directors who shuttle successfully between the stage and screen, people always badger him to explain the difference between directing pictures and plays. Some of the differences are recorded in the notebooks.

"Stage operates through illusion. There's nothing between the actor and the audience. Only he—without help—can project the idea to the audience. In movies, the camera helps out—moves the idea along. Sometimes it can talk, as it closes in or backs up, helps express emotion, what a character is thinking; or it can anticipate action. The more words, usually the lousier a movie script. Movies must be the real thing. Camera gives the plot an assist, helps the story get there."

The use of real-life characters instead of bit players ("nobody knows the difference") is one of his methods to achieve the "real thing." In filming *Zapata,* John Steinbeck's script of the life of Mexico's last revolutionary on horseback, Kazan sent his cameras roaming over the sunbaked mesquite hills of Mexican Texas, panning into the adobe shacks and faces of the Mexican border dwellers. To give Marlon Brando a dirt-caked look, he personally massaged Texas dirt into his cheeks.

At heart Kazan knows he owes his creative birthright to his feet-on-the-ground sense of reality and acts like a man suspicious of losing it. His impatience with protocol probably reflects such suspicion.

He bores, not easily, but suddenly. An overdose of lacquered conversation will send him into a corner with his notebook or on the rug for an escapist snooze. Like many creative people he demands his solitude. To deprive him of it would be like depriving a fighter of his between-rounds rest. It charges his batteries, and restores his normal affability. "At liberty" from plays, movies and scripts in his Connecticut farmhouse, he relieves his inner turbulence by running a tractor with reckless enthusiasm or, for hours at a stretch, swinging a sickle and ax in a few forest-locked acres.

With Mollie, a great factor in his success, and their four children, he lives like a man who enjoys his earthiness, shaking loose from any attempts to whisk him into the columnists' bistro society. His quick affection for almost anyone he meets, bus drivers, cabbies or total strangers, is complemented by an enveloping curiosity about them and the way they live.

During the war the army sent him to the Pacific to do an entertainment survey. He gave command cars and brass hats a wide berth, hitched a ride to the bloody Ville Verdi trail in the Philippines and there spent twenty-four hours without a hitch in a battalion aid station as a GI orderly, assisting surgeons, serving the wounded and preparing dressings. None of the GI's of the 32nd Division knew who he was, nor did they know that *A Tree Grows in Brooklyn,* the picture shown that night down the hill, was directed by the little man carrying bedpans in the surgical tent.

Sharpened by such experiences is the strong sense of balance that enables him to draw deeply, and at will, from the reservoir of his talents. The neurotic pressures that tie others into knots seldom inhibit him.

On a movie set recently a producer spotted him in contemplation in a corner and remarked, "There's a man who can put sixty per cent of his potentialities to work at any moment, where most of us would gladly settle for half that."

"Then what do you suppose he's worrying about now?" asked his assistant.

"He's probably wondering what's happening to the other forty," was the answer.

An aversion to waste, probably traceable to his utilitarian upbringing, Kazan imposes on his friends as well as himself. A paternalistic compulsion to uncover the best in everybody causes him, like a football coach at half time, to fire writers, actors and directors to dizzying peaks of ambition.

"He's so wonderful, it's awful," a young actress recently said. "After you're exposed to that enthusiasm for a while, you begin to believe you're Duse. Then you suddenly fall on your fanny and you darn soon discover who you really are."

Partial explanation for his ambition for others must certainly stem from the nostalgic Group Theatre days. The Group was a society where everyone taught, learned and worked together for common purpose in contrast to the theatrical jungle where actors bit and clawed for parts. Kazan has never lost his indebtedness to the Group for what it gave him. Its theatrical idealism stuck inside him like a youthfully learned gospel message.

To manifest continuity between the Group and the present, he recently organized the Actors' Studio, a free invitational dramatic school open to professionals with talent. Old Group hands, Lee Strasberg, Bobby Lewis, and Clifford Odets, with Kazan, teach classes in acting, directing and playwrighting.

Deficits are quietly, and without too much pain, made up by Kazan; his idealism has never interfered with certain self-taught lessons in practical finance, which enable him to command fees well in the six-figure bracket.

An old Group associate, ruminating about the short, muscular man with the explosive laugh and the supercharged energy which seemed all he had in the old days, related a W. C. Fields story that indirectly applied to Kazan.

"Years ago, when I was poor and hungry," twanged Fields, giving an interview in his shiny black Cadillac, "I swore I would make a million dollars, buy a Cadillac, fill the back seat with box lunches and distribute them to the wretches who are as hungry as I was."

The reporter turned around and commented upon the empty back seat.

"Y'damned fool," exploded Fields, "I've *got* the million."

Kazan's old friend let the words sink in, then said, "In a manner of speaking, Gadget's got the million, too. But the promise he could never forget."

A Quiz for Kazan

THEATER ARTS/1956

IN THE FOLLOWING QUESTION-AND-ANSWER interview, Elia Kazan discusses aspects of both stage and screen direction.

Q: *As an outstanding director of both stage and screen, what do you feel, from the director's point of view, is the major advantage and disadvantage of each medium as compared with the other?*

A: With films: the contact with reality. The inspiration of reality. The obligation one feels when working close to it. There is also great poetry in films and enormous scope, not of the CinemaScope variety but real scope. Films seem to me the most modern medium; they can move with the speed of thought. Their variety and complexity reflect the world today.

With stage: the freedom of expression. Censorship is a serious limitation in films; the stage is still free. Under the present way of producing and marketing films, the artists working in them have to make it possible for a very broad audience to see them and find them acceptable. There is tremendous pressure in films to "please everybody," and no matter how this is fought, the pressure is still felt. The stage today is the freest medium in the performing arts.

Q: *As the foremost director of Tennessee Williams' works on the stage, and of* A Streetcar Named Desire *and the brand-new* Baby Doll *(Warner Brothers) on*

From *Theater Arts*, November 1956. © 1956. Reprinted by permission of Routledge, Inc.

the screen, what do you think is Williams' greatest appeal to the audiences of each medium?

A : His emotionalism. Williams is a great artist. He has a positive genius for dealing with subject matter that is on everyone's mind and part of everyone's experience, but which has not been dealt with by other writers. All his characters are felt for. No one is a heavy. All are wrong and right, magnificent and foolish, violent and weak. In other words, Williams deals with real people. In his work you will not find the lily-white hero, the noble protagonist, the self-righteous moralist, and the other absurd stock figures of much of our drama. People recognize people. Audiences instinctively feel Williams is writing about their real problems — personal, social, whatever. There is also no infringement on the area of mystery and confusion that is part of every human soul. He doesn't tend to clean things up, clear them up, straighten them out, oversimplify, or the rest of that kind of dramatic claptrap.

Q : *Since* Baby Doll *was written especially for the screen by Williams, does the film script make special use of advantages offered by that medium?*

A : It does indeed. Tennessee has an increasing feeling for films. Actually he still relies too much on the power of the spoken word, but this "fault" is only a reflection of his talent for eloquence. Williams hasn't as yet tried his substantial gift for visual eloquence. Buried in the stage directions of his plays are many startling visual images which lead me to think that if he were ever to write directly and seriously for films, he could develop into a great dramatic film poet. Unfortunately for film directors who might work with him, his main interest is still the drama — and perhaps it should be. Williams is certainly our best playwright at the moment, but, if you ask me, he has a unique talent for films. Part of it can be seen in *Baby Doll*, but only part of it. I hope some day to intrigue him into more work in motion pictures.

Q : *What was the most challenging aspect of directing* Baby Doll?

A : Everything about *Baby Doll* was challenging to me. One thing, of course, was trying to make my work and the work of the actors fit into the violent, colorful, tragicomic setting of a Mississippi Delta small town. I hope we have succeeded in part. I love the South and its people. I'm terribly moved by their problems and their attempts to meet them. Under an

onionskin-thin surface is a titanic violence: That is drama. I don't think
Northern people, especially Northern intellectuals, know much about it. I
didn't until I went to the South and lived there. Now I hope I did justice to
it, both in what I had to say that was good and what I had to say that was
critical. I tried to "capture" the South in the microcosm that is this film. I
know I only got a bit of it, but it was a great challenge to try to get this bit
and to try to get it accurately and fairly. I believe the chief obligation of
films and any other art is to convey honestly the impression upon an artist
of his environment.

Q : *What was the most difficult problem?*
A : Everything about making a picture is difficult. If you try hard, nothing
is easy.

Q : *What was the most satisfying aspect of directing* Baby Doll?
A : One of the most satisfying things was working with eager, fresh and
really talented actors like Karl Malden, Carroll Baker, Eli Wallach and
Millie Dunnock, and in trying to make them one with the community of
people within which they worked. We were met in the Delta at first with
considerable distrust and suspicion. I think we learned a lot. I don't believe
we compromised our viewpoints. Both the company and the people of the
community were better at the end of making the picture for having known
each other.

Q : *Do you feel that certain actors have special qualities which make them ideal
for portraying Williams' characters—in this case Karl Malden, Eli Wallach and
Mildred Dunnock, all of whom you have directed in Williams' plays?*
A : Yes, I do. It is the talent for tragicomedy. It is the ability to capture
inner contradictions. It is an appreciation that nobility and foolishness
can come one on top of the other, and that this coincidence and juxtapo-
sition may be close to the essence of human character. You will see better
what I mean when you see *Baby Doll*.

Q : *Stage actors seem to predominate in the leading parts of the films you direct.
Why?*
A : I like them. But I think the difference between stage and screen actors
is narrowing a great deal. Tony Quinn, for example, is a magnificent screen

actor and a magnificent stage actor. The same can be said of Marlon Brando, Karl Malden, Eli Wallach and a host of others. Actually one has to act "truer," if anything, on the screen. A camera is that close: It is, in fact, a sort of microscope. False acting, stagy acting, shows up much more painfully in motion pictures. Of course, stagy acting is terrible on stage, too. There is a distinction to be drawn between the stagy and what's known as "big" acting. Shakespeare need not be acted in a flamboyant, artificial manner. Fullness is a more apt description.

Q: *Do you prefer to shoot on location, as you did in* On the Waterfront, *and in the case of* Baby Doll *on a Mississippi plantation?*
A: Of course. Much. Some of the greatest experiences of my life have come during work on a location. I have worked on the Mexican border and on the Czechoslovakian border. I have worked in New Orleans and northern California. I have worked in Hoboken and in the mountains of Tennessee. I remember each location as a rich experience, an experience that was an education in who lives in this country and what they are like. I have always felt terribly patriotic on leaving a location. America is a vast undiscovered country, full of themes, full of stories, full of drama. Our films haven't begun to touch what's here. Only a few stage writers really try to write about it. One of the penalties of success in our work is that one gets to know Romanoff's, Sardi's, Downey's, the MCA and William Morris offices, and all that, but one quickly loses contact with the real sources of inspiration for good work.

Q: *What are your future plans, and do they include directing on the stage?*
A: Of course, I am eager to get good plays to direct. I love to work on the stage. I have a deep interest in the Actors Studio and its work, but our stage today is essentially the playwright's medium. A fellow like myself can only sit and wait and hope that a good play will be offered to him. In the movies I work differently. I try, in collaboration with good authors, to create motion-picture scripts. I am a film maker, not merely a director. I'm a self-starter, so to speak.

Q: *How has your training for the stage and your work as a stage director helped you as a screen director?*

A :   Well, it has helped in the handling of actors. But when I began to work in films, I had to learn an entirely different craft — that of the film maker. Actually, despite the ten pictures I have done, I'm just beginning to direct like a screen director. There is an awful lot I still have to learn. The two mediums are very different, and they should be. In each, the vocabulary of expression is almost opposite. I think I have learned something from films for the stage, too. I try to be more theatrelike, even more theatric, in directing for the stage.

Gadg!

FREDERIC MORTON/1957

IN THE MOVIE INDUSTRY which is, according to the latest contract, fabulous for exactly forty-four hours a week, heroes arrive by special
delivery, like publicity releases, and die of dropsy of the option. But every
ten years a lasting legend emerges. One of these is a man whose name
evokes beauty and box-office blooming as a twin boutonniere from the
brutality of a leather jacket: Elia Kazan.

Early last year I went to visit him at work. The master's magic was
coming to pass on Avenue M near 14th Street in deepest, most domestic
Brooklyn. The building looked like a staid cross between a hospital and a
barracks, not like the Warner Brothers' East Coast studios. The hand-lettered
sign on the door, Newtown Productions, Inc., promised some bourgeois
textile activity instead of the independent company of a famous movie
maker now completing an Oscar candidate called *Baby Doll*.

But the moment I entered, I recognized glamour by the fact that it was
policed. I had to pass a number of vaultlike doors hung with posters that
hissed *Silence!* and manned by policemen who emanated as forbidding an
air as is compatible with absorption in the *Daily Mirror*.

When I finally reached the inner sanctum of the sound stage, all was
gaiety and chaos. Dozens of spotlights focused on a mildewed attic that
had been erected in the middle of the set. A window, complete with shutters,
hung surrealistically in the air, and a member of the camera crew maneu-
vered it against a baby spot, shouting for better shadows. Carpenters

hammered, electricians strung cables, a girl in a pink slip gestured to herself, a booted bravo whom I recognized as Eli Wallach murmured lines at his whip, pigeons whirred through the air and stagehands swung through the high scaffoldings to wave huge nets after the birds and trap them with triumphant howls.

The attic was a replica of the one in Benoit, Mississippi, where the bulk of the picture had been shot. The Tennessee Williams script (derived from, but no longer resembling, his short play, *27 Wagons Full of Cotton*) had Karl Malden, a middle-aged cotton-gin operator, living in the town with Carroll Baker (the pink-slipped, muttering girl) as his wife, twenty-five years his junior. Eli Wallach not only romances Baby Doll, but also sets up a new-fangled cotton gin which puts Malden out of business. Malden, in turn, burns down Wallach's gin. The scene now to be shot (the script girl explained to me) was to show how Wallach chases Baby Doll through the crumbling attic and forces her to sign a confession of her husband's arson.

Just then a man darted out from under the roof trestles. He wore Brooks Brothers pants and a Stillman's Gym sweater. He was small, but his hammer-brandishing hand was sized and muscled to fit a stevedore twice his weight. His hair was black Mediterranean thistle, and his stubble had the look of belonging, as though it had often flourished on that hard jawline before. He could easily have been tagged as a tough Sicilian fight manager. And yet the way he dropped the hammer and accepted a saw, the way he stood pensively sovereign for a moment amidst the steady bustle before vanishing again—all that suggested swarthy and informal royalty, a slightly shaven hobo of a Haile Selassie.

He lacked all the panoply of directorhood, from black beret to bossy bark. Yet this was Elia Kazan, called Gadg by friends or candidate-friends, Pasha by Sir Laurence Olivier, and Elia by nobody; owner of two Hollywood Oscars and director of plays which were awarded three New York Drama Critics' Circle awards; catalyst to fame for Arthur Miller, Tennessee Williams, Marlon Brando, James Dean, Jack Palance, Eva Marie Saint; top dog, in terms of money magnetism and critical esteem, on Shubert Alley as well as in Beverly Hills. The average show-business genius needs a lifetime to reach any of these eminences. This Turkish-born son of a rug manufacturer breezed past them all before leaving his middle forties. But a man's personality isn't as accessible as his statistics. What was the connection between the rumpled figure and the marquee magnificence? And why did the sorcerer perform in a sweat shirt? To escape the sterile glitter of the summit—the "catastrophe of success," as Tennessee Williams has styled it? Or only to establish a useful professional façade, a deliberate and lucrative trade-mark? I would watch and I would wait—first of all for him to crawl out again.

Which, a moment later, he did. He went to the girl in the pink slip and put his arm around her confidingly, like a sorority friend. "We just notched this attic beam a little more for you," he said, "so the whole thing is going to give a little more when Eli gets mad. You're not going to fall through, honey." He kicked the solid but invisible floor beneath the "attic" surface. "But it's gonna give you a better feel of falling."

Carroll stretched herself trembling along one of the few solid beams visible and clung to it.

"You poor darling," Kazan said, and with a playful stroke brushed a bit of her hair into her face.

"I can't see, Gadg," Carroll cried.

"That's why I said you're poor." He laughed, and suddenly shouted hoarsely at the stagehands, "All de boids caught?"

"Yes, Gadg."

"Ready to make with the dust, Logan?"

"Ready," said a stand-in with a bowl of dust.

"Lock it up, fellas," Kazan said, throwing a piece of wood up into the air and catching it.

"Lock it up!" yelled Charlie Maguire, the first assistant director, and the red light flashed on over all the doors.

"Give us three bells, huh?" Kazan said.

"Three bells!" shouted Artie Steckler, second assistant director.

A buzzer sounded three times. The hammering ceased, the talking died, even the faint clicking of the typewriter from the office upstairs stopped like an abruptly broken watch. Everybody froze into silence and immobility. Only the sweat-shirted little man who now stood next to the camera was alive. The entire building, with its high-powered personnel and fantastic illusion-making machinery, was in the palm of his hand.

"Action," Kazan shouted, and opened his arms wide, winglike [three stagehands released nine pigeons], and then made like a pitcher [the stand-in started to throw dust against the attic roof]. And, amidst a flutter of

wings and rustle of particles and a moaning and sighing from the prostrate, blinded Miss Baker, Wallach, standing a few feet away from his
victim, began to stamp and earthquake the old attic and to demand that
she sign the statement. He tacked a piece of paper onto a nail at the end of
a pole, attached a pencil to it, and reached it over toward the girl.

All the while, Kazan repeated in soundless pantomine Wallach's snarls
and stomps, Carroll's squirmings and jerks. With finger motions he directed
the stagehands shaking the "attic" springs. He nodded to the sound man,
who moved the mike boom suspended above the action. He encouraged or
soft-pedaled the dust thrower. He was a demon in constant joyful contor-
tion, the very gremlin soul of make-believe.

Carroll meanwhile had signed the paper. Wallach retrieved it, kissed
it exultantly. Then suddenly the scene became less fierce, more tender.
Wallach took a long look at the girl; the dust drizzled down like gentle
rain; Kazan's lips moved in a sweet, slow, silent rhythm. Even the pigeons
flew about languidly, as though they were bona fide Actors' Studio members improvising wistfulness. Wallach tacked a clean handkerchief to the
pole, reached it to Carroll with a gallant gesture. She hesitated, gave a ghost
of a smile, took it and dabbed her eyes with it.

"Cut," said Kazan. He suddenly threw himself down headlong on an
attic beam parallel to Carroll's. "Baby Doll," he said as one prostrate person to another (he even pushed some of *his* hair into his eyes), "Baby Doll,
when he reaches you that handkerchief, it's like something very nice but
unexpected. It's like something out of your childhood, something beautiful and unexpected like an Easter egg you suddenly found. Even touch it
like an Easter egg—careful, so you won't break it, see?"

He stroked her cheek, then jumped up and called to Wallach in a rough
man-to-man voice, "Eli, you old bastard, let's do it like you kiss that piece
of paper not because you're grateful to her, but because that signature of
hers is gonna break her husband. That kiss means 'Now I got him by the
testicles!' And do some business that shows it."

"Some business?" Wallach asked.

"Yeah, you'll figure out something," Kazan said with a confident shrug.

Wallach kissed an imaginary piece of paper with a gloating growl that
came up from his guts, and then spat.

"Great!" Kazan said with jubilation. "Roll it!"

The scene was shot again. This time Wallach spat (and Kazan spat sound-lessly with him) and Carroll took the handkerchief with marveling wonder while Kazan's hands cupped tenderly to form an Easter egg.

"Cut!" Kazan said, and instantly began to throw tiny pieces of mortar at Wallach's feet. "I want to annoy you, Eli boy. I want to get you mad. Come on everybody, that first shot again!" He grinned and continued to throw bits in Wallach's direction. "I'm gonna bombard the hell out of you until you show us you're really fighting crazy for that signature. I'm gonna stone you. . . . Action!"

He kept up his fierce throwing motions while his leading man went through the attic-stamping part of the scene again, but more intensely now under the waggish volleys. "Cut!" Kazan shouted. "Perfect! Print 3 and 4. Lunch!"

"He's got a knack for making a fascinating game of it all," Karl Malden said over a shrimp salad five minutes later. "You forget it's a big business, a tough business." He lowered his voice a bit. "I'll give you a for instance: He's way above budget on *Baby Doll*. It's his own outfit; it's his own finances that are involved. Thousands of extra bucks a day. But it doesn't cramp his style at all. You'd never know it."

"He's a good actor," another company member said, slow and hard. "He puts up a good show, all right."

"Listen," Malden said, "if being a grand guy were all there is to him, he'd still be an assistant stage manager. Sure, he's shrewd and subtle. I'll give you a for instance. In *Streetcar* I played Mitch, the guy who gets sort of sweet on Blanche du Bois. At one point she asks him, 'Do you love your mother?' I'm a Mama's boy, of course, so I say 'Yes, very much.'

"Now, the first week of rehearsal I couldn't do anything with that, it was a nothing line. And one day I'm going through it again when I look up and see Gadg pull the most terrible teeth-gnashing face. I said, "What's the matter?' And he said, 'Did you watch me? That's how you should feel when you say that line. Because you hate your bloody mother. Sure, you have to say you love her—you even have to think you do. But deep inside you know she's got a double nelson on all your emotions and she's the rea-son why you can't develop and mature.'

"As soon as I understood that, I'd licked not only the line, but the whole character. He didn't bawl me out like a great big director because my approach was wrong. He just pulled a funny face like a buddy with a sense of humor giving me a tip."

"I suppose he's been a buddy to Carroll by wearing her to a frazzle," the other company member said.

"What do you mean?" I asked.

"He's been notching those attic beams a little more with each take. The girl's been getting hysterical, she's so afraid of falling."

"It's a pretty intense scene," Malden said.

"He doesn't have to squeeze the intensity out of her by torturing her," the other company member said. "Did you get how he pushed the hair into her face?"

"Take it from an old pro," Malden said, "she'll have forgotten the physical discomfort long before the picture is released and she finds herself a star. In *Waterfront* I really got belted as the priest. I don't remember my black-and-blue marks. I remember my Oscar nomination. And I'd rather a director inflicts physical discomfort on you than indignity. With Gadg you can be sure indignity won't happen. Did he ever let Carroll know that she's a newcomer? No, he only let her know that she has loads of talent, which she does. The same with me. Before other directors I say to myself, 'I'm a professional. I've got to watch out for my reputation.' With Gadg I don't mind falling on my face. He'll just say, 'Okay, let's try it different.' With him I take chances."

"That's how he gets more out of you," the other company member said.

"Time!" Artie Steckler shouted from the next table.

We went back to the studio. The attic lay deserted. Camera crew and stagehands now populated a set representing the worn, greasy interior of a Mississippi café. "He's rehearsing the farmers," Malden told me.

The farmers, I found out, were Mississippi planters who had been flown up from the Delta country the day before. Until *Baby Doll* they had never acted in their lives. Kazan had come across them on location, liked their looks and made actors of them overnight.

"How?" I wondered.

"Watch," Malden said.

The four of them sat around a café table, and Kazan sat on top of it, legs dangling. "Jeez, fellas," he said, patting his stomach, "they sure can't make pizzas no more in New York."

Apparently he had been to lunch with them to warm them up. He did not condescendingly imitate their speech. He talked as if he had been raising Delta tobacco all his life.

"Now, this here thing is just gonna be a run-through, fellas, just to see how the damn thing works out on the set. You-all know your lines, and anyway we'll start worryin' 'bout that tomorrow when we shoot it. Now just get the feel of it. Charlie-boy, you go to the door and stay there a-leanin'. The rest of you stick. Ease back into the chair a little more, Eades—you're the sheriff. Now, when he comes in—" Kazan called out loud in his Eastern voice, "Eli!" and Eli Wallach entered. "Now, when this interloper comes tryin' to stir up a fuss just 'cause his cotton gin's burnin'—why, you set back and smile and give him nothin'. Go ahead."

Wallach came up to the "café patrons," demanded justice, was blandly refused, went up to "Charlie-boy," became more incensed, stalked out.

Kazan straddled his legs across a chair. "We'll go at it again. Now, when he comes at you-all, you know what you're thinkin'. You're thinkin', 'Why, that little outsider bastard! Speculatin' there's somethin' wrong with the Delta police force! Now, ain't that mighty cheeky!' Go ahead—No, wait, hold it a spell." He went up to Charlie-boy at the door. "Charlie-boy, somethin' botherin' you?"

"Well...." Charlie-boy said.

"Somethin' bothers you when Eli says, 'Everybody's so happy it's like a rich man's funeral.' Right?"

"Well," Charlie-boy said, "he's holdin' my jaw while he's sayin' it."

"You just keep grinnin', Charlie-boy. You grin right through him."

"But I feel like doin' somethin'."

"That's the boy; always tell me what you feel like doin'!"

"Push his hand down," Charlie-boy said.

"Sure," Kazan said. "Push his hand down. Good idea. But keep grinnin'." He turned to the script girl, resumed his Eastern voice. "Charlie-boy pushes Eli's hand down. Put that in, Bobby."

"We are ready for the singing scene," Boris Kaufman, the cinematographer, said.

"Great," Kazan said. "Let's watch Jennie sing."

We all walked to the other side of the "café," where the spotlights, huge black cuckalorises (shadow-throwers) and mike boom bore down on a tiny colored woman.

"Jennie!" Kazan said, and took both her hands in both of his. "We're goin' to have some fun now."

"Yessir," Jennie said.

"Hey, Jimmy, Bob—" Kazan shouted at the light crew and shielded his eyes against the glare. "How about taking it down a couple of points? I wanna go easy on Jennie." He turned to Kaufman. "Think we'll still have enough definition?"

The two began to work with light meters and camera finders. Meanwhile I asked Jennie how she had gotten into the movies.

"Mr. Gadg," she said, "he have dinner at Mr. Charlie's, yessir." Every statement came complete with yessir and careful smile.

"You mean Charlie-boy over there," I said.

"Yessir, I'm his cook," she said. "And Mr. Gadg, he hear me sing."

I asked her if she had ever been in New York before.

"Never been away from the kitchen more'n a day," she said. "Yessir."

Kazan came over. "Jennie-girl," he said, "remember, just like the rehearsal. When I say, 'Action!' he—" Kazan pointed to the "sheriff"— "he's gonna say, 'Come on, Jennie, sing us a song.' Go on, say it, sheriff." The sheriff said it. Kazan continued, "And then you're gonna give him the pizza—that's right, like that. And then—No, you're not goin' to look down, you're gonna look straight at Mr. Charlie. I'm settin' him on the camera stool for you, and then you're goin' to sing your song with all you've got. Okay?"

"Yessir," Jennie said.

"Fine," Kazan said. "Let's lock it up."

"Lock it up!" Charlie Maguire yelled.

"Three bells!" Artie Steckler shouted. The buzzer sounded three times. The world fell silent.

"Roll it," Kazan said.

"Scene 35, take 1," the second assistant camera said.

"Smoke it up!" Kazan hissed, and everybody—stagehands, prop men, actors—blew cigarette smoke around Jennie to give the scene a café haze.

"Jennie!" Kazan whispered, and held his clasped hands above his head in encouragement. Jennie took the pizza from the kitchen man.

The sheriff said, "Come on, Jennie, sing us a song."

Jennie put down the pizza and sang her song.

Kazan put his forefinger over his eyebrow and waited till the song was finished before saying, "Cut." He came to Jennie, put his arm around her, "Jennie, you ain't singin' the way you did down in Benoit. You got only half of yourself in that song. You're among friends, Jennie. There's your Mr. Charlie right here. Don't look down, look at him."

"Yessir," Jennie said.

Once more the scene was shot. Once more Kazan put his arm around her. "We're gettin' closer, Jennie. Gettin' more used to the lights. But we haven't got it yet. This time we'll do it, honey, right?"

"Yessir," Jennie said.

This time Jennie had barely finished the first five bars when he yelled, "Cut!" He went to Charlie-boy, took him behind the set, came back alone. Then he led Jennie to her chair again. She sat down and he knelt in front of her and, as before, put both her little hands into his.

"Jennie," he said, "listen. Mr. Charlie went down for a pack of cigarettes. I'm gonna sit where he used to sit. And you're gonna sing that song for me. I'm not your boss. I'm your friend, and I need you. I wanna make a good movie, and I just can't do it without you. When you sing that song, think of that. And think of all the poor friends you have. Some are sick, some are sinners, some are just plain in trouble 'cause things ain't always so easy for your folks down where you live. So sing for them. The song's for them, and a little bit the song's for me too. So don't look down when you sing it. Look at me. It's such a beautiful song."

"Yes, Mr. Gadg," Jennie said. For the first time I saw her lips move.

"Action!" Kazan said, sitting on the camera stool.

Jennie received her cue, put down the pizza, and all of a sudden she lifted her head, and her pretty, slightly wizened face inclined toward Kazan and gleamed alive. Her voice was small and flat, but it rang out unafraid. She began to make small emphatic gestures with her hands— probably the kind she'd been taught in the church choir—and her voice swelled and encompassed all the formidable apparatus around her and all the high-powered people, the least of whom earned more in four days than she could in six months. Her small voice queened it over all of them, and I saw a watchman at the farthest door drop his newspaper and listen.

"Cut!" Kazan shouted when the last notes died away and, as even the stagehands applauded, he ran up and kissed her.

The following night the whole company moved to Long Island in order to shoot the exterior of the Delta Café. The real-life café down South had been so excited by the prospect of their property's celluloid canonization, I was told, that they had redecorated themselves out of the background-for-Tennessee-Williams-movies business. Dick Sylbert, the art director for *Baby Doll,* had to comb the metropolitan area for two days until he found a café with a Mason-Dixon chimney and suitably shabby slat walls—in Floral Park, near the New York City line.

When I arrived around midnight, the generators on the company trucks were humming; the huge spotlights beat down on the carpenters finishing the false door, on the false neon sign, and on the extras rehearsing for their street-fight scene with Eli Wallach. All around, the sleep-roused citizenry of Floral Park pressed against police ropes and rubbed eyes at the wizards' invasion. I went into the café. Kazan was playing the pinball machine, with grave concentration. Then he shouldered his way out. He made straight for Charlie Maguire and said something to him. At a gesture from Maguire, the extras disappeared.

"The hell with the fight," Kazan said. "Bobby, change the script. There's just going to be Eli coming out of the café, like this." He acted it out. "And finding Lonnie [Lonnie Chapman, Wallach's side-kick in the picture] beaten up. And leading him away like this. And we won't even show all of that. We'll have a lot of people rushing out the door, a lot of shoulders and heads blocking the camera. A lot of pressure and intensity. Like this. The hell with another silly movie fight."

And, "like this," he began to orchestrate extras and actors. At one in the morning, the company was finished.

At eleven in the morning, I was sitting at Burl Ives's bedside, discussing the improvisation. Ives was perfectly healthy, but thought it indecent to be out of bed at so early an hour.

"Improvisation," he said, "that's the boy's specialty. I'll tell you about a hell of an improvisation in *East of Eden.* I was the sheriff in the picture, and at one point I had to stop a mob from lynching a German. So we were setting up the scene, with me coming in, gun drawn, when all of a sudden Gadg says, 'Goddam! Goddam! I hate to have you come in with that equalizer sticking out, acting Lone Ranger tough. This isn't that kind of movie. This mob consists of people who have respect for you. There's something else you ought to do.'

"And then he stops, and he says an amazing thing. He asks me, 'What would your father do in a situation like this?' It stunned me. There was no reason to drag my father into it. The only way I can explain it is that Gadg must have read my autobiography, where I kept writing about my father without knowing that I did. Anyway, he asks me, 'What would your father do?' And I told him that he would have said, 'I think that'll do.' And Gadg said, 'Put it into the script.' And that's how it worked. I come in while they're brawling on the German's lawn, and I say, 'Hello, Mr. Smith, Mr. Jones. I think that'll do.' Quietly. It stops the riot. It's one of the most effective scenes."

When I visited the set next morning, the press had been admitted, and the air was festive with solid ties from the *Times,* brisk bow ties from *Time,* and suavely cynical pipe smoke from *The New Yorker.* Kazan nibbled a popsicle while Mildred Dunnock was on camera, and I abducted Carroll Baker for a drugstore sundae. The place was awash with teen-agers, and nobody gave her a tumble. "Several months from now that won't be possible any more," I said.

"I know," she said. "I don't want to think about it."

"How did it all happen?" I asked.

"I don't know," she said. "Gadg is so weird that way. I still have no idea how he picked me. He saw me in one little part in *Giant* and in a featured role in *All Summer Long,* which was a Broadway flop. And I ran into him once when I took Lee Strasberg's private classes. Then one day he asked Jack [Carroll's husband, Jack Garfein, now directing Ben Gazzara in Sam Spiegel's film, *End as a Man*] if I could act. Jack said, 'You'll have to find out for yourself.' The next week he calls me and says he has a part in mind for me and why don't I come to his office. I do, and he tells me he's seen me in a kind of sophisticated part in *Giant.* Could I do a naïve girl with my hair all mussed up? I said, 'Sure.' He said, 'Good.' He gave me the script. After a few days he calls me and asks if I've read it and if I want to come talk about it.

"I come up, and he asks me, 'What kind of girl is Baby Doll? Talk to me as if she were a girl friend of yours.' Well, I'd developed all sorts of ideas about her, and I discussed them. Then he became a little more specific. He said, 'Does Baby Doll respond to Vacarro [Eli Wallach] just physically or does she have real feeling for him?' And I said, 'She's all mixed up, but she does have a real feeling for him.' He said, 'Wonderful.' And only then did

Mile End Library

Self Payment 18/02/2012 22:58

XXXXXX4988

Amount Outstanding £0.00

Amount Paid £9.50

Part 17 (06a) Pay Library Lft £0.62

PLEASE NOTE
If you still have overdue books on loan
you may have more fines to pay

it come home to me. I said, 'You mean I'm in?' And Gadg said, 'Sure.' It was just absolutely incredible. I mean, I had read for four months for the small part in *All Summer Long*. And here was Gadg starting the first movie of his company, with hundreds of thousands of dollars of his own money involved, and putting me into the title role! Staking all that on someone without a screen test, without an audition, without me even reading one line for him . . . I was dazed."

On the wings of Miss Baker's amazement we returned to the studio. The final scene (in the shooting schedule, not in story continuity) was filmed. Baby Doll accompanied her husband on a medical check-up that ended in comic confusion. There was mounting comedy on the set, but no confusion. Kazan produced a monumental cigar and barked guttural commands: "Aaakkktion!" or "Rrrroll it!" in imitation of a German movie director. Malden, cued to stick his head out of the doctor's office, stuck out a skeleton instead. The crew kept erupting into muffled guffaws.

"Charlie," said Kazan, "tell the gang to pipe down or at least tell clean stories. The dirty ones are too copulating distracting."

More guffaws—and an even more successful take of the doctor scene.

"There's nothing he doesn't exploit." The low voice came from the cross-grained company member. "He left that merry sequence to the end so he can use the end-excitement to milk every drop out of the scene. That animal trainer! Uses their emotions like they were animals. He plays democracy with them like a trainer puts his head into the tiger's mouth—for the good of the show. It's all calculated. He lets them pat him on the back—and each time they do, they're working for him."

At the moment, though, Kazan looked more like a conductor than a trainer. With his baton-length cigar he slashed the air in a Toscanini caricature, then pointed it straight at the "doctor," who had just gone through the scene with his shirt half unbuttoned.

"I'm gonna stop shooting, John, because your cleavage is showing. Wild track!"

Then they sat down on adjoining stools—Wallach, the whip-bristling brute, and Kazan, his longshoremanlike director—and mooned and moaned at each other with a sweetness Juliet might have envied. Carroll explained to me that this was a "wild track"—the sighs would be woven into the finished sound track of the picture.

"Ohhh," trebled Wallach.

"Uuuuh," trebled Kazan. "Give me an 'Uuuuh....'"

"Ouhhh," said Wallach. They had to stop because everybody roared.

"Uuuuh," from Kazan. "Ah, mine was perfect." He laughed and slapped his knees with childlike glee. "Print mine." He rose. "Yeah," he said. "That's it. Wrap up the picture."

The shooting phase of *Baby Doll,* which had kept cast and crew working together daily for three and a half months, had ended.

A great shout went up. Everybody rushed for the drinks table. Everybody took snapshots of everybody else. Next they all made for the director. Kazan took them on one by one. And then a pixilated posse of the crew swept him up out of the studio, into Izzi's bar across the street. There he drank, yarned, reminisced, laughed and rib-poked for an hour. He was a little smaller, stubblier and more muscular than the rest of them, but you couldn't tell him apart in language or deportment until they took the Sea Beach subway express and he clapped his chauffeur on the shoulder and climbed into the Cadillac limousine. When he slumped down next to me, he looked his forty-six years for the first time (he's forty-seven now).

"Not really tired," he said. "Sad, I guess, to see the boys scatter. And wondering, as I always do when I finish shooting and all that press-and-publicity muck is over, whether it's all been worth while, whether I've got at least a handful of truth in half a mile of film. Because there isn't only the press muck you've got to fight off. There's the technical muck, the filters and light meters and cameras and spotlights. While all that matters is the actor. That little human thing you want to get at—that little moisture in the girl's eye, the way she lifts her hand, or the funny kind of laugh she's got in her throat—that's what matters. And you never know how much of that you've caught until you see it. Sometimes you don't even know then."

He had lost the folksy authority he maintained on the sound stage. He spoke in a small dreamy voice.

"Did you notice the fellow who played the doctor? He's no actor. He's a lawyer, John Dudley. I don't care what they are, little colored cooks, big-time real-estate lawyers like John, or a kid like Carroll. If they've got something—the shine and shiver of life, you could call it, a certain wildness, a genuineness—I grab them. That's precious. That's gold to me. I've always been crazy for life. As a young kid I wanted to live as much of it as possible, and now I want to show it—the smell of it, the sound of it, the leap of it. 'Poetic realism,' I call it when I'm in an egghead mood. Like the doctor's scene we shot. I didn't want just another consultation-room scene. I had the doctor play checkers—not even play it, but just have a lost game set up on his examination couch and brood over it. Because that's the way an office is down South—people just waiting, outlasting the heat, looking out across the street and watching the saloon door swing in and out. I wanted to get all the Delta air I could into that little scene in the consultation room." He sat up. We were stopping before the Astor Building, where his office was. "Hell, I must be tired," he said, "running off at the mouth like that. Give me a ring in a couple of weeks. I'll show you my favorite place. A better place for talking than this—" He pointed at the bright caldron of Broadway which, a moment later, swallowed him up.

His name, though, gleamed from the marquees through day and night. The following week its mention roused Deborah Kerr from a ladylike repose in her hotel suite.

"Gadg?" she said. "The next thing to God. He's an angel to his actors. No rank-pulling, you know, no ridicule—and ridicule is our deepest fear. He's quite a bit of a psychologist too. D'you remember the final scene in *Tea and Sympathy*? I'm beginning to unbutton my blouse to commit heroic adultery and show the boy he's really a man? Well, it's a pretty delicate business—the thing I was most afraid of in the show. We were all astonished when Gadg didn't even talk about it the first weeks of rehearsal. But after a while we forgot about it because we were so busy with the rest of the play.

"When we finally came to the end, he said, 'Go ahead. You're inside your characters. You know what to do.' So we did it, just by obeying what was inside us, John Kerr and I. Without direction. And Gadg said, 'Fine. That's the way it will stay.'

"You see, Gadg made me realize that in some ways my role was literally me. I don't go around saving young men all day, as the heroine does in the play, but I'm full of compassion for stray dogs, lost cats and lame pigeons, and I didn't even know it until Gadg told me so.

"I didn't even know that I could handle an American part. In *From Here to Eternity* I played an American wife, but in a film you can always dub out a Mayfair syllable and dub in a Minnesota twang. You can't cheat in a play.

But all Gadg said about my accent was, 'Oh, that. Forget it.' He's got an attitude of taking you by the hand, and leading you inward to yourself, into what's important for the play and for you."

Kazan's genius has been something of a time bomb. It was around for a considerable time before it went off. Constantinople-born, of a Greek family that has been living on and off rugs for generations, he arrived in this country before reaching school age. After graduating *cum laude* from Williams in 1930, and after a term at the Yale drama workshop, he drifted through seven unspectacular years with the Group Theater, stage-managing and walking-on.

In the late Thirties and early Forties he began to act with sting and success, notably the taxi driver in *Waiting for Lefty* and Fuseli in *Golden Boy*—both plays by Clifford Odets. But all that ended when he directed Thornton Wilder's *The Skin of Our Teeth*, the Broadway miracle of 1942. He had become a big-timer. Yet the plays he staged immediately afterward were still not the kind one associates with his name today: musicals like *One Touch of Venus*, comedies like *Jacobowsky and the Colonel*.

Enter 1947. Kazan directed *All My Sons* and *A Streetcar Named Desire* in New York, filmed *Boomerang* and *Gentleman's Agreement* in Hollywood. In that year the bomb exploded. Elia Kazan became Elia Kazan. He not only displayed a stunning ambidextrousness by gathering for this year's production an Oscar on the West Coast and, simultaneously, a Best Broadway Director award in the East; his work also defined the qualities that have become his singular imprint—the shattering, clawlike fierceness of his stagecraft, the fine translation of social texture, his hard-muscled and yet lyrically susceptible realism.

From then on nearly every production in his charge left behind the impact that was his signature. *Death of a Salesman* arrived on Broadway in 1949, *Camino Real* in 1953, *Tea and Sympathy* in 1953, *Cat on a Hot Tin Roof* in 1955. He put *Streetcar* on film in 1950, *On the Waterfront* in 1954, *East of Eden* in 1955 and, finally, *Baby Doll* in 1956.

When I visited him some three weeks after our limousine ride, his office had already been turned into a preparation mill for his next picture, *A Face In The Crowd*, based on a Budd Schulberg short story. I asked him if this was the "favorite" place he had mentioned earlier, and he said, "Hell, no. I'll take you to it."

Ten minutes later a taxi had brought us to his remodeled brownstone house in the East Seventies. There he vanished, typically supersonic, while his handsome wife Molly showed me through three floors.

We passed the master's study on the top floor, featuring a huge drafting table, a big bulletin board, even bigger pictures of Kazan's grandparents, and no Oscars.

"The real, get-away-from-it-all work he does in Newtown." Mrs. Kazan pointed to a picture of their 113-acre Connecticut farm.

On the way down we encountered Nick, aged ten, and Katy, eight. The big two (Judy, twenty, and Chris, seventeen) were away at school.

Just then the summons of the paterfamilias filled the house.

I found him in a darkroom in the basement. "I got a photographer buddy, Roy Schatt," he said. "I built the whole damn room with him. He's teaching me photography, printing, fixing, enlarging, the works."

By this time my eyes had gotten used to the red light. Kazan was bustling about like a boyish poltergeist. Sometimes the dark bulb caught in his face an exuberance I had never noticed before.

"Look at my mother's picture!" he said. "Last time I printed it, I couldn't realize that wonderful arm of hers because the background was too white. Now look! I just shaded the enlarger image a bit. See all the values that come out?"

"Call from Mr. Lastfogel," the maid said from outside. (Mr. Lastfogel is the president of the William Morris Agency.)

"I'll call him back later," Kazan shouted, and said to me, "Still wondering what my favorite place is?" he asked.

His voice had suddenly become lower. It had the limousine tone again, soft and visionary. "There's nothing like a darkroom. It's so pure. No lawyers, no agents, no production managers, no telephones. Just you and your work. Funny, when I'm all alone down here, I find I haven't even started to do what I want. I want to do more movies than ever. In the theatre the director just serves the author. But a movie director can create. The camera is such a beautiful instrument. It paints with motion. Why, this whole country is still undiscovered in terms of the motion picture. Take the South. I could make five more pictures on it. Not the intellectuals' South. Not the Sardi liberals' South. But the South where the Negroes sit in the street all day long —"

"Call from the MCA conference room," the maid said from the outside. (MCA is entertainment's other giant agency.)

"I'll call back later," Kazan said in the darkness. "Hell, I'm just beginning to loosen up, with all my Oscars. I've alternated violence and tenderness for too long. I'm beginning to break out of my own formula—as in *Baby Doll*. I used to sit down and work out things in advance. Now I shoot more as I go along. I shoot as I feel. In the old days I had no confidence. Determination, sure—the determination kid, that was me. But I used to wait, to look for the good things to come to me, good jobs and good contracts. Now I'm beginning to *reach* for things. I'm coming to writers with ideas. I wish I were a writer so I could start at the rock bottom of creativity. I want to do a picture about immigration which has never really been done before. I want to do a picture on my people, the Greeks. I'm getting impatient. Maybe because I've got more confidence, maybe because there's less time every day—"

"Long distance from the West Coast," the maid said from outside.

He turned on the light. He sighed and blinked for a moment, like a little boy flushed from his hide-out. The next instant he was composed. With powerful steps he bounded past me and up the stairs.

"Well—darling," he said into the receiver.

Candid Conversation: Elia Kazan

SHOW BUSINESS ILLUSTRATED/1962

ANY HISTORIAN EXPLORING THE contemporary world
of drama would have to devote a whopping slice of space to Elia
Kazan. Originally an actor (one of the mainstays of the Group
Theatre), he turned to direction, co-founded the Actors Studio,
and sparked his first critical hosannas staging Thornton Wilder's
The Skin of Our Teeth. Other critical and box-office hits fired by the
magic Kazan touch: *A Streetcar Named Desire, Cat on a Hot Tin Roof,
Tea and Sympathy, JB* and *Sweet Bird of Youth*. His success as a motion
picture director has been no less significant, winning him acclaim
for, among others, *Baby Doll* and *On the Waterfront*. In this *Candid
Conversation* about the world he has dominated and served for 30
years, Elia Kazan is articulate, passionate and outspoken about
everything from Marlon Brando's mumbling to the plans for the
new Lincoln Center for the Performing Arts in New York City.

SBI: *There's been a lot of talk about your giving up the commercial Broadway
theater and devoting your time to Lincoln Center. Is that true? Are you really
leaving Broadway?*
ELIA KAZAN: I sure am.

SBI: *What are you going to do at Lincoln Center?*
EK: Well, we're going to do classics that mean something today, that say,
"this thing has something for contemporary people," and we're going to
do, I hope, the best new American plays.

From *Show Business Illustrated*, February 1962.

SBI: *How are you going to compete with Broadway in getting good new plays and good writers?*

EK: Well, we will. I can tell you that.

SBI: *Can you compete financially?*

EK: No, we can't, but we can give them enough so that they can make a good living. And furthermore, we will keep their plays alive, which is one thing that interests them a lot. If we tackle *Death of a Salesman* which we hope to produce at Lincoln Center—it would play not eight months, which is all it played on Broadway, but six months the first year, three or four months the second year, two months the third year. Then it would be revived every four or five years. See, the great thing about the Brecht Theater in East Berlin is that Brecht has a living monument there. Those plays are seen; they're not on a library shelf.

SBI: *Are you going to have a repertory company there?*

EK: Yes. And the repertory company is really going to play repertory. In other words, there will be a group of actors that's a permanent company.

SBI: *Are you going to work with young actors or hire established ones?*

EK: Both. We're going to have, I hope, 20 actors—really good ones. We'll offer Chris Plummer and Gerry Page a place. Whether they take it or not is their business. Karl Malden said he wants to come. I'd like him there and Pat Hingle—actors like that. And then I'm going to have 20 young people. We're going around this country and holding auditions and taking about 20 young people in, and also training another 20 so we'll have 40 young people in training—out of whom will come the people who'll play the leading parts in future plays.

SBI: *You were one of the founders of the Actors Studio—do you still consider it has made an important contribution to the theatre?*

EK: The Actors Studio is a place where actors go to work, where they get their training, where there's an opportunity to try out parts they haven't played before. For example, I would never have cast Gerry Page in *Sweet Bird of Youth* if I hadn't seen her do something at the Studio. She did a scene, I saw it, and I said, "Gee, this girl can do this part."

S B I : *Hadn't you seen her before?*
E K : I'd seen her a lot. But she always played fidgety virgin ladies of 40 . . . you know, fluttery and helpless.

S B I : *There's been a lot of criticism of the Actors Studio and the so-called Method technique it stamps on its students. You know, the scratching, the mumbles and so on. Does that bother you?*
E K : No. Who gives a damn? How could that bother anybody?

S B I : *But doesn't the Studio take itself a little too seriously once in a while?*
E K : We all do. Sometimes those kids over there do, too. We all think we're the only ones that know this or know that, but you grow out of it. A lot of the feeling about the Studio has come from Brando and Dean. Well, Brando hardly ever went there. He was in my class once for a year — that's all — he went about 20 times. And he did some work. He directed a scene once, which started him off on his desire to direct. Dean was there two or three times. He sat in a sort of poutish mess in the front row and scowled . . . you know, active narcissistic and so on. He was never really there. Both those guys mumbled . . . scratched a little. Brando is trying to get out of it, but that doesn't mean that Karl Malden or Gerry Page does it . . . it doesn't mean that Kim Stanley does it. I don't pay attention to all this.

S B I : *What about Marilyn Monroe?*
E K : She never went there in her life. She watched some classes — she never was a member — only did one scene. And I didn't see her.

S B I : *Will this company you're building up at Lincoln Center be in any way an extension of the Actors Studio?*
E K : No, it's another venture entirely. There will be some people from the Studio in it, but the Studio is not organized as a theater. It's organized with 150 people who have a life membership there and go in and do whatever they want; it's a place to work, but it's also a clubhouse, a place where actors meet. It's like Israel is to the Jews. When I was an actor, an actor was homeless, he had nowhere to go. An actor has standing room down at the Studio now. I've gotten him out of that goddamn Walgreen drugstore.

SBI: *What about the caliber of the drama critics today?*

EK: Kerr knows something about the theater. Kerr is a writer and a director—he knows what he's talking about—he's worked in the theater. I wish more of them had.

SBI: *Do you agree with him a good deal of the time?*

EK: I don't think that's the point. I think there's one area where the critics are mistaken—this right and wrong game that I don't give a damn about. I mean...if you were at a cocktail party you wouldn't rush up to some of these critics and say, "What do you think?" You wouldn't give a damn what they thought. There's one real use a critic could have—to make someone in the audience, or in the potential audience, see more in the play or in the motion picture than he would if he hadn't read the criticism. A critic at his best can be a very creative force. I mean, for example, Atkinson did one marvelous thing—he made Off Broadway important. Atkinson got behind certain plays like *All My Sons*. He made it a hit. He put *All My Sons* over by staying behind it. But I think the best of the critics are embarrassed by their power. I thought Atkinson—before he resigned—was embarrassed. He didn't want to have the power of life and death over plays.

SBI: *What about the movies? Are you moving more and more into the motion picture field?*

EK: Yes, I'm trying to write my own now. I've been working with authors like every movie director does. See, a movie director, whether he likes it or not, is part author in the sense that he chooses the images. A movie is a succession of pictures, and he's telling a story through a succession of pictures. Well, as soon as he starts to pick what is told, he is part storyteller. You work extremely carefully on a movie script because once you go on the thing you can't pull back. It's like going into a tunnel—you can't get out of it once you start. It's murder if you're not ready. If you haven't got the script right, you shouldn't start. That's one thing you learn through painful experience. I've worked with every goddamn author—intimately and carefully. In many cases, I transposed their scripts into screenplay form.

SBI: *Haven't you really contributed a great deal to Tennessee Williams' plays?*

EK: No, I really haven't. That's not true. That's all been built up—I've never written a word of one of his plays—I wouldn't fool with him at all.

I've made suggestions to him. What I always do with him is to send him a letter—a three- or four-page letter—telling him at the beginning what I think of the play, what I think needs to be done, and what attitude I would take toward the play if I directed it.

SBI: *What about your latest movie,* Splendor in the Grass? *Are you satisfied with it?*

EK: I'm very proud of it. I understand SBI didn't like it. I liked it very much. I think it's a very good movie...not a great movie or anything like that, but then I don't use that word much anyway.

SBI: *What, of all the things you've done, are you most proud of?*

EK: I don't think that way at all. I mean, I think the best thing I've done in the theater or in the movies is that I've kept a continuity of work going on my own terms. In other words, I do thing after thing that I like. If there's anything wrong with *Splendor in the Grass*, you don't blame any-body else—you blame me. I chose the script—I worked on the script—I cast it like I wanted to, and I chose the story because I saw something in it. Failure or success, it's my own. I'm a true independent. All that happens is that Warners gives me money. I give them a picture. They don't even see the rushes. They contribute nothing to it except the dough. And they're happy.

SBI: *What about audiences? Have they changed any?*

EK: Well, they're smarter. The audiences are smarter than the people that make the films, I think. I've been on this tour, you know, for *Splendor* and I've talked to a lot of college kids. They're bright as hell. They're *way* smarter. They're better read, more knowledgeable, more "with it," more understanding, funnier, more alert, more eager than the people that make pictures. They're way ahead of them.

SBI: *Who are some of the people and what are some of the things you admire in this industry?*

EK: I regret it's an industry altogether because I don't like the word indus-try. I think they made an industry out of what should be an art. The great people in films are the directors. In Japan, there's Kurosawa who did *Rashomon* and who has done a series of films including one called *Ikiru*, which is marvelous. There's a guy in India named Ray, who did that trilogy. I think that trilogy is just marvelous, wonderful. There's a guy in Argentina named Nilsson; there's Bergman, whom I admire; there's Fellini and Antonioni and De Sica. I think De Sica is a hell of a good director, by the way. I think his *Umberto D*, his *Shoeshine* and his *Bicycle Thief* were wonderful contributions. I think Antonioni is a fine director, fine artist. We know more about Italy from the work of these three men than through anything else. We love Italy because of that. The image of America overseas is shameful.

SBI: *What about American directors?*

EK: Well, I think Zinnemann does good work; I think Billy Wilder does good work; I think that Stevens has done good work. I think it's tougher out there because they're unconsciously part of an industry, of a way of work. It even penetrates through all the technicians; it penetrates to the color laboratories that develop their films. Our films are too glossy, the color is like candy. You want to lick the screen instead of watching it.

SBI: *Who are the really good actors?*

EK: I just don't have a hell of a lot of interest. I wouldn't name any actor. I just don't think that way. I'd have to make it up. What's the use of making it up? What I always do in my films is to try to get new people, you know, that have never been seen anywhere before. What I don't like about actors is that they look like actors. In the few years when they're still "people" instead of consciously becoming actors—that's when I try to use them.

Elia Kazan on "The Young Agony"

ROBIN BEAN/1962

OLD MORAL ORDERS HAVE decayed, and young people
have been in a wilderness. Now youth idealistically looks for
something valid to replace the past. This agony of youth has
been a recurring theme in the majority of the films of the distin-
guished American director Elia Kazan. In this interview with
ROBIN BEAN, Kazan discusses his philosophy . . . and how he projects that philosophy through his actors on to the screen.

During the past three weeks you have been working with William Inge and deal-
ing with America in the 'twenties. Is this to express criticism of the social system
as it exists by comparing it to the period of great prosperity in the 'twenties with
the warning that the collapse of 1929 could happen again, and are you drawing a
parallel here with the disintegration of the old moral standards?
There is a parallel in *Splendour in the Grass* between the collapse of the old
moral order of absolute puritanism (i.e., sex equals sin) and the collapse of
an economic order which is also contained in the film. The two are felt by
William Inge to be related phenomena. In the last five minutes, the author
makes the point that the important thing in living is to find out who you
are and live by your own lights; neither to follow a social attitude of success and ambition, an accepted social moral attitude, nor the strong demands
of an authoritarian person such as your parents on you. You should accept
your own nature and shape your life from it. I think the notable thing in

From *Films and Filming,* March 1962.

Splendour in the Grass is that at the end of it the author says "I forgive my parents."

We've had ten years of self-pity in which juvenile delinquents have said "Oh yes, I killed this man, but it was because my father was mean to me." This is a boring attitude.

You know, I was never very appreciative of Jimmy Dean becoming an idol of teenagers, and I rather disliked it. He's not an idol of mine, and I didn't particularly like what he was. I think I told the truth about a character like that in *East of Eden,* but I didn't like the result which was to blame your parents and the way you were brought up for everything. I don't go for that. I think that if your parents raised you wrong, you should realise this as soon as possible and go your own way. In *Splendour* I think Inge has taken a step forward to say "I don't care what they did, I'm going to do what I want." Of course, in the picture the father has to die before the boy does it, but still it's there.

There's been a whole decade, both in American stage plays and films, of the self-pitying hero who blames all his misfortunes and violence, all his deeds of hatred, on someone else. I think it's time to stop it . . . that's enough.

Would you say that this attitude grew from a genuinely serious social condition, or would you say that it has been greatly magnified by writers?
I think it was really in the air after the war. I don't mean to say it wasn't important; it was true. As I said, I think *East of Eden* was true, and after the Second World War there was a very understandable and correct disgust felt by the younger generation for the generation that had caused the war. There was a genuine feeling that the moral standards of the old generation were hollow, that they no longer meant anything and weren't valid for us any more. So there was a very genuine questioning of the values of their parents by the young people.

But the first manifestation was this one of "Pity me, I'm too sensitive for the world. I'm too good for the world. Everybody's wrong except me. Look what my Daddy did to me!" It was a fairly universal attitude.

That's why Jimmy Dean was an idol everywhere. You see all these little boys around the street still looking as though "I'm a homosexual because my mother did this to me," or "I'm a neurotic because this happened to me." They should shake this off and go on to solve the problem, so you have objective problems and very complex ones.

To what extent do you try to put the author's feelings on the screen? In many cases characters in your films have been identified as being created by you rather than the author. Is this intentional or do you think it is because of certain similarities in the mannerisms and actions of the characters?

I think that's inevitable. I can't be aware of those, someone else will have to judge that. But there must be some similarities in my work because no doubt I have strong inclinations, tastes, and a definite personality. But it's hard for me to see these similarities. But by an understanding of the nature, temperament and feelings of the author, I try to put him on the screen. The French have a wonderful word for a director, they call him a *realisateur*. And I try to *realise* the author.

I think there are certain things that are repeated in my work and the way young men behave, which I suppose is the way I remember myself as behaving. But I don't think that's bad. I don't demand that Goya paint like Rembrandt, I think he should paint like himself, because the more you are yourself then the more honest you will be. The films that I don't like are those where I don't feel any personality. It doesn't bother me that all Bergman films are alike, they should be because he made them. If he's behind the camera I want to feel him, as I do in his films. The same with Antonioni and Fellini. I want to feel their own individual personalities; I don't want to be more eclectic or have fewer mannerisms (which I don't *try* to have). But I do think that you can see that all my films are made by me, for better or worse I do the best I can. I don't think any of them are perfect or wonderful, and some of the failures I like as well, if not better, than the successes. I think one of the best films I made was *Viva Zapata!* which was a complete failure, and one of the pictures I liked best was *Face in the Crowd* which only a few people went to see, although I think I could now make it better, which I feel about everything I've done with the possible exception of *On The Waterfront* which came out pretty well.

But I don't mind faults in things either, I think there's nothing wrong in that. The important thing is that you be truthful, that you put on the screen what you feel.

Has your association with writers Steinbeck, Inge and Schulberg been intentional, and fitted into your pattern of exploring more fully the Cinema as a medium of expression?

Yes. One of the feelings that I have is that in order to make films it is important to bring in good writers, and also to write directly for the screen. I've done more of that than any American film producer. *Viva Zapata!, On The Waterfront, Face in the Crowd, Wild River* and *Splendour in the Grass* were all written directly for the screen.

The screen doesn't need a long story, but a single strong incident that is explored, expanded by penetration. Also, the whole sense of writing about contemporary issues, whether or not the story is contemporary, is my own temperament. I see things around me or feel things in my life which I think would make a wonderful subject for a film. Since *Viva Zapata!* in 1952, I've initiated all my own subjects, good, bad or indifferent, success or failure. Each one was my own and anything that's wrong with any of my films since '52 is my own fault. I've found a subject, interested a writer in it, and created a script. It's a long process, but to me a much more satisfying way of living in films.

How important are actors to you in putting these subjects on the screen?
I don't prefer to work with one actor rather than another, I don't have a troupe like Bergman has in Sweden. I'm interested mainly in the story, and I cast to realise that story. I don't know who I shall use in my next picture, which will be made in Greece, but it will probably be somebody brand new again, only because it's more real to me that way. An actor is a person who quickly becomes "an actor," whereas there's a simplicity and unselfconsciousness and mystery about a new actor that an experienced actor often loses quickly. A person when he feels something in life would prefer to hide it, whereas an actor is in the habit of showing it. I'm not saying this is a general rule for other directors or that it is right for anyone but me, but it fits my own temperament and my own feelings about a film.

A star undercuts a story in some ways; you know he's not going to die in the second reel or going to do anything unpleasant and that he'll get the girl in the end, and if he doesn't come out well, the audience is disappointed because they've gone to the cinema to see him. I don't want an audience to come to see a star. I want them to see my story.

Very often recognised actors in a very subtle way condescend to a part; they clean it up, and make it more pleasant, glamorous, brave, courageous or resourceful than it is. There's nothing more boring than the bravery of an actor, and when you get a person that's new, he's not on the lookout to always be brave or be cleaned up.

I can't stand a hairdresser on the set, and I try not to have one. But if the unions force one on me, I tell her to go in a room and play solitaire or something. If I see one fussing with the leading lady's hair, I have a fit the first day, and then they don't come round again. I mean I like them personally, but I don't want the hair in place. One objection I have to most costumes is that they obviously look like they were made for the film and have never been worn or used before. It's a very hard thing to fight unless you're terribly determined and persistent; everybody's trying to clean everything up on you.

The set is full of many charming and very friendly enemies, people who are in the habit of making things pretty and more comfortable. This is the whole technique of Hollywood, to make everything more digestible. My whole effort is to bring the impact of life to the screen, so you don't ever know quite what's going to happen.

You were yourself for some time an actor which must be an advantage. Because of this, what kind of responses do you want from an actor?
I've gotten a lot from some actors; there are some who really do contribute things. While a director must act cock-sure as though he knows exactly what he's doing, the process of filming is so quick that any interplay is stimulating. If you come with something you think right and they have a slightly or completely different attack on it, whether or not you use their ideas, they're very stimulating.

I don't particularly like obedience or servility in an actor. If an actor is terribly reverent or agrees with everything I say, it's liable to be a punk performance. So I try early in the procedure to encourage them to say what they think and come forward with their own ideas. I tell them frankly: "I probably won't use one idea in twenty, but don't just come here with your lines learnt. Tell me something about the content of the scene, how you'd like to play it, and don't be discouraged if I say no." But every once in a while, I'll take something. As a matter of fact, I'll take it from the doorman or property man, because some members of the crew have pretty good ideas. [*Kazan now uses the same crew on each film, which has been built up during the past eight years he has been working in New York.*]

The set should be a place where imagination has been freed, where everyone is working together on a project. I try in all my early talks with actors to make them interested in the picture as a whole. And so if you get them interested in their own part, they'll stop worrying about the other performers too, which is a help.

You say you often prefer to work with an unknown actor as they are more real for the part. Do you find that they are able to offer very stimulating and creative ideas on their characters?
Usually when they're just starting, they're so nervous and dependent. But the interesting thing about beginners is that they have not yet assumed a public image. Usually stars have a sympathetic public image which they are unconsciously defending, and are not keen on doing something that might make audiences hostile to them. But beginners are usually specifically interested in achieving the part as I see it, and so they will work much more boldly and directly.

Is this also the reason why you have rarely worked with an actor more than once?
I'm out of the New York Theatre. New York is the grass roots of acting in America. For instance, Barbara Loden and Zohra Lampert in *Splendour* are out of the New York theatre; no one could find them in Hollywood. If they did find them, they would not know what they could do. I only know because they're in the New York theatre, and it's exciting to see new talent coming up; you suddenly find someone absolutely fresh.

There are actors I've used several times. Marlon Brando I used in three films, but he's an exceptional person, an exceptional talent. I wouldn't have worked with Dean again, in all likelihood. Marlon I can't touch now because he costs too much, and I'm not going to pay any silly figure. But I have a great admiration for Brando, and it's because of the subtlety of his feelings, the violence that's in him, and the surprises that are in his nature. It's the human quality that is attractive to me, not the acting technique.

There is a difference between film and stage acting, I think at bottom the problem in both cases is to be psychologically true.

Now on the stage I have to take what is in the inner event, and try to project it into external behaviour that is large enough so that it becomes visible or even eloquent to an audience. In film you can photograph a person thinking, you can photograph thought. The camera can also be used as a microscope; it is a penetrating device by which you can photograph the inner experience of a person, particularly a sensitive person. Things that wouldn't count on stage are most precious in film. The essential job is to get the truth of the experience going on in the actor; if he will really experience what's happening truthfully, then it's worth photographing.

I am trying in all the films I do to either eliminate as much dialogue as I can or to make it an embroidery on the outskirts of action. Part of the behaviour *is* what they say, but not the essential part of it, and in that sense I think my work is getting more cinematic.

What effect does the fact that you continually look for new actors for roles have? Do you find that people are continually expecting them to have the same effect as say Brando or Dean?
It hasn't affected me at all as far as I can see. I think its maybe been a burden on Carroll Baker, ever since she did *Baby Doll,* everybody's expecting her to do *Baby Doll* again. Andy Griffith was pushed ahead into a star part a little before he was ready.

Now Warren Beatty, however, has made it very quickly, and he is at the moment the most in-demand leading man in the States.

You are probably the only producer in America who is consistently able to obtain financing for films which have no recognisable box-office or star attraction. Why do you think this is?
I think I couldn't do it unless I had made money somewhere along the line. Now *Splendour in the Grass* is a great success in America; I don't think it will be in Europe, although I hope people go to see it. But that's not my problem. As long as I can make what I want I will do so, and when I can't, I'll simply cut costs and go on doing it anyway. That is, I've made enough films that made money, like *East of Eden* and *On the Waterfront.* But *Baby Doll* has still not made its costs back; *Face in the Crowd* and *Wild River* were disastrous failures. Fortunately *Splendour in the Grass* has made a lot of money already in the States, and I think it'll end up doing extremely well. But every once in a while it is helpful if one of your films goes well. I think Hollywood feels about me that every two or three pictures, "He's going to do one that's going to make us some money." But I don't have that in mind when I do a film.

Your successes in many cases have been much imitated by other film-makers. On the Waterfront was imitated a great deal. I even felt that The Angry Silence with the whole idea of Coventry was very similar, although I don't say those fellows imitated it. *Waterfront* did start a whole series of labour pictures going to a formula; Martin Ritt directed one. *A Man Is Ten Feet Tall,* which I thought terribly imitated my picture, embarrassingly so.

East of Eden was imitated. The whole Jimmy Dean phase was started. It's sort of flattering in a way, but it also makes you feel uncomfortable. I think *Face in the Crowd* had quite an influence, there's been quite a number of films like that, in fact some more successful than mine.

Do the companies insist on seeing the script and advising on it before you commence shooting?
I like to do that. I don't like to take a million and a half dollars from a company without them knowing what I'm going to do basically. There's no harm in them giving me a memo or two before I start although I usually don't pay too much attention to them, but they may even have a good idea here and there. I invite initial comment on a script, but I don't get any notes from them during the course of production, and I don't alter anything unless I feel it's right myself. In that way I can have a strict independence.

But I don't like to go with a company simply because they have a contract with me, and then make a picture that they don't want. I did it once with *Wild River,* I had one more picture to make under my very first contract in pictures, with Fox, and the very last picture of the contract was *Wild River.* I don't think Fox wanted to make it. I think it's regrettable because they didn't advertise it and showed no interest in it. The film didn't go into the West End in London and was never even shown in France, which was outrageous. I said to Skouras, "Put it into a small theatre, a 300-seat house, put it *somewhere.*"

I think there are some excellent features in *Wild River.* I thought it was a fascinating story, and I also thought the end of it was excellent, that it was one of the best things I'd done—the old woman moving off the island to a new house. I resented the way they treated that picture. But they only did it because of the contract, but they didn't want to make it, showed no interest, and sort of hated it when they saw it.

Jack Warner didn't like *Splendour in the Grass* when he saw it, but we had this thing of the one-day previews [*The film went out on one-day showings at certain cinemas several weeks before release to test audience reaction*], and the audience caught on to it . . . and there it was.

Look, There's the American Theatre

RICHARD SCHECHNER AND
THEODORE HOFFMAN/1964

ELIA KAZAN IS PERHAPS America's foremost director. Among the plays he directed are *Death of a Salesman, Streetcar Named Desire, Sweet Bird of Youth, Dark at the Top of the Stairs, J. B.,* and, most recently at Lincoln Center, *After the Fall* and *The Changeling*. His movies include *On the Waterfront, Baby Doll*, and *America, America*. Kazan and Robert Whitehead are the directors of The Lincoln Center Repertory Company.

QUESTION: *What about the first season at Lincoln Center?*
ELIA KAZAN: On the whole, I'm pleased with it. We made a lot of mistakes, but we learned. And I think the company liked the experience. Very few are going. Jason Robard's taking a leave with our blessing to get his bills paid. Ralph Meeker is a damn good actor and we're anxious to get him back. They've all worked and . . . well, put it this way: for the first time in my memory after an opening night the actors were back at noon the next day to rehearse two other plays.

We have a theatre which cost under a half million bucks; excavation, building, seats, the whole thing. I think it will be imitated all over the country. We designed our stage on the premise that nothing would change: no flies, no wings, nothing but a turn-table for *Marco Millions*. We learned that it's not ideal for all presentations. Take the Behrman play — *But For Whom Charlie* — which is wise and witty and beautifully written. I don't

From *Tulane Drama Review*, Winter 1964. Reprinted by permission.

think it's the greatest play in the world, but I think it's the best play he's ever written in this sense: it's the most committed. It's the first time he's admitted he's a Jew. It's the first time he has stuck up for a type who's "incapable," like himself. I think there are many cogent things said in that play. And it's a charming play. It charms me. People ask: what the hell did you do it for? I did it because I like it. You don't like it? That's not my problem.

Its theatre values are simply those of two people seated together and talking beautifully. Sometimes there are three people sitting together and talking charmingly. Now you must put an intimate frame around these conversations. Well, I tried, but intimacy is difficult to get on our stage. Perhaps I should have set it differently. At the same time some of our critics complained, "He didn't use the stage boldly." If I had, as I did in *After the Fall*, I'd have done Behrman's play an even greater disservice. And then they'd have said, "Oh, he uses the stage brilliantly, but what a boring play."

Q: *Are you happy with the audience reaction?*

EK: I don't go entirely by audiences, but I like ours. They're not the uptown audience. They're younger, brighter, more questioning, more eager. They come because they *want* something, not to pass the time between dinner parties. I bet they're fifteen years younger than uptown. They're not sleepy men their wives have dragged to the theatre. And they're not men who go to the theatre with a girl just to kill time before they go home and screw. They're not half-drunk. They're not buyers. It's a different group of people, and I have great hopes from that. I watched the Behrman play, the least successful of the plays we did, and they applauded lines on opening night. At the end of the run, they were applauding exits. I've been around the theatre a long time, but I've never seen a play get as many bravos as *After the Fall*. Whether an audience likes it or not, they *are* having a theatre experience. They sit there after the play's over. I've walked down the street among them and often they're having intense arguments about the play, about Miller. A year ago, you couldn't pick a fight about anything in the theatre. No one gave a damn about it; it was kaputt. Now people are fighting all over the city about Miller's bad taste.

Actually there's more moral posturing about the "bad taste" of Miller than I've ever seen in my life. You can say what you want about the play, but to question whether he has the right to put *anything* on the stage is horseshit. Strindberg wrote about each of his three wives right after he divorced them, and while they were still alive. And if you read Chekhov's life you realize he was writing about people he knew intimately. Dostoevski's the subject of his own books, and he talks about people he brushed shoulders with the night before. It doesn't offend me. As a matter of fact, I'd like more of it. I wish to God people were more candid, not less; more personal, not less; more direct and involved, not less.

I believe in passionate objectivity; but I also believe in passionate subjectivity. Now Miller—whether you like him or not—is trying not to lie about himself. The character that comes off worst in the play is Quentin. The person you have the least patience with is Miller. "Stop it!" you want to say. So he's not romanticizing himself. He's not presenting a sentimental hero. He's *not* building a dramatic structure that says, "Look at the difficulties this poor guy is in. I want you to root for him." And you know damn well Quentin's *not* going to come through his difficulties and wind up with a little lift at the end saying there's hope in the world. The old liberal plays had a sentimental hero. "Pity this poor son-of-a-bitch," they said, "he's up against a terrible social dilemma." But you knew damned well he was going to mostly solve it; not entirely, because then there couldn't be a third act message of hope saying, "Someday the world will . . . and so on," after which you say, "Good, someday the world will . . . and so on," and then go home and say, "Shit" because you're still up against the world the way it really is.

Q : *Did the ten-week rehearsal period help?*
E K : It was crucial in the Miller play. I didn't really know how to direct it. I worked the set out as I went along. It got more and more economical as we went along and finally I evolved the idea of the boxes. After a couple of weeks, I said to myself, "All we really need is five boxes!" I told the assistant stage manager, "Go to the grocery store downstairs and get some soap boxes." He said, "I'll build them for you." So he built the boxes we're still using, now covered with dark blue velour so they fit into the set. I wanted the attitudes of people, not their physical environment, only their psychological environment. The boxes are moved to slightly different positions— and that's all there is to it. The architecture of Quentin's mind doesn't change. Originally, I thought of doing the set differently, with certain physical elements torn out of reality, like a collage—a bit of this and a bit of

that, a bit of the staircase he remembers at home, etc.—the significant elements that he remembers. But in a theatre like ours, without any way of changing scenery, I finally couldn't do it. Only the extended rehearsal period gave us time to find the right solution.

Another thing happened during our rehearsals that saved the play. We started to rehearse while Miller was still writing the second act. He brought it in after I had been rehearsing the first act about a week. We then rehearsed the second act about ten days. At the end of the act, there was a very long and quite realistic scene between Maggie and Quentin. We both knew it wasn't any good, and the actors knew it. Miller said he wasn't satisfied with it. I said, "Take your second act and go up to the country and don't come back again until you rewrite it." And he did just that. He disappeared for ten days. Meantime, I worked on act one. I didn't see Miller until the day he brought back the second act that's now playing at the ANTA Washington Square. If he hadn't done that, if we had used his original second act, the play would have been a disaster.

You can't do that on Broadway. *J. B.* was done in nineteen rehearsal days and in nineteen days *you don't go back on your tracks*. You commit yourself to a style of production, and you've got to go through with it right or wrong. I went back on my tracks once—I did *Jacobowsky and the Colonel* in '45, rehearsed it for about six days, went to the company and said, "I screwed this up. I've directed it too heavily. I want your patience and your forbearance." So I redirected it and got the first two acts pretty well, but the third act was still no good. I just didn't have the time. But, as I say, in nineteen days I had to wear blinkers. I couldn't consider any other possibilities than the one with which I started. With *After the Fall,* I'd do it one way, and two days later I'd do it a different way. I experimented. Whether or not I satisfied anyone else, I did have a chance to partly satisfy myself.

Q : *How did the actors respond to it?*
E K : Very well. You know, people feel safe in the face of candor. They don't feel safe in the face of invulnerability, because it's false. If a director *has* to be right at all times, you've got to distrust the man. If you feel something's wrong with the scene, and the director says, "Don't worry, it's fine"—he's full of it. But if a director says, "I don't know—let's try it this way," and then he tries it that way with full conviction and full feeling, and then he says, "Let's try it another way," and he tries that way as fully as before—well, the actors respond because they feel he's honestly searching.

Q : *Do you think you'll develop a specific style out of this kind of work?*
E K : If so, it just has to evolve. I think there is something in *After the Fall*
that's new. Barbara Loden acts differently than the veteran pyrotechni-
cians—if there is such a word—of our theatre. More realistic, more pitiless,
more un-self-favoring. There's no sentimentality in her portrayal of Maggie.
She's tough, and her performance is hard and true, true to what Miller
wanted. I think we are developing performers like that. But I don't want to
speculate. I'd say my aim is not formalistic, but organic. I hope so. I'm not
going to say, "We're going to develop such and such a style of acting."
There's more bullshit in the theatre! I've lived through a lot of it. You know,
"Someday we will—we will *someday*." "Someday" comes and goes, and all
is the same.

Q : *What's Miller's relationship to the Lincoln Center Repertory Theatre?*
E K : Miller is our playwright. This is his theatre, he's part of the guiding
group in the theatre, he's part of all decisions, he knows everything that's
being done. This theatre is his outlet. But that doesn't mean we only do
Miller plays. We'd like to do the same thing with other playwrights, so
that their work comes through us. The big disappointment I had last year
was that we didn't get to do the Baldwin play, *Blues for Mr. Charlie*. I gave
him the idea for that play—"Do a play on the Till case." I told him what
the climax of the play was, and we even talked about the set. I corresponded
for two years with him about the play. He said he couldn't give the play to
us because there are no Negroes on the Board of Lincoln Center. But I don't
believe that was the reason we lost the play. I feel the play could have been
much better. Baldwin wasn't tough enough on himself. And no one was
tough enough on Baldwin. The end result was not what it should have
been.

   Now Miller is very self-critical. He keeps learning. His new play, *Incident
at Vichy,* was written in a single surge, an absolutely direct line. *After the
Fall* is here and there and all over the place, but *Vichy* is in a straight line.
At the same time, it's very rich. Miller is very determined at this moment
in his life. He's had his bad years. He's not going to waste any more years.

Q : *Some people think* After the Fall *didn't come off very well; it was too traditional.*
E K : I think the play is highly experimental. I've never seen a play like it
on Broadway. Have you?

Q: *What do you think of the criticism the first season got?*

EK: In America, you're a success or you're a failure. Any halfway ground— where you say, "Well, this is our first season, and we thought this and this would happen, but it didn't, something else did"—isn't recognized.

I've had and enjoyed bad notices all my life. Some people like certain things and some don't. I'm in the theatre, and I do the best I can. I've made mistakes. I hope I have learned. I hope we've all learned. A good deal! But the *degree* of critical venom directed at us does need explanation. You can say, "I didn't like the Miller play." That's legitimate. But a lady named Hard-wick says we produced three dead bugs. At the same time, every single per-formance of the Miller play has been greeted with cheers. The audience often stood up and cheered. I've done a lot of successful plays, but I've never had that before. Then another critic said, "They're not a repertory company." This troubled me until I looked at what this same critic does approve of.

Once I got to know the critics personally it changed my attitude toward what they wrote. You're bound to think *ad hominum.* You say, "Come on, friend, what the hell have *you* done? Come on, do something. You don't like this? Let's see *you* get one play on somewhere for one moment so I can see what you think is good."

Many of our critics have that sort of absolute certitude possible only to the non-performer. So actually I don't give a damn about most of what's been written. But if an actor or a director did one scene in such a way that I would open my eyes and say, "That fellow did some work that's new, that's valuable, that moves the theatre ahead a little bit," then I'd have respect. Now, in *After the Fall,* we did do a few things that I've never seen before. I don't think the theatre will be quite the same again. Because of Miller, it will be a little bolder. That's an accomplishment.

You asked me what I think of the critics. It's easy to sit on the side and say you should've done this or that. But that doesn't help the theatre. The only valuable criticism comes from someone who's actually confronted the problem and dealt with it. If one of my actors down there comes to me and says, "Why didn't we try this?" I'll listen like hell to him. I'll listen to my actors because they're in it and working at it, and they know what they're talking about.

Q: *Do you think you've got a repertory company?*

EK: There's a thing called process, which isn't understood in this country. I said when we started that you can't cast thirty people and have an acting company. A company is created. Not everyone's suited to it. Damned good actors have no place in it. It's a way of life, really, and it needs a special kind of person as well as a special kind of talent.

We didn't set out to do what the critics said we failed to do. We weren't trying to create a typical repertory company, the kind that uses Canadians or Americans to imitate Englishmen. We're not interested in that. We're trying to make a company out of our own kind of actor, our own kind of talent. We'll finally do classics and plays of the world repertory in our own way with our own voice and vocabulary.

Q: *What about the famous acting unity of the Group Theatre?*

EK: The stuff I read about that really has little to do with the Group. They talk about the unified style of acting. At the beginning—Christ, there were all different kinds. Carnovsky was from the Theatre Guild, Luther Adler from the Yiddish theatre, Russel Collins from the Cleveland Playhouse. I was from Yale and from the street, and Garfield and Bromberg from Eva LeGallienne, and so forth. The unity of the Group, to the extent that it was achieved, came from years of work together. But it also came from the circumstances in which the theatre evolved: the Depression. And the emergence of what used to be called the Common Man. Remember that phrase?

It wasn't protest theatre in the political sense, but it had an underlying spirit of protest. "Humanity's being pinched and squashed down," the Group said, "and the aspirations of people are important. And the social system that's produced this state of affairs is intolerable."

Q: *What sort of new talent do you expect to develop? Barbara Loden's your discovery, isn't she?*

EK: Yes and no. She was unknown. Whitehead hadn't heard of her. Miller never saw her before *After the Fall*. But I had her in two movies. She did an awful lot of work. She studied with Paul Mann for years. She did a lot of dancing, a lot of voice work. She's actually had more training than any of the young people in the company. And she's had a lot of experience in her life that deepened her. Yes, she's a talent, but there are many developing talents in our company now. Talent is not *only* something you're born with. It's what you allow yourself to go through; what you permit yourself to experience and perceive. And the work you do. Barbara's voice isn't what it should be; her speech is definitely not what it should be. But she's one of the most conscientious members of the company about that. She's tired as hell playing Maggie, that ball-breaking part, and still she goes down to classes every morning. So do others. They're down there every morning in voice and speech classes.

Q: *Is Barbara Loden a star?*
EK: She's sought after. I can say to an author, "We've got Barbara Loden," and he says, "Oh, great." It isn't that she's a star but she's an asset to a repertory company, someone who's a character actress—all parts are character parts anyway; there's no such thing as ingenues, straights, or heroes in Rep. She's an artist, she's working on herself. That's an achievement for us, because we've given her an arena in which her development means something.

This second season the young men in our company will have equal opportunities to work and to be seen. There are some fine new talents coming up.

Q: *What training did the younger actors bring to the company?*
EK: They were all trained differently. And all in some respects are woefully untrained. For instance, they are not trained vocally—not as they should be—nor in speech, nor physically. But why blame them? Full training in the American theatre isn't necessary. With type casting, a producer wants a series of "characters"—like kids use the word "character"— a clear, *single* image of a certain kind, a near-eccentric physical and speech image. Training isn't necessary, a waste of time, boring, and even possibly hazardous. It might blur the salable image. It's more important to stay home by the telephone in case your agent calls. In the professional theatre, if you have a failure, it's a disaster, and you have to run and find another job to pay the rent. And if you have a success, it's a disaster because it means that you play the same part for another year and a half, and you're going to go nuts. So, then, you say, "What am I going to do? I'll have to join the Actors Studio and do lab work or class work or something far-fetched like that." In this climate of quick success, young people want to have fame and a home of their own and a place in the country, and they want a hefty bank account. And sometimes that's achieved quickly. Elizabeth Ashley does *one* show, and she's a star. Why go on naming them? Look for yourself! But if Barbara Bel Geddes had not become a star in *Deep Are the Roots*, she might really have grown. But this very talented girl's going nuts

now because she's asked to do the same thing over and over: the blinky-eyed ingenue.

In time a company should become comparatively homogeneous in technique. If they work with the same sort of director, in the same spirit, and with each other, they develop the same goals. You can talk all you want, but until these goals become theirs, represent their own yearning and their own experience, they don't mean anything. Now, this is a problem. When we started, our actors were all trained differently. The American Academy taught certain people in our company techniques quite different from the Actors Studio or Sandy Meisner's work at the Neighborhood Playhouse. I've always tried to keep the same group of actors together. Karl Malden and Brando at one time, and later Pat Hingle and Milly Dunnock and Lee Cobb. I've stuck with the same kind of actor. But now the problem's much bigger than holding a few actors together. We're trying to make a company.

With the younger actors we've made a start in training. The problems of our stage are difficult. Actors have to project in a fearless and bold way. They're more exposed! You need the courage to say, "This—my experience—is important, and you better watch it." We're training for a kind of work which is based on psychological reality, but which becomes bigger through our emphasis on rhetoric and poetry and largeness of conception. Bobby Lewis started with fundamentals and gradually built his work into scenes of a more poetic kind. Paul Mann has been working in that direction too. We finally have a voice teacher in whom we have confidence, Kristin Linkletter, and an awfully good speech teacher, Alice Hermes, who is reaching her mark. It's difficult to get actors to want to improve themselves badly enough. But I think progress has been made. The American notion of progress is quick. Progress is *not* quick in the arts. A painter goes along for ten years, slobbers and fusses, and fails and fails till finally one day he becomes who he becomes. It takes time to develop actors and there's no tradition of patience here.

Q : *What has Stanislavski's influence been on the American theatre?*
E K : Enormous. It affected in one way or other everyone who came out of the Group. That includes a lot of directors. If you start following the tree branches: Lee Strasberg, Harold Clurman, Bobby Lewis, Joe Anthony, Alan Schneider, and the fellows they taught who taught others, and so on.

In his own career, Stanislavski changed a lot in his attitude toward the

System. He even kidded it a little at the end of his life. He began to dislike the word "system." He definitely changed in regard to technique. His work became far less based on emotional association and far more on simple external and physical things. He began to teach that if you understood a physical act thoroughly, like putting on a coat, you would, from that, also learn about the whys and wherefores. Now the New York people who work in the Method—"The Method" is a big industry here—push different things, ranging from the teachers who stress psychological objectives to others who work more to make physical acts meaningful and clear, and finally to the ones who still work mostly with emotional associations.

What everybody agrees on is the importance of asking what the person on stage wants, what the circumstances are which he is working in to get what he wants, and why he wants it—and *how* to make all these important to the actor. But within these basic common features, there are all kinds of emphases, depending on the individual. I've seen one well-known Method director say to the actors, "Your job is to justify the readings I give you." Other so-called Method directors—all this Method stuff is *"so-called"*—say "You have to be in exactly this attitude." And the actor says, "Why?" and they say, "Because, just *because*! You figure out the reason. Justify it for yourself."

If an actor is smart and tough-minded, he'll demand certain things of *any* director. He'll say, "Where have I been, what have I done just before, what do I want here, what do I do to get it, what is he to me?" He'll inquire into relationships in a way that any alert, intelligent person, whether he's Method-trained or not, will do. The basic elements of Method, really, are just horse-sense. They humanize acting. You know that you've just been somewhere which makes you come into a scene in a certain way. You know you want something of the people you're playing the scene with. You know that *want* can be achieved only under certain conditions. So, the director has to set the conditions under which that *want* can be achieved. Well, if you use these elements, someone asks, "Are you working in Method?" Why ask? Any good director uses them. You have to use them with an actor like Jason Robards who says, "Method? Shit! Just tell me what button you want me to push! The angry button? The sad button?"

Q: *What about the much talked-about Method techniques: improvisation, sense memory, emotional recall, the Private Moment?*

E K : I think improvisation is a technique whereby, freeing yourself of the lines temporarily, you can find behavior that is truer and more original and more meaningful and expressive of what's happening. But improvisation without objectives is useless. Improvisation hinges on the word *want*. Once you set *that*, you can move. On the basis of that psychological impetus you can improvise in every other way: behavior, props, circumstances, character elements. And the director will get great value in his effort to find the best *mise-en-scène*.

I use improvisation with young people. They're not tied to lines as much as older actors are. On the other hand, one of the faults young people have is that they sometimes tend to throw the lines away. Well, the lines are what the person is *saying*, whether they express what he's doing or not. The lines are there. I've seen Shakespeare performed where the actor seems to be thinking, "I have to say this damned speech — get it out of the way — but what's really happening is my experience inside." That's not the answer, especially where there's poetry, thought, and intellectual value in the lines. Where the lines are literature in their own right you have to give them full weight. And that's the task: to get both the experience and the poetry.

Sense memory and emotional recall are two entirely different things. Sense memory is a training technique to make the qualities of objects and of the total physical moment more alive and vivid. In acting, it's much better to use real props. At the end of his career, Stanislavski came to that. His ideal theatre would have the set and real props available all through the rehearsals, from the first day.

Q : *What about emotional recall and Private Moments?*
E K : Emotional recall is a simple thing, just a psychological trick, the way most actors use it. You think of something and it calls back an emotional memory. But the problem is to make the emotion specific and make it grow out of the scene. The emotion should really come out of what happens in the scene. To recall some personal event in your life and go in and play a quite different scene is not good. It's false. You see the worst misuse of emotional recall in actors who are really playing with something in themselves — not with the person in the scene. There is this glazed, unconnected look in their eyes, and you know they're somewhere else.

Private Moments are hard to appraise. And easy to parody. The parodies are sometimes deserved. But preparation for a scene is critical. You can't walk on cold. Something happened before the scene started. You can choose the events that preceded the scene and so choose the emotional meaning the scene has for you. All those choices, when they're made by the director together with the actor, affect the way the scene turns out. People who kid about preparation are foolish. All the great actors prepare some way. Just to walk on cold and pretend you can play a scene is nonsense.

I don't use group warm-ups because every actor needs a different preparation. Each comes on from a different set of circumstances, a different environment, a different physical environment. In rehearsal I change preparations quite often. I start one preparation, and then I say that we ought to do something else. I say. "This happened right before you came in," or, "Yesterday this happened," or, "You haven't seen this person for so long." Then I start changing the circumstances under which the scene is played. I say, "You have to catch a train in ten minutes," or, "You have to do this so that no one hears you." I set the circumstances under which the scene is played. The thing about preparation that hurts is that often it's "general." An actor whoops himself up, gets excited and aroused—and this preparation has no specific quality, nor does it relate to the scene that's coming, and therefore it doesn't develop in the course of the scene that follows.

Q: *Tell us more about how you work.*
EK: I put terrific stress on what the person wants and why he wants it. What makes it meaningful for him. I don't start on *how* he goes about getting it until I get him wanting it. And then I make clear the circumstances under which he behaves; what happens before, and so on. Then I try to find the physical behavior without preconception on my part if possible, but from what the actor does to achieve his objective under the circumstances.

I do whatever I think will be efficacious, whatever will be valuable. I often do improvisations on what happened before the play begins. Improvisation is part of the director's process of finding how he is going to do the play. It's a way of leading an actor into the typical or true behavior of a role, which he can only get when he is freed from the necessity of saying lines in the sequence in which they were written. It often brings sudden illumination to a role.

Q : *Do you type-cast?*

E K : You always type-cast in one sense. Not for externals, but because you say to yourself, "That person has the role in him." You find a little river of experience in the person that's like the thing in the part. Then the actor knows the part experientially rather than logically.

It's also important for a director to know a lot about his actors as people. Not that you talk about their lives, but you begin to find out what affects them, what they love and hate, what's meaningful to them, how they react, how they do things. And that's the advantage of a company. As it becomes permanent you get to know the people you're working with. You don't need to say so much to them.

Anyhow, you create values around the events of the scenes that are meaningful to the actors. Gradually you touch elements in their lives that make the scene so real and specific to them that it takes on a life of its own. Like the bottle scene in *After the Fall*—I don't really know what Barbara Loden did there. Good actors make the problems meaningful for *themselves*. You watch the process. When they don't need help, you simply set the problem for them. You say, "You must get involved in this need to hold on to that bottle." And Barbara did that brilliantly. How she did it, I never inquired. It was none of my business. It's only my business if she can't do it. Once she did it, I knew it was personal and real to her. I didn't ask where and why and what happened and all that.

The life of a play is in behavior. Generalizations are always dangerous. But if you say that part of the job of directing is to convert psychology into behavior, you have to find the unique way of behaving for all the characters. I find I can make it up to a certain extent, but I discover most of it when I start working and see what I want in the actor's behavior. For example, a boy is flirting with a girl, and I have a feeling that she'd resist showing that she is being affected by him. He'd be reaching her, but the more he reached her, the more she'd put up a barrier. The fact is, however, that if someone courts you, you're flattered. So first you have to work so the actress recognizes that basic thing experientially. Once you've established that with her, then you can say, "When he comes on with you, the more you want to give in to him, the more you feel, 'I musn't, I shouldn't,' and the more you hold off." But you establish the basic thing that she *is* aroused and flattered before you get to the scene as it is to be played.

Then, a second step. Maybe you have a prop in mind that you're going to use in the scene; say this scene should be played in a swing, as in the movie, *Baby Doll*. Well, you do an improvisation in a swing that has nothing to do with the scene you're going to play. But when they do get to the swing, she knows *why* she sits in the swing. It's a comfort to her. It rocks her, and it relieves her of her humiliating and embarrassing home-life. It strengthens her. It's a romantic thing to her, and before you know it, you get to the scene and that swing means something.

Stanislavski said at the beginning of his career, "Say 'as if' " — as if this, that, the other. But now we talk more objectively. We deal with the actual meaning of the specific action, not with parallels. It works better for us because it's more alive from moment to moment. It's not something parallel; it's the thing itself. I think that's what Stanislavski was trying to do at the end of his life. He was saying, "If you really investigate the moment itself — what's actually happening there — you'll get all the emotion you need." And that's what I believe, too.

Q :   *How did you use improvisation in* After the Fall?
E K :   I'll give you an example. It's very important that the father, played by Paul Mann, feels that his wife is treacherous in regard to Quentin; that his wife somewhere in the past has encouraged Quentin against the interests of the father. In the second act, the father comes rushing on saying, "What the hell? Who are you? What are you doing?" He just has a few lines there, but I had to get him on a level of betrayal that I thought was correct for that character. He discovers, after many years with his wife, that she is deeply and completely treacherous. So I did an improvisation where he comes home and finds out for the first time that his boy is going to college rather than into his business as he had hoped. I arranged the improvisation so that he finds out also — and Paul didn't know this, he didn't know what I was after — that his wife had encouraged the boy not to go into business but to go to college. I then set the circumstances so that Paul was starting up a new business and had plans for his son so that when he comes home and finds the boy is not going into business and then he finds that his wife has encouraged this change in the boy — it left an indelible mark on Paul. And the way Paul does the scene in the second act came out of that improvisation.

Q :   *Technically this is a very well-plotted improvisation; the circumstances are very clear. Did you run it just once or did you run it several times until Paul felt he arrived at the emotion and the situation you wanted?*

EK: You never run the same improvisation twice. But with this one I deepened the circumstances and added surprises, particularly ones Paul didn't know about. Actually, at one moment in this improvisation, I remember vividly, Paul got white.

Q: *Did each of them have an objective in the improvisation?*
EK: Yes. But I don't tell Paul what I tell his wife because in life you don't know. You just come home to talk to your son, and you hit something you don't expect. So the thing has the impact of life or as near as we can get to it.

In the early scenes with Quentin's first wife, I did a lot of experimenting that had nothing to do with what is usually thought of as experimental. I changed the business and movement. What I found was that I was playing her too harshly; so you wondered, "What the hell did he ever marry her for? What was he ever doing with her?" So then I thought, "My God, I knew Miller's first wife, and she had strong, positive, good qualities." So I did the whole thing over and started them much more in rapport and developed the relationship so you felt the conflict and antagonism increase. When it broke, you felt there was a development. Then I showed it to Miller. He said that the inner structure of the play necessitated a certain obduracy in her character. For example, I had Quentin touching her. He told me Quentin would not touch her often. She should stiffen when he touched her. In other words, the conflict she had in her relation to any man and in relation to Quentin—I'm talking about Louise now—would make her un-yielding. It was important that Quentin found that what he could get from Maggie he could never get from his first wife. We played that relationship three different ways until we got what we have now.

Another thing developed in rehearsal. I became convinced that the show should not have any "lights up, lights down, blackout, lights up" pattern. I tried to make it flow like the mind. In your mind you don't black out one thing as you do another. For instance, now I'm talking to you, but in the back of my mind I'm thinking about rehearsals. The mind is a continuum of many things going on at once—some come to the forefront, others wait their turn. In directing, I found a way of doing it so the scenes overlap. One scene doesn't end completely before another begins. A scene starts while the first scene is still going on. For instance, Mickey comes on and stands around the back talking with Louise while the previous scene is still going on. You know while he's involved in the previous scene, Quentin's thinking, "I've got to get to the subject of Mickey with the analyst." Finally, I worked the play out so that there are no blackouts. When you read it, it says, "lights go off on him, so and so appears." But what happens on stage is truer.

Q: *So reading the play gives you an entirely different impression?*
EK: That's why I said *After the Fall* is experimental. I've never seen that done before, putting the way the mind works on stage.

Q: *What about working in three dimensions?*
EK: Well, that stage puts much more of a burden on the actor and director. I learned a lot about it. I'll be bolder and freer now. But I didn't feel anything odd about our stage because I work in movies. This stage is like that: deep, and everything goes to and away, not across. Movies are always in depth; the movement is towards the camera and away.

Q: *How about the* After the Fall *set? Do the actors pretend the scenery is real?*
EK: I don't try to give them any false problems: pretend you're in a house or anything like that. The fact that the mother runs up and down the stairs is important because Quentin remembers her as always running upstairs, downstairs, supervising this, looking after that, worrying about this one, taking care of that one. A sense of harrassment. You've got to create that. And going up and down the stairs helps. But I don't say, "Imagine it's the stairs in your house." I try to stay away from imagined objects. I chose things very sparely. For example, in Miller's script it says Paul Mann is in a hospital bed. I didn't want that. So what I did was put the scene on a hospital porch and make Paul play with sunlight. I said, "You're brought out onto a porch, one of those sunny porches where they bring invalids—and you have a moment of peace. The sun warms your face." Now that's a sense memory he gets very well. That's important because he's at peace before the bad news is brought to him.

Q: *What about the subway scene?*
EK: That's there to give the sense of people all together in some sort of motion. Everything in this play is as Quentin remembers or imagines it. And the quality of his imagination, his memory, has to do with what he feels about the object: guilty, or whatever. He just thinks of this man in the rush hour, bursting through the people on the edge of the platform. It's all mixed up. These men are hanging, reading the paper—you actually can't

jump through the side of a subway car. It makes no *logical* sense. But *illogically*, as a memory, it makes sense. Well, it's just like painting—people paint seemingly discordant elements together, because they're part of a psychological reality.

Q: *What kind of theatre do you think your work on the open stage will lead to? Some critics say you can't leave movie realism.*

E K : There's no such thing as realistic theatre. The very presence of the audience, the fact of selection of any kind, the very taking off of the fourth wall make it not realistic. I'm not interested in what's called realism. I don't believe I've worked "realistically" or "naturalistically" either. What our stage does is put a strong light on a person, on the inner life, the feelings of a person. These become monumental things. You're not seeing the characters in two dimensions. They're out there living right in your midst. It puts a terrific emphasis on what's said, too. You can no longer pretend a character is talking only to the partner he's playing with. He's talking in the midst of eleven hundred people and they're there to hear him. They can hear his breathing, so right off the bat, the theatrical exists. You can't duck it.

I was busting out of the goddamned proscenium theatre uptown. In *Cat on a Hot Tin Roof*, I had everybody address the audience continually. Every time they had one of those long speeches, they'd turn and say it to the audience. Nobody thought anything of it once we opened. But there was a hell of a lot of bitching about it before. Williams said, "I hate the set. What are you doing?" He wanted the play done realistically. But he had some superstition about me, so he went along with it. After it opened, no one said anything, and people are doing that kind of thing much more often now. The whole second act of *Cat* was a long address by Burl Ives to the audience. I had him address various members of the audience. This is the way I think soliloquies were done in Shakespeare's day. I think Hamlet stood out there and said, "What do you people think I should do? Should I kill myself? What would *you* do?" And "what would *you* do?" is implicit in this kind of staging. It sucks the audience into the experience and emotion of that moment.

QUESTION: *You're doing classics next season. How do you plan doing them?*

KAZAN: It's a problem we addressed ourselves to at the Actors Studio and that I've been dealing with in many plays: *Death of a Salesman, J.B., Cat,*

Sweet Bird. When people say, "You're not a repertory company yet" it's a laugh, really. Who says we are? The point is that I don't want us to be like Stratford, Connecticut *or* Ontario. I'm going to try to combine the psychological penetration of the best tradition of American acting—which is the tradition that came down the line from the Group Theatre through the Actors Studio—and combine this with the size and eloquence and rhetorical clarity and freedom of the best elements of the classic tradition of acting. I don't want to create a tradition based in any sense on the English. If we do classics, the relationships have to be as psychologically deep as we can make them. At the same time, the acting has to recognize that poetry is being spoken. Poetry takes moments that in life would be an instant and enlarges them into a song. The moment is enlarged and deepened and felt through, and then you're speaking poetry. In other words, you're doing what movies do through a series of quick cuts and close-ups. You're enlarging a moment. A novelist will describe something, like in *The Death of Ivan Ilyich* Tolstoy will describe what his hero is thinking, lying in that bed, and go on for three pages—but actually in life, it would go past in a flick of time and the man would hardly know what he felt.

Q: *How do you get believability in poetry? People don't speak poetry.*
E K: I can only answer that theoretically. I haven't done a play in verse except *J. B.* You have to create in the actor, through psychological means, a level of experience that will force him to speak in poetry. Just like directing an opera. If you do opera organically and truly, you get the circumstances so violent and personal that the performer has to come out with more than, "Oh, the hell with you!" or more than, "I love you!" He has to erupt into a fully expressive aria. Now that does happen in life sometimes; it happens, for instance, in fits of anger.

If I can get the actor to a point where he says, "God damn it, I don't know whether life is worth living, because it is so treacherous and so long and so uncertain and so unappreciated, and the finest people go first and . . . so on," I finally get him to a point where he can say, "To be or not to be, that is the question." And mean it, because he has to talk and talk at length about it and in an elevated way because his feelings are elevated. Now that's a tough thing to do, but that's the only way *we* can do Shakespeare.

At the same time, the experience of poetry is partly in the meter and rhythm. You can't do what some of our young actors do and say, "Screw the rhythm," and turn verse into talk. Part of the experience is contained in the fact that the author writes it rhythmically, because there's something in moments of elation, whether in love-making, anger, terrible melancholy, self-doubt, or self castigation, that is rhythmic. I mean we all have had moments when we feel either worthless or elated or avid or furious or something like that. Well, you have to direct the play so that before you engage the poetry, you're at a point experientially where poetry is *necessary*. That's a theoretical answer to a theoretical question. Now doing it is something else again. You need a certain kind of actor. You need a trained company.

Q : *What plays do you want to do?*
E K : I want to open the theatre uptown with the *Oresteia*. Barrault's *Oresteia* was the worst production of a major thing I ever saw. It made me feel, "Look, even if I don't do it entirely well, at least our effort itself will count." Planchon's the greatest director in France today, a force in the theatre. The three best productions I saw in Europe were *Mother Courage* and *Arturo Ui* in East Berlin at the Ensemble and Planchon's *Georges Dandin* at Lyon.

We're starting the second season not with a big work of Shakespeare's but with something where the blank verse is rather simple. The verse in *The Changeling* is terribly direct and spare and strong. It is within the range of the young people in the company, and we're casting it mostly with the people who were in the original training program. I like *The Changeling* very much. It's not a tragedy but a "black comedy." It's an ironic, realistic, hard-headed view of the way humans behave. It deals with double-face. People present one face in order to get along, and it's always a violation of their true face, their spontaneous and true feelings. The whole idea of *The Changeling* is that people wear masks in order to get by when their real impulses and their real feelings are something else. And the "something else" erupts every day on page four of the *Daily News* in violent and desperate actions. I think there's a terrific schism in our society between the way we pretend to live and the way we really live. There is a terrific amount of pretence depicted on TV, in most films, news articles, and most all magazines. There's no truthful revelation of the pressures people feel, and the way they behave due to the pressures they feel. *The Changeling* is very modern in spirit.

Q: *Does the same go for* Tartuffe?
EK: Yes. We chose these plays because although they are part of the world repertory they shed light on our own lives. They're not just "classics" or rather, they *are* classics. Our theatre is committed to comment and reaction to the life around us. I like Anouilh's *Antigone* very much because it discusses the problems of the person in authority and throws light on the complexities of his life. It exists in any time. It exists now.

The third season will be the first great challenge for us. We'll be doing plays which are immense and very difficult. The *Oresteia* and de Musset's *Lorenzaccio*. But if we'd started with them, I wouldn't know where to begin, who to cast, how to direct. The *Oresteia* has choral work, singing, great rhetoric. It would have been a mess. So, we've always planned this, step by step, moving into the world repertory. Some of our critics have demanded, "Why didn't you start with *Hamlet*?" But who the hell would we do *Hamlet* with, and how? We won't use guest stars. We're committed to the company idea. No drop-ins, no floating company, no favors between movie commitments.

Q: *How would you relate the identity of the Lincoln Center Repertory to the Group?*
EK: They're terribly different. The Group was a real outgrowth of the thirties. We were all unemployed underdogs in revolt against everything that was being done in the theatre. We now have a big challenge because we have money, some power, good actors. People say, "Now that you've got it, what are you going to do with it?" We have better actors potentially than we had in the Group. We need time. Everyone thinks of the Group as *Waiting for Lefty, Awake and Sing, Golden Boy*. That was 1935. The Group started in 1928. Seven years! Do you know how long seven years is?

I know how long it takes. I went through the Group Theatre experience. Not until 1935 with *Waiting for Lefty, Awake and Sing,* the year after that, *Paradise Lost,* the year after that, *Golden Boy,* the year after that, *Rocket to the Moon: then* we had our own playwright, and *then* the Group had its identity, not before.

We'll get better as we go along. Bob [Whitehead] and Arthur [Miller] and Harold [Clurman] and I have a brotherly feeling about the problems around us. We're not just a theatre. We're not asking the audience to judge us on that basis alone. We're saying to the audience, "You will see something here that will somehow have meaning for you. You will see something that will touch you some way or other, will relate to your life." That's what we say when we sell subscriptions. In four or five years we'll produce two or three shows that will be emblematic. You'll say, "Look, there's the American theatre."

Interview with Elia Kazan

MICHEL DELAHAYE/1966

SINCE SPLENDOR IN THE *Grass,* there have been *Wild River* and *America, America,* but Elia Kazan is still in purgatory, no more accepted in Europe than he is in America, still jolted about by his flair for misunderstandings and maledictions. It is the aim of the present offensive once more to stress the importance of this youngest of the grand old men and oldest of the grand young men. Our efforts join those, notably of Roger Tailleur, who has just devoted to Kazan one of the rare books in cinema worth the trouble of reading (and rereading), one of the best that has ever appeared (Editions Seghers). But however necessary they may be, these efforts are never anything but secondary assistances to a thing that already, in any case, asserts itself: a prodigiously stimulating and fecund body of work that ceaselessly follows and asserts its way, more and more. It is merely a question of time.

But everything is a question of time with Kazan, and time is a question of everything. It is the measure of the entire body of work, as it is of each film, time which, from confrontations to confrontations — victories or defeats, wears, restores, enriches. Time that makes everything move.

Time — equally the price that one must pay if one wants to leave, at each age, the *toga praetexta* of the one before, to destroy a world that risked shutting one in, in a reassuring but debilitating enclosure; the price that

From *Cahiers du Cinéma in English,* March 1967. Reprinted by permission of the British Film Institute.

one must pay if one wants, beyond these necessary transitions to a further stage, to preserve one's roots and one's fidelities, to resist the opposite fascination of annihilation.

It is, too, the price that one charges others (as they charge it to you) at every change and every permanence, whether one wants to keep, or to change, oneself or another—for the better or for the worse.

This perpetual movement, from progressions to preservations (and which at each of its stages secretes the antagonistic reaction), is that very thing that all puritanisms, of moral, social, or political order, deny—all orders established on the permanence of involutions or revolutions. From that comes the reactions of all orders and provenances which the work of Kazan has always provoked—work that always emphasizes, unseasonably to the fashions, movement and permanence, in the same way that it incites you to judgment through a process that implies the annihilation of all reassuring forms of judgment.

People will overlook, I hope, these unexemplified generalizations, since on the one hand, I am brief, and on the other, the examples are there, abundant—those that we have already given, those that we give here. And the films are there. Notably these last three, which now I stress, and which form the most astonishing trilogy of cinema: *Splendor in the Grass*, *Wild River*, and that *America, America* which gathers together and extends all the elements of the earlier films, and which is, on this level, as on all the others, a summation.

For *America, America* is the story of the birth of a man (with, in filigree, the birth and the stages of a work), through the very process of the birth of a nation and of the birth of a man to that nation. It is, too, the birth of an idea—freedom, which always returns with Kazan on the thread of its different ways, individual and collective.

America, America is the modern incarnation par excellence of the tale of apprenticeship, in which one passes through the physical and moral trials that forge a being for his final form, and the adventures or transformations of intermediary forms, from better to worse, that one must take, before being born—sound or weak.

America, America is the final form—the most extensive and the most open—taken by the story—always the same—that Kazan tells, the story, if there is one, that best deserves to bear that title of *The Greatest Story Ever Told*.

CAHIERS: *And shall we begin with the actors? It seems that, little by little, you have guided them from exteriorization toward a certain interiorization.*

ELIA KAZAN: I believe that that is true. In the films that I was making twenty years ago, I had, I chose, more flamboyant actors. They were the engines of the film, and the film was the vehicle of their expression; it was always a question of expressing, of exteriorizing what there was "in" them, and the free course that I left to this flamboyance made me tend sometimes almost toward opera. But, little by little, I lost interest in this expression as such, and in fact I almost turned against it. I began, too, to restrain my actors, in proportion as I saw things in a truer, calmer fashion.

At the same time, I became more and more interested in what happened to them, to the actors, human beings, characters—in the way in which they reflected or reinforced something, be it unconsciously, in the way in which they let something grow in them, come out from them. Now, ten or fifteen years afterward, I see the gap that separates me from the first manner, when my actors were moved by the most violent feeling of life, which they rendered directly and unconsciously. Now I no longer "feel" people through an acting technique. Life is not like that. People ordinarily do not know or realize the why and the how of their beings, whence they originate and whither they lead them. In any case, very few people know exactly what they want, and there are fewer still who can go straight to what they want. That is why I direct my youngsters in a more supple, more complex way, I abandon myself more to imprecision, to the nebulous, and I accept more readily the ways of contradiction. I believe that that is the only way to approach the truth.

CAHIERS: *Your films themselves are made more and more on the complexity and contradictions of life.*

EK: At the start, my films were always written by scenarists, sometimes theatre men [Tennessee Williams, William Inge]. Even then I worked on them myself, but little by little I collaborated more and finally I began to write my stories myself. I was present at the birth of the film, instead of being, as before, the conductor of cadences and solos. In *Streetcar*, there are entire scenes that I would do differently today. I would have them happen much more calmly, unconsciously, and that would take much more time as well. I still think that dramaturgy is essential in theatre, but one must rethink the thing completely when one approaches the screen. That too is why, as I grew older, I felt more and more acutely the difference between theatre and film, and, little by little, I lost interest in the theatre.

CAHIERS: *But the fact is that you originally acquired much from the theatre. Perhaps something of it still remains today in your films?*

EK: I agree absolutely. I took something from the theatre and that something is still there. But, regarding that, let me be more specific about some points. The essence of the Stanislavsky method, and the fundamental interest that it had for us, in the way in which we learned it as students and used it later, dwelt in the action. That is to say, when someone felt, experienced something, our feeling—and our theory—was that this emotion would never become "of" the theatre, unless it were expressed as a need, a hunger. And it is of this need, of this hunger, that such-and-such a precise action sprang incarnated as expression of this hunger. The play became a series of progressions, each of which consisted of the fact that a person did a certain thing that responded to a certain want. We stressed the word "want," and we did our best to emerge on the word "do." In short: To do. To want. To do.

We sought to attain the infinitive: To conquer, to love . . . infinitives emerging on "To want" and "To do." The result was that our performances in the theatre, especially in the form in which I expressed myself at the start, were extremely violent, violent and amusing. But today, when I observe life, I see it takes much less direct paths, circuitous paths, subtle and subterranean. Moreover, when the actor is aware of his aim—because the director has pointed it out to him or he has analyzed it himself—he cannot but distance himself from life to the extent to which, in life, people are uncertain ultimately as to what they want. They oscillate, wander, drift, in relation to their aim—or they change their aim. In short, they want this, then that, but . . . but *that* is life, and it is there that the poetry of life dwells, in these contradictions, these sudden deflections, these aspirations that spring up and disconcert. In short, while I once had a unilinear approach to life, I now interest myself more and more in the complexity of things.

CAHIERS: *In fact, complexity became the very subject of your films. Your characters confront one another in that some represent a more or less simplified view, and others, a more or less complex view of the world. That is the entire subject of* Splendor in the Grass *and of* Wild River.

EK: Yes, and that responds to another thing that happens perhaps everywhere in the world of artists. In the thirties, when I was a student, there prevailed in our milieu a kind of puritanism, which manifested itself in the belief that the course of things in the world that we saw, as it concerned words as well as politics and society, was the only right one, almost. Now this puritanism—whether under its Soviet or its American form—has broken down. We absolutely no longer believe in it, the young especially. They doubt their parents, they doubt the established moral code, they doubt the State, they doubt their country, they doubt themselves, and things are infinitely more complex now than they were then.

But in the thirties, the period when I was forming myself—still a young man and a young actor—we were certain about what the values were, certain that America must progress, even, in the end, to leaving the control of the country and of all its institutions to artists, and in particular to Communist artists. For America would become a Communist state, and, at the time, I myself was a member of the Communist Party. Then, when I turned against the CP—and I turned against it very soon and very violently—I began to question myself very severely, and I asked myself—what are the values that I possess? What is the real sound that they ring? How do they stand on their feet? How, and by what right, could they be respected? I discovered then that none deserved it. But that was a real search. For years, I questioned everything and everyone, and especially, starting from the moment that I began to doubt, I began to watch people. Starting from there, I lost the habit of thinking in the mode of judgment. I stopped saying to myself, "This person is good; this person is bad." That is grotesque! absurd! infantile!... I said to myself then that the facts did not follow that line, and that, perhaps, the scale of values was a little more subtle.

In the course of the thirties, I lost, little by little, that habit that we had of saying "This person is reactionary; this person is progressive." That is nonsense. All the more because a thing can always evolve and change itself into another, in its nature or in its functioning. There are derivations or mutations, but everything changes and continues to change. In the period after the war, as you know, things continued to go that way; there was *this* way, and that *other* way, but nothing else. It was then that I began to make films against puritanism. *East of Eden* was an anti-puritan film. The character whom everyone could believe a good son and a good boy ended by turning into a monster from egotism and complacency, while the one whom everyone could say was a very bad boy ended by showing that he possessed, in depth, more of real goodness than the first.

And I think that I went much farther in *Baby Doll*, for in that film, the business man—the man conspicuous for his material possessions—the middle class citizen, the one who is a model for the community and who is liked by everyone (and who himself is, in a sense, worthy of being liked), that man is insulted in all possible ways, beginning with his wife, who refuses herself to him, then sleeps with another man in his own house. Moreover this man is, in reality, a lyncher.

But there is something laughable in the way the French and the English treat the ridiculous things about us; they make all the Whites who oppose the Blacks into the Wicked, into the Villains. That is, in fact, very far from the truth, as I discovered when I went down to the South. From all other aspects they are often discerning men, charming, fascinating, born story-tellers, closely linked to the land and to the men who live on it, to the animals, to the trees and the rivers, and they understand the way in which life evolves. It is that kind of man who was to be in *Wild River* later, and who really appeared for the first time in *Baby Doll*. I thought for a long time that I had made, with *Baby Doll*, what one could call a black comedy, but now I know that I was orienting myself particularly in the direction that I have just told you! For the characters, grotesque, absurd, as they all are, are in another sense, true, human. Because in the film there are not Good and Evil, justice and injustice, but all that at the *same* time, mixed with the people, and capable of taking several directions—which is the very way in which that happens in life. Sometimes a gesture is enough to reveal this passage from one world to another. In *America, America,* for example, when the boy takes his coin, tosses it and catches it again, you say to yourself immediately—that is an American gesture. He has just grasped the style; an American is in the process of being born before our eyes. We are in front of a new table of values.

Everything that this boy undertakes is motivated by this sole aim—to bring his family to America. He arrives at his ends by means that seem bad, yes. But who can say whether they are good or bad? Do the categories mean anything? Is there a Value that lets one ask those questions?

CAHIERS: *In the confrontation of* Wild River—*the two worlds incarnated by the old lady and the young emissary—we see that both, in the end, understand the motives of the other and enrich themselves by this understanding.*

EK: Exactly. And this old lady, who is the incarnation *par excellence* of Reaction, who combats social progress, is heroic, yet stupid in a sense, but humanly, who knows?...One can never say. That is the complexity of life, the very thing that made me change, too, the behavior of my actors. For it is not only a question of the subject; it expresses itself at all levels, even in the casting.

Hold on—there's a thing that just struck me. It is *La Guerre est finie.* I like Resnais' work; it never leaves me indifferent, and often interests me very much. Only, something in the film put me ill at ease. It is the actor's shirt—Yves Montand's—always clean, from the beginning to the end. After all, he makes love with the girl, completely dressed, and when he gets up, his shirt is absolutely as before!...Then, I said to myself—well! Just look at that!...All the same, that is an idiotic objection, infantile... and I protested, I grumbled....Yet Resnais has felt certain things in a rather desperate and confused situation very well indeed, and that is what I liked in the film. But at the same time...I could not keep from coming back to that man's shirt, and I said to myself—but after all, is that how one wears a shirt when one is a man in his situation? Does he always conduct himself as he is supposed to be? That defines the part of the film in which there is nothing. Another point that struck me and amused me— the sex scenes. You see the girl's legs separating gently, progressively, like that....What is that supposed to represent? Either you are frank about sex, or you are not. But let no one say that this is the way that things happen! It is not a virgin with her beautiful legs separating for the first time like a flower—for that is the tone of the scene. Yes, I suppose that it must be hard for Resnais to imagine what she was going through in those circumstances. I do not know, but a man is there who decides to take her, so one can think that there will be a certain aggressiveness on the part of one or the other. I mean—I do not know exactly how that would have happened, but it seems to me that, in a way, the life has been taken out of this scene, and that a schema, a pictorial schema, has been substituted for it. Life, in any case, would have been full of contradictions and diverse interests, and if he had sought to render what really happens, instead of thinking about his schema....

CAHIERS: *A little while ago you mentioned the gesture with the coin, in* America, America. *That makes me think of some other details—the old woman*

on her chair, in front of whom Natalie Wood passes when she comes out of the
clinic; the road that is being tarred in Wild River, *exactly in front of the house*
into which the old lady is moving—followed by the shot in which one sees two
cars pass each other on the road (in both cases the detail is there to emphasize
the painful aspect of the situation), and, in America, America, *the handshake*
between the boy and the woman, through which the difference of the two worlds
is revealed. Now the question is—in this kind of detail, what is the share of
preparation and improvisation?

E K :   In fact, that is really what I wanted to show. But in the scene in
Wild River, there are the feet, too—the heaviness of steps that stick....
How does that come to me? During the periods of shooting, I have the
habit of working between 8 and 9 in the morning to begin what has not
yet been written nor photographed—the behavior of the people and what
there is behind it. I examine what I have, and if I am not satisfied with
it, I try to find the thing that, in the simplest way, will make appear the
very essence of such behavior, in such a situation. In *Splendor in the Grass*,
when the girl leaves the clinic, I wanted to obtain a strong feeling of relief.
Fifteen years ago, I would have shown her face, and then I would have
added a sigh, an Ah!... or a Whew!... anyway, something of that sort. But
by showing an old woman, and the young one who merely glances at her
in passing, from the mere fact that the old woman is there and that the
young one looks at her, you hear her say to herself, Thank God I have not
become like that! I am delivered from all that! I am free!... In short, where
before I would have relied on Natalie Wood's acting, today I leave it to
the audience to take part in the acting itself, that is to say, to experience,
starting from what it sees, something analogous to what Natalie Wood
experiences.

Another thing (I am still on the same subject—anyway I believe so)—I
no longer believe now in easy respect from another person, but in another's
respect painfully acquired. I believe that it is not really easy to love someone in life, but if you persevere on and on, finally in spite of his flaws, in
spite of your own prejudices, in spite of your aversions, in spite of the way
life goes, you end up loving that person. For what he is, what he will be,
everything. You do not see his goodness or his badness, where he is wrong
or where he is right; you value him as a human being, for his vividness,
and not for his perfection, for his humanity, and not for his conduct. In a
sense, it is the details that lead back to that, which I seek, details that will

be able to reveal what a human soul is, instead of pointing out to you—this fellow is right, or—this fellow is wrong.

CAHIERS: *And the tarred road?*
EK: I thought of that the night before, and I said to my assistant, "Get a tar spreader and put it in front of the house tomorrow, so that people will see the road in the process of being made." And I wanted a great deal of smoke, so that the audience would smell the odor of the tar. You know, that was one of the most familiar odors for Americans between thirty and forty years old. Now they use concrete, but at that time it was old black tar, and it gave off one of the most memorable odors of all. Today that odor brings with it, or, really, makes an entire era spring up again around it.

Ordinarily, that is how things come to me. But it depends on the period in which I work. In general, it comes at the moment when I am in the process of immersing myself in the work, of imposing myself upon it as a creator, and not while I am conceiving it or while I am preparing it. Then, the details are still nothing, but when one approaches the shooting, one begins to think about them, and sometimes, even, one introduces into a scene something that came to him the day before. For my part, I have this kind of idea especially at the moment when I begin to work on the scene on the set, where it seems to me that nothing else exists any more, where I no longer think except of one thing—to render everything in the truest, most exact way possible. For example, that moment in *East of Eden,* where Jimmy Dean defies his father; he is on a swing—you remember that?—and he swings, back and forth. I thought of that the night before. I wanted everything in him to express to his father—I could not care less what you think of me, you will not be able to reach me, you will not be able to touch me, you no longer control me, you no longer have me in hand; look—I am escaping you, you think that you have me, but you do not have me, you have me, but you do not have me.... You feel the movement? the swinging? I had only to put it in concrete form.

CAHIERS: *And the handshake?*
EK: That was prepared beforehand. I worked much more and much longer on *America, America* than on my other films. On the script too. That was the first film that I wrote entirely, all alone, the first film that was entirely mine, that is why I worked particularly hard on it.

About that scene in Wild River *of which we were speaking a little while ago, in a* ciné-club *someone said you were exaggerating in the accumulation of details. What have you to say to that?*

EK: There is no exaggeration; there is the truth, that is all. But I believe that the audience grasps the idea of the scene, and that is the essential thing. I made that scene with what I am, with what I love, and perhaps that is where I am at fault; I love vividness, I love to make it possible for the audience to feel something with all their senses, with all their memories, with all their associations and their experiences. And I do not like tenuous experiences. Because, too often, we go through things at flying speed. Bam! Poof! It is past, finished; nothing has reached us. And it seems to me that what an artist should do is stop! come! stop! look! just look at that! just feel that! That is not a fleeting moment that leaves no trace; it is an experience, and human experience means something. What is there ought not pass— poof!—like a breath in front of your nose. It ought not pass through your body as if you were transparent! It is something that happens, that is in the process of happening, to that person, there, in front of you.

The audience now, especially the American audience, watches television, it is a habit, an eye in the corner, all the while talking, in back, in front, or yacking.... Then what you show them means nothing at all, if you do not succeed in provoking them. One must almost shock them, give them a turn, if one wants to make them aware that something deep can happen, that it is in the process of happening. It takes that for the audience, they need that, otherwise it will be—Well! nothing is happening... hold on! pass me the beer!... and there is the war, and the boys who get themselves killed, and the civilians who get themselves killed, now in Vietnam, but that passes, everything passes... a form of habit, a form of distraction; that is television. Then one must provoke them, shock them, so that they feel that people, today, are bleeding, dying. Otherwise, if you merely "show," they will say—well, it's still television... so pass me the beer, and let's change channels, we will try something else. You know, at that rhythm, nothing, in the end, has meaning any longer.

What ought an artist to do if it is not that—to force them to feel, since they do not want to or cannot discern any longer by themselves?

One of the things that explains the commercial disaster of Wild River *is that you are among those directors who go "too far" (and what is more, within a framework—scope, color, actors—which the audience tends to associate with a conventional form of spectacle). The love scenes, for example, about which people have said that you were exaggerating. What shocks, there, what comes from that to the audience, is that either one goes very far and one is being "sexy" (even if being "sexy" lets you do so without going very far), or else one is not being "sexy," and then one hasn't gone very far. But if one does go far—as far as you do—without it being "sexy," then the audience feels itself completely lost.*

EK: That is it, I think. But, in relation to that scene, I'd add one detail; the first time that the hero embraced Lee Remick, I directed him as I felt him. He is an intellectual, and, consequently, he feels himself above life, he lives a distilled life in which things never affect him too much. In fact, he is a little bit of a snob, and in the bottom of his heart, he thinks himself superior to this very common girl. Starting from there, what I tried to render is that love is the first equalizer, the first thing that makes them equal. That is why, if you remember, I made them go on the floor. I made him go there, with her, and one sees there, on the floor, something like two animals. . . . They are down at the bottom, brought back to the base of things, so that his mind, more educated, more subtle than that woman's, at that moment no longer makes any difference. Is that sexy? In any case, my intention was not "sexy"; it was to break and to lay low his snobbery.

Let's take Truffaut. He is extremely sensitive, and I really do like his work, which is very exciting, especially *The Four Hundred Blows*. Now, *Jules and Jim* interested me greatly, but in that film he did something that I would not be able to do, because I do not believe that it is true. I do not believe that after four years of war these two friends could meet each other again on the same level, united by the same bonds, their faces unchanged, along with their attitudes.

What! . . . Four years have passed, four years of a horrible war, and the men reappear in quite as good health as before, quite as plump, quite as courteous, quite as friendly as before, without any physical mark, without any moral tension. . . . I don't believe a word of it! It is like the other man with his shirt—I just don't believe in it! That is an attitude before life, it is theory preceding facts and simplifying life.

CAHIERS: *Again people have said—still about* Wild River—*that the photography was too exaggerated, was false. What do you think of that?*

E K : I feel that the photography was very good, especially in the exterior scenes. But I am not as fond of the photography of the dramatic scenes shot close up in interiors. I said to myself—his face is too orange, it looks too pleasant—especially that of the hero. As for Clift—who is dead now, and who was a great artist—at that time Monty Clift's skin was in very bad condition, and consequently he used too much makeup. Therefore the colors were at once too crude and too healthy. So I said to the camera-man—this man is an intellectual; he has never seen the sunlight before coming here; he has come down here among us straight from his office. Thus I want him to have the air of a bureaucrat, to have a touch of the bureaucrat about him. But that did not work very well. . . . Oh, I do not want to blame anyone; merely, I failed and I regret it. All the more because I would have liked very much to get the contrast between his pallor and the wholesome glow of the girl.

I have never really made a success of color, up to now. At least accord-ing to my own criteria. Yet I approached each of my color films saying to myself, —this time, I am going to make something magnificent. And I have tried everything. I have even gone to the point of painting the entire set to try to deaden the colors, to leaving just a few splotches of them, here and there, but whatever I did, I never completely succeeded. The only film in which I approached what I call a success was *East of Eden,* in which the colors were really beautiful, not prettily so. Now, before starting to work again in color, I am going to wait till I have studied the question thor-oughly. I do not want to dash into battle before having prepared everything, tried everything, experimented on everything, and very carefully. Before beginning my next film, I am going to make a great many tests, which I am preparing at present. I will make them in 16mm, and then have the film enlarged to 35mm, so as to obtain gradations and study their quality. That is what I seek: the gradations.

The trouble is that color has imposed itself on cinema as an amusement value, and that people are used to having pretty colors before everything else. Moreover, color is a very difficult thing to control technically. The material is manufactured by Eastman Kodak or some other large corpora-tion, and it is manufactured as determined by what most directors want. There are the laboratories, too. I cannot control them; they do things their way; they develop the film following certain norms established in practice; they have orders, they follow them; they are not there to please me, they

are there to please the people who are going to make the next two hundred films. So, no matter what your argument or your protests, you may as
well beat the wind or strike out with your fists, nothing can be done about
it. No doubt they will end by saying—Yes, yes, of course...and then, as
soon as they are all alone, they will always do a little more, or a little less,
than what you asked, and afterward you can go chase yourself....

CAHIERS: *We will come back to the actors, but taking another track—some
people say that one must employ professional actors; others, that one can do
nothing with them and that it is better to use amateurs.*
EK: It is very difficult to work with actors. Because the life that most of
them live is a life of cafés. There is the school, the café, the stage, the studios....Life cannot leave its marks on their faces. They do not live the
despairing life that human beings live. They are for the most part childish,
spoiled, plump, their faces have not been distorted or illuminated...in
short, they do not bear on them the marks of life lived. It is very rare to
find an actor who has that, and still more rare to find one who can play
that. Let's take Brando who is the best actor I have ever worked. At the
time when I made *On the Waterfront*, he was a much better actor than he is
now. I do not mean that talent can be lost, like that, all at once. Only at
the time he was an unhappy young man, anxious, who doubted himself,
and he was solitary, proud, oversensitive. He was not someone particularly
easy to get along with, and yet he was a wonderful and lovable man,
because one felt that nothing protected him from life, that he was in the
midst of it. What is terrible with an actor is that it is hard for him to prevail over success. As with all artists, success is more difficult to prevail over
than failure. They all use success to isolate themselves, to keep aloof from
experiencing life, so that the more success an actor has, the more he
acquires the look of wax fruit; he is no longer devoured by life. Now, most
of the characters that he has to play must be. That is why I must always
find new actors for my films, among those who do not have—not yet—
success, among those who still have a passion, an anxiety, a violence that
they will almost always lose later. For I have never employed "stars," even
if my actors sometimes became stars after that. In *Wild River*, Lee Remick
was not yet a star, and Monty Clift had lived a terrible catastrophe beforehand, and he was miserable. When Natalie Wood made *Splendor in the
Grass*, she was at the end of a career, and people said generally that she

was finished, washed up. . . . Since then she has indeed come up again, but one had to see her then, she was in despair. In short, I try to catch my actors at the moment when they're still, or once again, human. And if you have a human actor, at that moment, you can slip your hand inside, touch him and wake him.

But a star. . . . Success protects them; their space is different; they float, distant from everything. Nothing that happens touches them. And I'm forgetting Jimmy Dean; he was a beginner in *East of Eden*. He had never yet acted. He was just a young fellow who prowled about the front offices. But he had violence in him, he had a hunger within him, and he was himself the boy that he played in the film.

I never choose actors by having them read the script. I do it after having talked with them, a great deal, to discover what they are really like. And when I have discovered that the essence of the acting that I want to obtain exists somewhere within them, at that moment I know that I can use them.

CAHIERS: *To what extent do you think that what there is in an actor (an actor who is suitable for you, whom you have chosen) should be able to express itself, or left free to express itself?*

EK: I am convinced that what there is in the actor, starting from the moment when it is there, somewhere in him, (and even if it is protected, covered over, buried), you can go after it, and you will end by obtaining it. In *A Face in the Crowd*, for example, my actor had the first part of the film in him. But not the second half. There was nothing to be done. It was no longer anything but a facade, a mask, and the interpretation became superficial. Yet the first half he had done magnificently, as a man of talent, and quite simply as a man. Only, that second half—he did not have it in him. I tried everything; but there was nothing to be done, even on the days when he was drunk. No use to force, to push; you will never get a thing from someone who doesn't have it. An interpretation must be built starting from that and from nothing else—from what lives within a man and which should nurture the role. The current must pass through the actor. The river that is the story of the acting has its own current; you must feel it there in order to be able to capture it. In *Splendor in the Grass*, the boy—Warren Beatty—was new then, and I think that he has never been better since. There was a girl, too—the sister—who was wonderful.

But I knew her personally beforehand, I knew what was in her—but you would never have guessed it by looking at her. You had to know that there was something inside. I knew it; I caught it.

If one examines what one can do with an amateur, one quickly discovers that it is very limited. But sometimes one must use them, and I have done so. Only I think that *America, America* would have been better if I had had a professional actor endowed with the same qualities that my young amateur had in him. But that special form of virility that was his, no actor could give me. That young man had gone through the Greek civil war; his father had been wounded and had died in his arms. That boy, at fifteen, found himself the head of an entire family, and he acquired a kind of hardness, of avidity, of force of soul. And he was unshakeable; it was impossible to make him deviate from his road. It was with such qualities that he succeeded in protecting his family and in allowing it to survive.

But, on the other hand, he had serious limitations, because he was not an actor. You see, on the one hand you gain, on the other you lose; it is for you to establish your own balance. As for me, I tried to obtain the thing that seemed primordial to me—the life that he had in him that should pass into the role. That is what I want, and it matters little to me whether I have it with a professional or with an amateur. At the same time, I am very flexible, very detached, very careful, too, not to use what would not be suitable. That is another trouble with stars—they distrust the story that you are telling. The character is already familiar to you, and, thereby, the story itself is familiar to you; you know in advance that some things can or cannot happen, and what would spoil everything. Thus, I would have liked *La Guerre est finie* better if I had not already seen Montand elsewhere. He is a good actor, and I have nothing against him, but I think that this story of resistance, very special, would have been infinitely richer for me if I had not already seen that face. I do not defend that at all as a theory; I do not trust theories, they do not interest me. I only say my taste, the way that I am, my own feeling of life.

CAHIERS: *At the start you mentioned Inge's name. Even when he works with mediocre directors, his scenarios always succeed in giving the films that result from them a certain personality. . . .*

EK: William Inge has a real talent, but that talent is more that of a miniaturist. That is his true field. I do not mean at all that this is a form of talent less worthy than another, only, that this is the special form that his talent takes. He keeps everything and everything serves him—his childhood memories, his parents, his mother, the house, the home town, the people whom he has known, the fellows, the girls... And all that is put to use through a quite authentic talent and an exceptional sensitivity. But his talent is so linked to what is banal, ordinary, that a slight lowering of tension or a very slight share of failure is enough for his work itself to appear banal, ordinary. Does that answer what you were asking? In any case, that is what I think.

Inge is someone who can easily come off well starting from anything, but he is very perceptive, sometimes astonishingly deep. I think that the best thing in *Splendor in the Grass* was not so much the love story or anything else, as the portrait of the mother. At the end, when she says, "I have done my best... How can I have done wrong? Tell me...." That was the result of a very deep vision. But, you see, that is not a big effect, it is one of those little effects that one can quite well let pass without noticing. Yet it truly expresses reality, and not only that of the mother, but that of the entire era behind it, an entire style of life, seen through a certain America, static, anchored in the past and refusing change.

CAHIERS: *Two questions now about two directors whom some people think have certain points in common with you either because of their relations with the theater, or because you have influenced them, or, quite simply, because they have met you at certain points—Richard Brooks and Arthur Penn.*

EK: I hope indeed that I have influenced no one. For I do not believe in schools; I believe in individuals. The more a man is himself, the more he is unique, the more he is true, the more value he has. I have not seen the movie that Brooks made from *Sweet Bird of Youth*, but I originally staged the play in the theater, and since he used some of the players I had on the stage the acting that they gave him can not have been very different from what they had given to me. If certain directors have been influenced by me, or say so (I do not know whether that is true or not), in any case, that does not particularly interest me. People say that about Martin Ritt, who was my assistant in the past, but, to tell the truth, I have not liked his films very much. In any case, I do not believe that to take something to oneself can give one anything. I mean—in one way or another, one must come to write one's autobiography. That I believe. At least it corresponds

to the way in which I feel things. And the sooner one rids oneself of influences, even of good ones, the better.

When I was young, I admired Eisenstein immensely, and most of all
Dovzhenko. He was my God. To me he was the greatest innovator in cinema. But I do not try to make films like him, and my films—I do not
know what value they have, but they are no one's but mine. If ever anyone has been influenced by me, I hope that he will rid himself of this
influence.

CAHIERS: *A few years ago,* Cahiers *asked you if you had seen the* Poème de
la mer *of Dovzhenko (with which* Wild River *has a point in common) and, at
the time, you had not seen it.*
EK: I still have not seen it. The film of Dovzhenko's that, in the past,
most influenced me was *Air City—Aérograd*—that struck me enormously. I
saw it again recently in Paris. There are, quite simply, admirable things in
it. Those two men, for instance—one of whom is going to kill the other—
who begin to recite a poem together. That absolutely antirealistic thing.
They stand beside each other and begin to recite the poem facing the audience.... That is magnificent.

I think that another great innovator is Godard. He has brought some
astonishing contributions to cinema. And all his films are extraordinarily
stimulating. There is another too whom I like, Jean Vigo. On the contrary,
I am not very interested in the work of American filmmakers. The one
whom I like best is John Ford, and his best films are films like *Young Mister
Lincoln* and *The Long Voyage Home,* into which he has put his form of
poetry, that is to say a poetry of the ordinary, of everyday people, a poetry
that springs from a combination of the hardship that is at the depth of life
and the beauty which, at the same time, emerges from it. But there again, I
do not think that I shoot my films like him. Except that I do not use the
dolly at every end of the field either. Ford puts the camera on the ground.
One point, that is all. Unlike the fashion that comes from television—all
the takes must move and swing! Go there in one direction, go there in the
other.... Those tricks distract me; they disperse the attention; I no longer
see the essential, the content.

CAHIERS: *I'll remind you of the other half of the question—Penn.*
EK: I think it still remains for him to find himself and define himself. I
do not believe that he really belongs to a cinema in which someone pre-

pares your script which you then have to direct. In *The Chase*, I think that he was submerged by Mr. Sam Spiegel, who is himself a very intelligent man, but not at all in the same way as Penn. There is something there that does not hold together. No director should have several faces. One cannot have the face of a producer, the face of an *auteur*, and one's own face. One cannot glue everything together. But Penn is a man of great qualities. Until now he has not, I think, found the opportunity to express his special gifts, but sooner or later he will find his own way. I do not much like *The Chase*. Moreover, the film simplified the Bad Guys, the Villains, considerably. I have been in Texas a great deal myself, and I worked there when I was a young man. I have traveled over it up, down and across. So, yes, I know very well that there are people there who are violent, full of hatred, but not all of them! and not all the time! And I know too there are people like them in Paris. No—nothing is so clear cut. Confronted with wicked people, you *should* say to yourself—this could be me. You *must* say that to yourself. You don't have the right to say—look at that fellow; he is someone of a different species, he is an evil man! No! That makes no sense! You just don't do that! One must say to oneself—that could be me, that could be me. People must not play the superior being. Now, I think that in *The Chase* everything was seen starting from a superior and snobbish point of view. I do not believe that that was really Penn's fault. Only, something did not work. The machinery was too heavy. There was a script to respect, and it was Lillian Hellman; there were the actors; there was Spiegel. . . . In the midst of all that he was only an executor responsible for transmitting.

CAHIERS: *These questions were perhaps not very exciting for you; in any case they were fruitful, for they brought you back to speaking of the simplification of life, that is to say, of its complexity. That is why I come back to that here by connecting the matter with the audience—for there, too, you trouble, you disturb people. Indeed, on the one hand you give them all the elements necessary for understanding reality, and, on the other hand, they feel the richness and the complexity of these elements as a hindrance to judging. Everything happens as if you were forbidding them judgement at the same moment when you seem to permit it to them. How can they judge the old lady of* Wild River? *And the boy of* America, America? *Is this a pleasant character with unpleasant aspects or the opposite?*

EK: That is exactly it, and I wouldn't want to say it otherwise. That is what I want to do. And what judgement can you bear on *Baby Doll*? And on the characters of *Splendor*? And that boy of *America, America*? Is he good, is he bad? And what do those words mean? Have they so much significance? My films are not judgements; they are events, and an event happens. So I do not want to give them ready-made judgements. No. When I show someone, I want to say—look! That might have been you! That might have been me! That is the way in which things happen.

The theatre, I think, does not prepare people for life. It represents a simplification of life that makes things easier to digest. One prepares the audience to receive them. But one must not prepare them. Or rather, one must prepare them for life, harshly. One prepares them for carrying on their lives, harshly or violently. One must illuminate them, widen life for them, through its real events. But in no case will you arrive at that if you bring people to say to themselves—I am good, very good, and I know everything, but that fellow, down there, he is a filthy slob...even if you bring them to say that in a slightly more subtle way.

So, perhaps I trouble people, but that is because I do not want to let them alone. And it is all the same to me whether they are contented or not! I do not mean that I rejoice if my films are not successes. Oh no! Very much the contrary. I would like very much for them to be successes, but I am not willing to pay any price to get it. The fact that *America, America* did not do well was very painful to me. I would have wanted so much for people to see it. If only it had had a minimal success!...But no, not even that. Nobody wanted to see it. On the other hand, if I were to do it again, I would not want to change anything. Except certain things that I could improve, but I would not change the pace, or the tone. And especially I will not change my way as a result of such reactions. What I like is to render certain experiences of life, as I see them, as I think it is necessary to render them. What I like is to do that in movies. But if I cannot do it in movies, I can write a book. And that is exactly what I did. It came to me after the failure of *America, America*. I felt down and out. I said to myself—I would do better to write a book, and I set to work at it. That is the book about which I spoke to you in New York. *The Arrangement*. How would you translate that into French?

CAHIERS: L'Arrangement....

EK: So I wrote the book, which is a very full book, very rich, very long, very frank. Very candid too. And everything is in that book, about what I think of America, of a certain sector of American life. I hope that people will read it.

Happily my standard of living is... low. I mean that I have no need for a Rolls Royce, no need for prestige, no need to have my name in the newspapers — I have had my fill of that — I want simply to do what I want. I hope that people will see what I do; I hope that people will like what I do.

Someone has said — I no longer remember who — that the work of art should correspond to nature, should present itself as a natural phenomenon, and that one should first be able to say — this phenomenon *is*.* And if it is like a phenomenon, like an event, it is certain that two people will very well be able to see in it two different things. It is like the mountain for the painter. It *is*, that is all. But that same mountain means one thing to Cezanne and another totally different thing to another painter. Each one imprints on it his own vision. But who is to say which of the two mountains is true?

What people reach in my films, they reach through me. Ultimately it is I whom they reach. They see life, but through my way of seeing it and of rendering it. If I do that honestly, they will be able to say — That is indeed *he*. That is the man. That man. That is the way he sees things. That is true. But others will say — I do not like that. I do not like that at all, I do not like that filthy slob. I want never again to see any of his films! Then... good! That is all right with me! Some are for, some are against.... That is normal.

CAHIERS: *This "arrangement" that is the subject of your book, and about which you have already spoken, is the subject too of all your films — the arrangement that is brought about — or that must be brought about somehow or other — between the ideal and the reality.*

EK: You would have to read the book. Everything is in it. It is the truest thing that I have done until now. It is everything that I see and feel about the America of today. I love my country, as you know, and my feelings often go towards it. At the same time, I have some other very violent feelings, and some fears. Not about politics, or other things of that kind, but

---

*Diderot: "Every composition worthy of praise everywhere and in everything is in agreement with nature; I must be able to say, 'I have not seen this phenomenon, but it *is*.'" (French *Cahiers* editor's note).

about the essence of the civilization that we express, and I have—I hope—shed some light on that. But those things are still too close to me at this moment for me to be able to talk about them. The book is written; they are in it...I show in that book that many things in American life are arrangements—in the bad sense of the word. They do not correspond to the truth; they do not respond to the true bonds between people; they are arranged bonds. Relationships adjusted so that they will be viable, endurable. Here I am speaking of the gulf that there is in America between the professed moral code and the actual moral code. In a word—America pretends to have a certain morality, but, in fact, it has another.

CAHIERS: *In* Splendor in the Grass *the father—within the puritanical moral code—says to his son that, besides the serious girls, there are others with whom one can amuse oneself. Yet gulfs of that kind between what one is presumed to do and what one does, exist—and not only in America.*
EK: For my part, I study this phenomenon as I know it, *where* I know it, in the country that is my own, that I love but which worries me. At the same time, each person will be able, through the phenomenon that I describe, to make the comparisons that he wants to make. To decide what is like puritanism. Through the form that it has taken in America, one can very well discover the form that it has taken elsewhere, the one that perhaps others have known. Puritanism—puritanisms—are a simplification of life. There are simplifications everywhere. That is why *Splendor in the Grass* can provoke in certain countries the same kind of reaction that it provoked in America.

CAHIERS: *You provoked that kind of reaction very early. With* On the Waterfront, *for example.*
EK: Yes. Certain films of mine have been detested, but that one particularly. In the case of *Waterfront*, it was the left that detested it. In the case of *Baby Doll*, it was the right...With *Viva Zapata*, they were in agreement. The communists hated the film, and the right hated it too. All protested—"What have you done?"—*Streetcar* had already brought me some troubles with censorship, *Baby Doll*, still more. The Catholic Church attacked the film very violently, and Cardinal Spellman condemned it. And he did that in the greatest cathedral in America. It was a shame! A slur! I was dishonoring America! And he forbade people to go to see it. Yet the film is very

gentle and very simple; it says just what it must, but not more. Only, as you say, it troubles, it disturbs. And when one troubles professed values—officially professed by a group, by a society—people no longer know at all where they are. They do not want to see life as complicated, as confused, as it is. They do not want to confront it as it is. Look at Dostoyevsky. He was a great man because he troubles people, he mixes up their thinking. I believe in confusion because confusion is true. I do not mean dramatic confusion—you must show clearly what you want to say—but confusion, contradiction in values.

Another thing—when I was a young man and went to California for the first time, to make films—to work on the first film of my life—I met a man, a producer, who had some influence on me. He is dead now. I was very much to the left, then. Now, I talked to that man, who was very much to the right, and I found myself admiring him, in some sense, at the same time that I detested him for his political views. And I could not make the connection between the two, and I did not stop saying to myself—you *ought* not to like that man! But there is something wrong there, when one comes to say to oneself—you *ought* not to like that person; you *ought* not to esteem him! One should not say that. That is why I think that my spontaneous reaction was truer than the other.

CAHIERS: *With* On the Waterfront *and* Viva Zapata, *there is a third film, a little of the same family since it represents another kind of struggle for a liberation—*Man on a Tightrope. *Which of the three do you prefer?*
EK: But why do people detest *On the Waterfront* so much? That I have never been able to understand! ... The most violent attacks! The hatred.... All the same I have the right to say what I think. What there is in *On the Waterfront*, I saw, I studied, I made investigations. And I was not the only one at that task. We spent months at it. We verified, we checked.... All the same we did not lie! I am quite willing for people to have different views from mine, but I am still waiting for someone who knows the New York docks as well as I do to come and prove to me that I invented out of whole cloth this or that thing that I showed. Many reactions were provoked by the priest, I know. Why? It seems that people were indignant because I showed him as a man who had goodness.

But as for *Man on a Tightrope*, I think that that was a failure. For everything concerning the personal lives of the characters, the love stories, was not really very successful. But what concerned the exterior adventure—the caravan, the passage of the frontier—that part was rather good. Certainly not as good as it could have been, but not a failure. In short, I think that I succeeded at the part of the film that I *really* felt, where I could bring to a successful conclusion what I wanted. It was a script that I had not worked on myself, afterward, I never did that again. The script was by Robert Sherwood. He had done it completely, and had never even talked to me about it beforehand. I came into the affair late and without preparation. Finally... there remains at least the passage of the frontier, which I think was, at once, amusing, interesting, and dramatic, and I think that starting from things like that, one could have made a good film.

CAHIERS: *It seems that, of these three, it is* On the Waterfront *that you prefer.*
EK: No! *Zapata!* I love *Zapata!* I think that that was a fine film. Of all the films that I have made, it is certainly one of those that are most dear to me. And the ending is very fine—the moment when he comes down from the mountains, and later—when they throw his body, and one hears the noise of the falling body. I love that... I have always liked that film very much. But I like *On the Waterfront* very much too.

CAHIERS: America, America *is a kind of summation of all your films. One finds in it* Waterfront, Zapata, East of Eden, Splendor in the Grass....
KAZAN: Yes, that is correct. There are similar situations in *America, America*. And there is, too, antipuritanism, which represents a very strong, very important current in me. You see, I am not, it seems to me, a very comprehensive personality. I am not very catholic, I do not have very diverse tastes, I cannot make films of very different kinds, and even, in a sense, I always make the same story (a little changed), again, and again, and again. That is all that I can do, it is what I know, it is what I have.... I am not many people at once. You see, I could not make a great spectacle, then a comedy, then something else, like Wyler. He makes a comedy, then he makes *Ben-Hur*. He makes a great many things. Me, I can come off more or less in my own register. Yet I develop; anyway, I think so. I change, but as if the same thing were changing, the same current, hollowing out its way, in proportion to different progressions. But I hope that I develop, that I improve. That I improve my style, too. Only I am not a magician, I cannot do this, do that—I cannot make the Bible, for example, and I will

Dorothy McGuire, *A Tree Grows in Brooklyn*, 1945

Gregory Peck, *Gentleman's Agreement*, 1947

Marlon Brando and Kim Hunter, *A Streetcar Named Desire*, 1951

Jean Peters and Marlon Brando, *Viva Zapata!*, 1952

Marlon Brando, Thomas Hanley, and Eva Marie Saint, *On the Waterfront*, 1954

Marlon Brando, *On the Waterfront*, 1954

James Dean, *East of Eden*, 1955

James Dean and Earle Hodgins, *East of Eden*, 1955

Carroll Baker, *Baby Doll*, 1956

Andy Griffith, *A Face in the Crowd*, 1957

Natalie Wood and Warren Beatty, *Splendor in the Grass*, 1961

Natalie Wood, *Splendor in the Grass*, 1961

Ingrid Boulting and Robert De Niro, *The Last Tycoon*, 1976

never be able to make a comedy—even if, as it happens, sometimes in my films there is, I hope, a certain amusement. No, I can only remain myself. Perhaps, in a sense, my films are boring. Because it is *he*, always he, always the same damned Kazan! And with *America, America....* Well! Commercial films are not my way.

CAHIERS: *Now let us take two other films of yours*—A Streetcar Named Desire *and* Baby Doll. *Both render somewhat the same atmosphere*—the South, sex, madness....
EK: Yes, but *Baby Doll* renders the atmosphere of the South in a truer way. In any case, *A Streetcar Named Desire* was shot in the studio, while *Baby Doll* was shot in real exteriors. But *Streetcar* is a beautiful theatre piece that I shot without softening it, without deepening it, filming it as it was because there was nothing in it to change. But I never set out to do that again, and I no longer believe in it. But I admired, and I still admire, the author of the play, Tennessee Williams, for whom I have much affection personally as well.

Baby Doll, on the contrary, had no theatrical antecedents. It is a thing that exists by itself and is like no other. It is, too, I think, the best film that anyone has made from Williams. And I was really able to put into it the atmosphere of the South, moral and social. It really corresponds to the way that the South folded in on itself, or developed. One interesting detail, for example—the Negroes. They are different now; they struggle, they organize marches. But at the time, they had no other outlet, to preserve their self respect, than to laugh—remember the Negroes of *Baby Doll* who laugh at the slightest pretext—to make fun of the whites whom they found vain and ridiculous.

CAHIERS: *Another pair now—we have already talked about them,* East of Eden *and* Splendor in the Grass, *both on adolescence.*
EK: Both, too, on puritanism. But in *Splendor in the Grass*, the two principal characters are much less active, they do not rebel because they are submerged in an environment that dominates them. In *East of Eden*, on the contrary, the boy rebels against his father, then after that forgets, and ends by forgiving him. *East of Eden* is more personal to me; it is more my own story. One hates one's father; one rebels against him; finally one cares for him, one recovers oneself, one understands him, one forgives him, and

one says to oneself, "Yes, he is like that"... one is no longer afraid of him, one has accepted him. But *Splendor in the Grass* is a sadder story because puritanism makes the youngsters weak. They lose something of their life. In a sense, it is a more true-to-life story, for it responds more to things that actually happen. Look at the end. They lose each other; they can no longer be together. Puritanism has wounded them, has cost them something, has killed something in them. The cost—that is something in which I believe a great deal. One must never believe that things happen without one's having to pay for them. Even in victory there is a price to pay. You gain one thing, but you also lose another. In the film, both gain, in a sense, but the price has been frightful, and this price is the point at which one is most sensitive.

CAHIERS: *In* Splendor in the Grass, *the young couple are victims of an environment, of a mesh; while the couple in* Wild River, *more mature, are able to face up to situations, in spite of the intermittent cowardice of the man in front of the woman. But to what extent do you think that the couple of* Splendor *appear as victims?*

EK: The couple in *Wild River* are, as a matter of fact, conscious, while the couple in *Splendor* are not conscious of the currents that drag them along, not conscious either of what they represent. They are not in a position to deal with reality. But can one say that they are purely and simply victims? To shift everything to parents, society... that can be a form of resignation, of complacency. My book develops certain things about that. I refer you to it. I cannot say everything.

CAHIERS: *And between* Wild River *and* A Face in the Crowd, *the point in common is that you describe certain aspects of American life in relation to politics.*

EK: I like very much the first part of *A Face in the Crowd*, but the second much less, as I told you. But not everything was the fault of the actor. We had not created a character as deep as we should have. It is because of that too that the film disappointed me. However, I am proud of that film, such as it is, because all the same it responds to reality. It is the first film that shows the power of the means of communication. The film shows, too, the moving nature of success, and of the one who sustains that success. And what it describes—the fact that a personality of little scope, but pleasant and stirring, takes the place of real intelligence—that fact represents the danger of democracy—one runs the risk of seeing a personality take the lead in a country, not because of his appropriate qualities and capacities, but solely because of his vividness. In spite of its imperfections, the film says a great many truths about America, in a way that is often amusing and striking, from a script very brilliantly written by Schulberg. At least in relation to the first part. As for the second, I believe that everyone was a little mistaken. He is a fine author, Schulberg. He is at present in California. He is the moving spirit of a group of young Negro writers; he works with them, he wants to make them able to express what they feel on the subject of the racial situation in the United States, the conflicts, Watts, and so on. I am thinking at this time of a film on the Puerto Ricans that I am going to try to make. That is one of the things on which I am working. The film would be shot in New York and in Puerto Rico.

CAHIERS: *You said that the character in* A Face in the Crowd *should have been deeper. So you seem to attribute your failure to the fact that you did not show sufficiently—at least in the second part of the film—the complexity of reality.*

EK: Correct! That's what I think. In the last part the character is too naive. He is an imbecile. And he becomes "The Villain." It is exactly that in which I do not believe. Exactly that which I refuse to make again. We set about it badly. It would have been necessary to make a much more complex character, much more intelligent, much more devious, that is to say, much more formidable.

CAHIERS: *Your first film, now*—A Tree Grows in Brooklyn. *Do you think that you put something personal into that?*

EK: Yes, I think so. And particularly into the way in which the personality of the drunken father is treated, and that of the puritan mother and the child. I remember the scene where the puritan mother says that life must follow a certain path . . . And the father is a bad man only to the extent that he is a drunkard, a man without value. Yet he gives the child more things, and more human ones, than the mother does.

CAHIERS: *Were you conscious of saying personal things?*

EK: That came to me quite simply because I was separated from my wife—because my wife and I had had conflicts. Also, I put into the film many of the feelings that I had then for my children, whom I had lost at the time, and for whom I languished. That was the personal note of the film. But I was not totally conscious of all that. I did not enjoy working on that script which someone else had written. At the same time, I did not dislike it. I felt a kind of fraternity toward it, in a certain way, I felt myself near it. When I see the film again now, I think, this is sentimental, but I also think that in it, there is much of the nostalgia that I had for my children, of my impulse toward them.

CAHIERS: *You were the first director who really worked in New York, and refused to work in Hollywood. What do you think of the New York-Hollywood opposition in its present form?*

EK: I do not think that an art can be organized like a commercial enterprise. In Hollywood, the entire organization aims at manufacturing amusement. Without any doubt, there are people of fine quality who work there, often conscientiously, and sometimes with talent. It is not they whom I question, but the whole of the organization. In New York, everything is smaller, and poor. You do not have facilities, but the mentality is different. In New York, you see, if you work starting from your apartment, you must indeed go to the corner of the street to buy yourself a pack of cigarettes, and you see something — life is there all around, you are inside it. In California, you are in a protected atmosphere, and at the end of a year, or two or three, you have lost contact with America, and even with everything that happens. Even Watts does not reach them. They do not see it. They have heard of it or they have seen it on television, but they do not have contact with it. Any more than with anything else.

In New York, yes, everything is more expensive. But there are ways of resolving the question. The question is first — to shoot in New York, not only in a studio, but everywhere that the film *should* be shot. One can succeed in that; it is feasible. Here, the demands of unions or cells of isolated technicians are greater, but you can form a small crew; that will let you gain time, and the expense will be less. And then, one can go away from New York, go where the expenses will not be so terribly high that you are strangled by them. It must surely be possible to make films somewhere else in America. In any case, the important thing is the small crew. I have seen Godard shoot, and it made me so envious. Everything was held in one small room. And his little crew was there, working around him, and Coutard did his lighting himself, tinkering right and left, fastening the lamps and lighting them. It was obvious that the budget was low but the expenses were too, and that he did what he wanted to because he did not have to endure the strangling grasp, the necessity of success.

That is what affects me now; when my films make a little—but not much—money people say, "Well! He is not commercial!" But I do not want to be commercial! That is not the aim of my life. But I have the big crew on my shoulders, and that represents obligations—it is all the more necessary to make money because it is necessary to pay for all that. I have been in Calcutta, too, to see Satyajit Ray shoot. He too had a small crew, and I envied him too. He has perhaps twenty people with him, that is all. And he arranges matters with his little world, in the small studios of Calcutta, or around it, in nature. One can put up a showing with that; it is not the big machine, as in California, where you have a crew of building contractors, where, on the simplest film, you have some hundred and twenty men. That is no longer a shooting; it is a safari! No. That does not interest me. I am not the commander of an army.

I had some successes in the past—two or three—but my best films, among them the last ones, did not make money. I no longer have the choice. I can no longer work here. It is the organization, the men, the material, everything. In the Hollywood organization, everything is connected. The method of work; the aim of work. Nothing in all that is right for me.

The cameraman whom I had for *America, America,* Haskell Wexler, was a man new to the field. It was his first job as a professional cameraman. He has made *Virginia Woolf* since. He is an excellent cameraman. He made *The Loved One,* too. But to me *The Loved One* is like a Hollywood film.

My aim, today, is to have small crews and lower budgets. One day I asked Ingmar Bergman with whom he made his films. He told me—with eighteen friends. He too made me envious. I know very well that in the past Hollywood has made some fine things, particularly the musicals, which I like very much. Only things have changed, and in any case, that atmosphere is not right for me.

I need to work in the very setting in which my films unfold, as I have always tried to do, so that everything in the environment stimulates me. *A Face in the Crowd* was filmed in the middle of Arkansas, and *Baby Doll* is full of things that I saw every day when I was in Mississippi. The wind, even, the rain, the dust, all that helps you, inspires you, and makes things alive. *Wild River* too was shot exactly where it should be, in Tennessee. And the river was there, and the trees were there, the fruit was there, and the people were there. Everything stimulated me and stimulated the others too. Each day we extracted some material from all that was there. And *America, America*. It is obvious that part of its value comes from its being a documentary on the near East. Even if it's only because of the faces, which are the poetry of the place. For the faces of the people, on the boats, had their truth. They were Rumanian refugees, Bulgarian—people come more or less legally from beyond the iron curtain, people who, after passing the frontier, had been put into refugee camps. And those faces, themselves alone, say more, it seems to me, than many words. No extra's face would have given me that. Those professional extras grown old and fat in the work, plump, glutted. People who have lived nothing, and who have no idea of what the people whom I used have lived. All that they know how to do is save money. And they have become cynics. Despair and cynicism are all that remain to them. They are still human, certainly, but that can no longer be seen, can no longer express itself.

C A H I E R S :   *But in New York there is another form of despair, another isolation. To take the young directors and the young technicians of today—they all react violently against Hollywood, and against America, but this devastating, uncontrolled reaction leads them finally to be against everything. Against life, even one would say; they flee it, with marijuana, and LSD. Film making itself is no longer anything but a form of escape. People bend their efforts to filming dreams, phantasms, obsessions, and contrivances . . . Do you think, given that, that anything can really spring from New York?*

E K :   It seems to me that the films to which you allude are the product of a very small group, very special and very isolated, who represent nothing and who mean nothing, except a fashion, a caprice, another form of snobbery, sometimes touching, sometimes idiotic. The fascination that LSD and other drugs exert on them, the fact that they use stimulants to bring themselves out of themselves, that is certainly revealing of something, it is not without significance, but until now they have always been unable to give form to this significance themselves. And the Hollywood-New York opposition is not situated there. Quite simply, what they do has scarcely any human interest. The great human dilemmas absolutely do not concern them. They are elsewhere, in a very narrow little world, very special, in which people cultivate sadistic or homosexual obsessions. For example, I have seen *Scorpio Rising*. But that is banality pure and simple. It is crap. Highly valued, but crap. Boring, moreover, and snobbish. To show boys who sleep with other boys has no special interest. It would have to reveal something profound. But first, we would have to know the real problems, those boys. If they revealed something true, something human, to me, at that moment, yes, I would be interested in what they were doing. Only, until now, I have seen absolutely nothing more than one boy in the process of having relations with another boy. What interest has that? What does one of those beings in those films reveal to me? I see in them only the expression of a world in which snobbery and phoniness prevail. There is Andy Warhol too, and many others, all who make what they call "cellar movies"—no doubt to change the name "underground movies." Those films that are shown in cellars. To show for hours boys or girls in the process of playing with each other does not seem to open extraordinary horizons.

Sometimes I happen to see certain films and say to myself—hold on! I had not thought of that! I had overlooked something! The day when they will make me say that, then yes, I will recognize that they have seen a thing that I had not seen. But not now, in spite of what the English magazines write about them—and *Sight and Sound!* There is, too, the cinema of the Maysles brothers. They are excellent reporters. And there is Ricky Leacock. He is without any doubt a great photographer, and even an artist of the camera. But never yet have I seen a film by those people that makes me feel reality more deeply. It is certain that if one considers this cult of drugs, sadism, and homosexuality, one must indeed think that involuntarily, or unconsciously it reveals something. It reveals sickness. And the study of those sicknesses would surely be interesting. But it is not the sick who will be able to do that. Indeed they reveal, in a sense, their alienation, their despair, their solitude, and so on. But they are not capable of giving them a form that would provoke interest, which would transform them into events. When an attitude is lived and shown as an event, then through that event you can discover that attitude. But you will discover nothing starting from an attitude statically and complacently described. This attitude, in itself, will never be able to provoke anything. They want to act on the reality? On America? But how could they? They have no contact with it; they are cut off from everything. What will they change? To whom will they speak? There is only the very narrow expression of a group of sick snobs. Because they are snobs. And because they are sick. When I say that, of course, I think too that it is painful to be sick. They have troubles, those little boys and those little girls; they are in distress. I would be quite willing to interest myself in their troubles, in their distress, but to interest myself in their phantasms, of that I am incapable! Especially those which they have with LSD. One can say what one wants to, but that kind of trick does not go very far. It reveals nothing to you, and those who practice it have nothing to reveal, except that they have escaped into a world in which they have had, for a certain time, strange sensations, sometimes agreeable, sometimes not at all agreeable. What more do you know of a being after that? Not much.

Now I must admit to you that it is scarcely possible to know exactly what can spring up in New York, and how. I said to you a little while ago that it was necessary to film outside Hollywood, that a solution could surely be found, notably thanks to the small crew. Perhaps among those disturbed young New Yorkers, there is someone with enough lucidity to confront reality. And enough talent to take something from it. That is possible, I hope, but I can say no more about it.

CAHIERS: *When you shoot in New York, do you have any special difficulties of a human, a technical, or an administrative order?*
EK: Yes, and one of those difficulties was that it was unheard of to let film-makers do what they wanted in the city. Now they are much more flexible. Instructions have even been circulated to the police to be more understanding or cooperative with film-makers. In any case, I never had insurmountable difficulties anywhere. One can always make some arrangement. And to begin with—one must talk to people, if they have worries. And one can always talk to them. One can always at least calm them, and sometimes even one can make them share one's enthusiasm. In any case, you have only to go ahead. They will not stop you. With *Waterfront*, yes, I had difficulties. And especially because I had trouble with a great many gangsters, who did not like at all what I was doing. I even needed a kind of bodyguard, a man who did not leave me and who watched what happened. There were also a great many young toughs who prowled around us or who played the fool on the docks. They also didn't much like what we were doing. Once a young fellow flung himself on me, and there was

the beginning of a brawl. But that got straightened out, and in any case it did not mean much. Those were rather like children's games.

It was with *America, America* that I had the most difficulties, in Istanbul. There were thousands of people who were furious at me because I showed the sordid aspect of the port of Istanbul, the degraded life of the workers, men heaped together like animals, or working like beasts of burden. Officially, the government did nothing against me, but I had constantly on my back, every minute of the shooting, a kind of censor who never stopped saying to me—you must not do this, you must not do that. And a great many people kept coming up, who hated me and created the worst difficulties for me. They ended by making work impossible for me. The government declared itself unable to protect me, and finally people told me that I had better leave the country. That was the worst crisis I had faced on a film. I had some trouble with *Baby Doll,* but that was less serious. For a week or two, it didn't go well, but finally it was settled. I did just one thing—I invited everyone to come to see us. They said to one another—if he invites us, he has nothing against us. So they came, and they watched us work. Those whom it interested watched us a long time; sometimes they came back. Those whom it bored stiff, cleared out. The difficulties were settled.

CAHIERS: *Your coming film, I think, will be another* America, America?
EK: Yes, but first I'm going to publish the book. Tomorrow I am leaving again for New York, where I have to correct the proofs. I've just learned that they are ready. I want to clear that out of the way immediately. But before doing that continuation of *America, America,* I am going to wait a little. A year or two, I do not know. Meanwhile, I am going to try to make another film. I'm in process of writing it. When you arrived, I was in the midst of pounding on the typewriter. Now I'm going back to work.

Elia Kazan

BERNARD R. KANTOR, IRWIN R.
BLACKER AND ANNE KRAMER/1970

ELIA KAZAN WAS INTERVIEWED in a small walkup
office on Broadway in New York City. It would be difficult to find a
greater contrast to the Hollywood suite he would warrant than this
writer-producer-director's working office. A warm personality who
had about him none of the trappings that usually adorn the presence of the "important man," Kazan seemed to be deeply involved
in what he was doing and how he was doing it. Too old now to
question the *why*—he had already made up his mind about that.

In New York, Kazan is a writer-at-work and not a director, but
his own strong feelings about himself and his work as a film
director dominate most of his thinking. Outside the office, the
noise of New York traffic, news vendors, and the confusion of the
city seemed to press in on a visitor, but Kazan did not seem to be
aware of the sounds. Several times the interview was interrupted
by phone calls—someone wanting a job, someone wanting to
offer a job, several personal messages.

The actor still appears when Kazan moves with a grace that
belies his years, and there seems to be about him the lightness of
a fighter on his feet, ready to weave and shift. Even in the simple
background of his office, he gives an interviewer the impression
of a committed man who is as much fighter as artist.

From *Directors at Work: Interviews with American Film-Makers,* Funk & Wagnalls, 1970.
Reprinted by permission of HarperCollins Publishers.

QUESTION: *Let's go back to the beginning. You started in theater. How did that happen?*

KAZAN: The thing that brought me into the theater was, oddly enough, films by Eisenstein and Dovzhenko that I saw in the early thirties. They made a profound impression on me. So before I was ever in the theater, I wanted above all to be a film director.

It was impossible in those days, or I felt it was, to say, "I'm going to be a film director," and start becoming one. So when I got a chance to go with The Group Theater, I jumped at it. There I met two men, Harold Clurman and Lee Strasberg, who did the same thing that the Eisenstein and Dovzhenko films did: made me feel that the performing arts, theater and film, can be as meaningful as the drama of living itself. And they made the theater, which was at that time in New York just a way to kill time, seem relevant to the social events of the time.

I was taken into The Group Theater, was a stage manager for a while, then an actor. But always in the back of my head what I *finally* wanted was to be a film director. During my early years with The Group Theater, I did make a couple of documentary films, one with a man named Ralph Steiner. He and I and another actor went out to the city dump, and improvised a two-reel comedy that was great fun to do. Then I did a documentary for an outfit called Frontier Films that—

Q: *Was that the agriculture film?*

EK: No, it was about coal miners in northeastern Tennessee. It was called *People of the Cumberlands*. I think my experience there, photographing non-enacted drama—day-to-day living behavior—was influential on the work I did later. I've always known since then that I could go into any environment and not only find interesting faces and people, but the drama and the poetry the simplest people have. What's poetic and what isn't, what's dramatic and what isn't, is in the eyes of the beholder, of course. Just being among these people with a camera was itself a dramatic event. It was a small camera and we didn't know exactly what we were going to do every morning; we simply went out and photographed what we saw that interested us. That for me was the beginning of what critics call neo-realism. That experience showed me that before and beyond a script there was life itself to photograph.

Q: *So story—script—has always been secondary for you?*

EK: No, I'm a great believer in having a well-constructed story. Story is the way character and destiny work themselves out in the lives of people. I like to watch a progression, one event influencing the next, and so on till the final climax. That's the way I feel life myself. What we do today is never erased; it determines what we do tomorrow. I believe in script too, and I've always worked very hard on mine. At the same time, I always try to leave the script free enough, open enough, so that the human material that's being photographed is not rigidly arranged to the point of choking out surprises, any unexpected possibilities. I think when you simply write a script, then photograph it mechanically, it is economically the practical thing to do and saves a great deal of money, but I think there's often a great deal lost. The process of shooting a film should be a creative one, not just a recording of what has already been determined before the shooting itself starts.

Q: *Do you think that your original acting experience in things like* Golden Boy *and* Night Music *has or did have a great deal to do with your working with actors?*

EK: I suppose so. I like actors and have great respect for the difficulties of their profession. I joke about it and say that the fact that I was an actor made me not afraid of actors. But it's more than that, really. Perhaps I understand their potentialities more having been one of them, and this allows me to use their creativity. In other words, I don't—perhaps because I was an actor—insist on a single interpretation. I somehow try to get them going and allow their own imaginations and their own reactions to the material to express itself. With a very good actor especially, I play for surprises. I set little traps and hope that he or she will do something that's better than what I had preconceived. In the case of the very best actors, the most gratifying thing about working with them is that they not only perform what I had in mind, they go further; they improve on what I had in mind, and very often they reveal things about the material that I had not imagined and for which I feel very grateful. "My God," I feel, "I could never have anticipated that!" or "Look what he's doing that I never knew was in this."

Q: *Do you think the Actors Studio which you founded has something to do with this? And the Method?*

E K : "The Method"—that term—has become a columnist's joke. There are
an awful lot of people who make teaching the Method a racket today, and
it's a very good living. Actually the Method was two quite different things:
one, a method of training actors, and the other, a method of rehearsing. It
was never, as I understood it, a method of acting, but a way of training
that takes many years. It's very hard work and requires tremendous devo-
tion. The other thing is that it's a method of rehearsing a play or preparing
a production of a play. The great Russian stage directors used this "method"
very well; that is, they would go on the premise that rehearsal is a process,
subtle, often long, a little mysterious. They scorned easy definitions and
oversimplifications. For them the "method" was neither a panacea nor a
quick, all-purpose stage trick nor an instant culture for sale.

Q : *In terms of working as a director both in theater and films, particularly with
the Williams plays and the Miller plays, what specifically did you do in terms of
adaptation from the stage to the film?*
E K : I only did one—

Q : *I'm thinking of* Streetcar.
E K : I only did one piece of work in both mediums. I had tremendous
respect for *Streetcar Named Desire* and for Williams himself, and I still do,
no less than I've ever had. I think he's *the* best playwright we've had in my
time. When I started to make a film of that play, I thought in the usual
terms. I thought we'd better open the play up, move it around a bit, make
it pictorially more varied and so on. After all, I thought, film is a visual
medium. We had better play some of the scenes somewhere else. So I
worked with a writer for about seven or eight months on an "opened-up"
script. I thought it was pretty good, put it away for a few days, then read it
again, and found it a total loss. I realized the compression in *Streetcar* is its
strength. So I went back and photographed the stage play as written. I
think that particular play merited that treatment, and I thought the film
came off pretty well.

Q : *In terms of your own adaptations and stories, you've really worked very
closely with writers, haven't you?*
E K : Yes, I have. I started working very closely with writers in 1952 when I
did *Viva Zapata!* with John Steinbeck. Of course, that's his work, and he

did a tremendous amount of research and knew just about everything on the subject. But I worked very closely with him, and I've worked very closely with every author since. Most of the things I've done, or that I did up until 1963—in that eleven-year period—were projects I initiated. I would suggest to an author, "Why don't we do this together?" Or, an author and I would get to talking and say, "Why don't we make a film out of this?" Then I would work closely with him. That doesn't mean I wrote the material. I did not. But I worked on the premise that I would be telling a good part of the story through the images I chose. It was understood without any declarations or anything of that kind that, since the story was going to be told through the camera, it was important that I be involved in the arrangement of scenes and sequences, as well as the images and the way the film was finally going to be cut. So I did work very closely with writers; nearly all good directors do. In 1963, however, I wanted to make films from stories that meant more to me personally, that were out of my personal past, or out of my own life experience. I wrote a script myself, an original screenplay called *America, America*, and I made that. Many people who've seen that picture feel that I would have done it better if I'd had a collaborator of some kind or a producer to tell me it was a bit long, and so on. But I don't feel that way. I think it *is* a little long, but all in all I was pleased with it and happy that I'd been able to do it. And, more important for me, I felt a great opening up of possibilities. Having had a taste of writing, I decided to write more, and I wrote a novel called *The Arrangement*, and am about to film it.

Q : *You did your own screenplay?*
E K : I had an interesting experience with that. It took me about a year to write the first draft of the novel. It's quite a personal novel. It's not autobiographical, but still, in one way or another I've experienced most of what's there, or people I've been very close to have. So when it came time to do the screenplay, I found that I had to do it. I could not get someone else to adapt it, even though I'd have liked that. And I could not use most of the material in the novel. So in effect I wrote an original screenplay which I'm now going to film. I had to retell the story entirely. I've never had such a sense of the difference between a literary work and a work that is essentially communicated by visual images as I had doing this job.

It was a shock to me. I started thinking, "Well, after all, I'm a film-maker. I wrote a novel, and it must be just a matter of picking a bit here and a bit there to tell the same story." But I couldn't do that. I tried, but it was cumbersome and vastly overlong, and it was formless. I had to throw it away and start on an entirely fresh tack. I think I've got an interesting screenplay now, but it's the same story told in an entirely different way.

Q : *Does the film grow out of Eddie's mind and body as much as the action of the book did?*
E K : Well, I haven't shot it yet, so I'd rather not talk too much about it, but a lot of it is presented as Eddie sees it; you are in his mind a lot. The luxury of writing a novel is that you can go into things and take off from things; the best parts of my book I thought were flights of thought, reflections and comments that I made on the scene around us. Those are the parts that I like best. But in a film, one quick image will often do it.

Q : *One quick image!*
E K : Yes. There's something magical about film. It's so elliptical, so much a matter of suggestion. And the vocabulary of film has developed so. Often it's better *not* to make things too clear, better to leave areas of mystery where an audience is tantalized or roused to thought and feelings of its own. All art is a shared experience. But particularly film. Whereas in a novel you're usually saying, "Here's how I see things, and how I think, and I'm going to convince you that you must think or feel the same way," in a film, it's quicksilver. You see a fish in the sea, it's there, then it's gone! One fault with *America, America* was that it was too explicit, too clear, therefore often redundant. I will try in this film to move more quickly and more elliptically.

Q : *It seems to me that in recent film there has been a great deal more complexity in human relationships. Do you think that that has had any influence on you?*
E K : Yes, I've been very influenced and I've been very moved by the new film-makers — I don't mean just the interest in style that the French are so devoted to, I mean all of them, the Japanese, the Italians, the English, and the great Swede, and Ray in India, and now Rocha in South America. All

over the world something wonderful has been happening, particularly in the last ten years. The whole vocabulary and idiom of film-making has come alive and is still expanding. I admire many of the younger men, those who haven't quite come out yet. They are exhausting every possibility in every direction, proving that artistic habits are only a rigidity of mind and must be broken. This is going on in every art form, of course, but the the-ater and films, till recently, were behind. Now films are the vanguard. These new film-makers have taken something that was *locked* in the American film tradition and opened it up. So all of us are much freer now in our use of techniques. We are here-and-now finding, as the rest of the world already has found, that we are just beginning to realize the potentials of this mar-velous medium.

Q: *Will you be doing that kind of thing in your next picture?*
EK: I don't understand.

Q: *Jump-cutting, subliminal shots—?*
EK: Jump-cutting and that kind of thing—those are just the externals. It's the whole attitude toward the material of films and the techniques of film that have changed. For one thing, film-makers are more aware of the dangers of overordering material. The danger in the kind of structure that by oversimplifying takes the contradictions and the poetry out of life. And we've become very leery of oversimplified messages too. I am wary of the man who is rigid in his viewpoint, a man who says to me, "You must think as I do. I'll tell you how you should think." We've messed up the world so badly that everyone is understandably very careful of the simpli-fications—political, social, or moral—of ten and twenty years ago. If a man preaches at me and says, "This is the conclusion you must come to from this material," when I feel that heavy hand on me, his cold moral fingers at my throat, I shake him off. I say, "Go preach at someone else." I believe that we are now attempting to find truths without robbing life of its contradictory elements and its complexities.

Q: *What about the kind of thing that's going on now in terms of "There should be no more violent films?"*
EK: A film that makes entertainment out of smashing a person's face in, or says that brutality is fun, and killing is sport, is reprehensible. That

doesn't mean I think all films should say how wonderful things are; they're not. It doesn't depend on whether there's violence or not, but on the basic use to which the images of violence are put. If the purpose is genuine, if a point has to be made through tremendous violence, I'm all for it. The thing is, to tell the truth. The film that reflects the violence that's now going on in this country truly and honestly has great value.

Q : *Do you think that the film-maker, the creative artist, has an obligation to make a film about something that he believes in?*
E K : An obligation? He does. You see, the thing about Hollywood is that it was basically organized, and is today still basically organized as an industry. No matter what you say about what a film contains, its artistic aspects and so on, the purpose of the people who put up money is to make more money. Quick. It's too bad that an art is used that way. The purpose of art is to make man confront his humanity. That's a very complex thing, and a very difficult thing. The large studios call themselves industries, and they're right. They *are* industries, and an industry is a profit-making effort first and always. Every year the people who head big studios get up and make speeches to their shareholders and tell what their profits were, as if that was the sole purpose of their efforts. And they're quite right. But that doesn't mean that that is the highest purpose to which this art should be put. That's why I think another great thing that's happening today is that there are other ways of making films, less expensive, therefore freer. After all, finally, film-making is a very simple thing. It's just a camera and an environment and the people around this environment and the drama that the film-maker sees.

Q : *Do you think that in terms of technology, just to get back to the big studios for a minute, that they will allow the kind of innovations that we really should be having in terms of camera, equipment, etc.?*
E K : I don't give a damn if they allow them or not; people are doing them anyway. The big studios got rattled a few years ago over the huge profits that some of the foreign films were making and how badly our films were doing. So they began to loosen up on their code of morality. Suddenly there was more nudity, more candor, and more freedom in subject matter. But the impulse to do all that was not to free the medium and the art; the impulse was born when the front-office fellows saw there were profits to

be made that way and, of course, they grabbed at that. If there is more enlightenment today, it's basically because the industry was shaken up.

Q: *Well, you've worked for all the major studios, but always for yourself, as producer, director, and writer. Do you feel you've ever had problems coping with the industry?*
EK: Oh yes, but I think the biggest difficulty an artist has or that a worker in the arts has is in dealing with himself. Those are the really subtle difficulties. I have no real complaints about the people that run the studios. By their measures, they've been fair to me and sometimes very generous. I like a lot of them, and I don't complain about them. It's just that their goal, their aim, is a different one than my own. I don't want to go into this because I am in no mood to complain about anybody. I feel very happy and not grumpy a bit.

Q: *So then you feel hopeful?*
EK: Yes. The great hope is that with faster film stock, with much lighter equipment, with much less equipment necessary, with film-makers who like to write, produce, and direct their own films (in fact, it's really one process) we are returning to a simplicity of working in the medium. I wish there was some way of getting the money necessary for films without going to the big companies. But even this is beginning to happen and in time—

Q: *What about the Hollywood unions? Do you think they can be handled so you can work with lighter crews?*
EK: I don't really know; I haven't made a film in Hollywood for many years. When I go to visit one of the big studios, I know a lot of the fellows who work there, and I understand their problem. It's simple—they *should* be assured a yearly wage. They have to be protected that way, and they're right to protect themselves. On the other hand, I think the solution of just saying, "You must have so and so many crew members on every picture," is a preposterous one. I think we're going to have to meet, in one way or another, the industry, the unions, everybody, the new circumstances. I remember one day I was making a film, and we were out on location, and all we were doing were a few modest shots of two people talking. Very few lights were needed. I looked behind me, and I saw over a hundred men,

the crew, all sitting there doing nothing, and they were all on my picture. That picture cost far more than it should have. I think the unions have to do something about that. But I can't answer the problem organizationally. I last made a film in California in 1955.

Q : *Is there a specific reason for not having made a film—because of your novel, or—?*
E K : Between 1962 and 1964, I worked in Lincoln Center, then I wrote my novel, then the screenplay of it, and I'm writing another book now. I decided to write on my own, so I've stopped making so many films.

Q : *It's a totally different way of living, isn't it?*
E K : I like that part of it, because you're essentially living within yourself. You're not responding to pressures: "Do you like this story? Do you want to make a film of this play? Answer me immediately! Here's a great novel, read it right away, it would make a good film!" You're not doing that. Instead you're thinking, "What do *I* want to say." You know when you're fifty-eight you shouldn't live the way you lived when you were thirty-eight. When I was thirty-eight, I was doing plays and movies, two or three a year; I never stopped working. But now I've reached the point in my life when I just want to do the few things I really want to do, and that's the way I try to live.

Q : *Do you find there is a different kind of feeling in terms of working in films and theater and writing? They are three totally different kinds of activities.*
E K : Oh, yes. As I said, when you're writing a novel, you're living within yourself. You have difficulties, but they're of your own making. You have limitations, but they're your own limitations, not organizational ones. I live in the country a lot, which is an entirely different way of living. I love privacy, to be by myself a part of every day, and I like working on my own material. When you've produced a book, and you hold the damn thing in your hand and think, "That's all out of me!" it's like a woman feels with a child, I suppose.

Q : *And as for critical reaction, how does that compare?*
E K : You don't really give a damn. You *hope* people will like it, but deep down you don't give a damn. Some of the critics and some of my friends

didn't like my book, *The Arrangement*. Of course I wished they had, but it didn't bother me too much. I feel what it contains is the truth; it was, one way or another, lived through by me, and I put it down as truthfully as I could. Something you do yourself is valid for you whether it is successful for others or not. When you work in theater or in films, directing a play or dramatizing a novel, you are a steward for someone else, you're hoping that Tennessee Williams or Arthur Miller will like what you do and that you're bringing their play off for the public and expressing what they, your authors, feel, being true to them. In the theater you must hope that this whole group that's collected around you is successful as a group, that you've brought their efforts to a successful conclusion. But when you write a novel, you look at it finally and say, "Well, for better or worse, that's me," and so you've got something that's much more satisfying and, in a way, invulnerable. I expect I'll have the same feeling about the films I do from my works. I did about *America, America*. I realize it had serious faults, people pointed them out to me, but I really didn't give a damn, I was so proud of it. I'm more proud of it than any film I ever did. *The Arrangement* means more to me than anything I ever did. And it has nothing to do with other people's reactions to it. As I say, when you're sixty, you begin to look inside yourself and ask, "Well, who am I really, and what am I like? What do I feel? What do I prize? What do I hate? What do I want to change? What is the way I want to live? Whom do I love?" And you begin to think that way. And when you write your book you have the luxury of living entirely with yourself which is a great and deep feeling. Well, you see, there are people who make films in Europe in this way—Fellini, and Ray in India, Bergman. Oh, a lot of others. There are a lot of film-makers in England, in France, and in Italy who—

Q : *Do you like Bergman's work?*
E K : Yes, I do. Every film is a piece of his autobiography. That's what I like about his work. It's oblique and subtle and personally seen; you can't quite put your finger on it, but it's a piece of him. He's a true artist. I think Fellini is, too. In *8½* there is a scene I will never forget: the one in which the hero imagines his wife and his mistress dancing together among the cafe tables. Every man's dream of "Why can't my wife love my mistress? Why can't my mistress love my wife? Why can't they like each other and get along together."

Q : *But let's just jump back to* The Arrangement. *How do you feel about cast-ing someone as yourself?*

E K :   I don't think of that part — Eddie Anderson — as myself. Not at all. It's like some of my friends, yes, and I've had some of the experiences he's had, yes, but I'm not like that. The basic thing about Eddie in *The Arrangement* is that he's finally and totally dissatisfied with his life. I've never been unhappy about what I've been doing. I've always wanted to be a director, I've always wanted to be an artist, I've always felt myself lucky to be able to work in the theater, and in films, and now as a writer. If I was unhappy for any length of time with what I was doing, I changed it. I've never been miserable, and I've never been suicidal. I've always been basically a happy person because I've always functioned in the area that I wanted to function in. Eddie hates himself; he's full of self-scorn and self-disgust. I've done wrong, but I've never been full of self-disgust. So when you say, "It's like you," you're wrong; it's not. It's like a lot of people I've known, and it's like a lot of people around me. Symbolically you can say it's like America now, in the middle of its course and not knowing what's gone wrong or where to turn next. I thought it had those overtones.

Q : *Will you direct the film?*
E K :   Oh, yes.

Q : *Will you produce it alone?*
E K :   I'm producer, director, writer, and I sweep the stage.

Q : *The whole thing.*
E K :   The whole thing.

Q : *What about the end?*
E K :   Well, I've got a different end. I think it's rather good. It has the same qualities as the old end. I've managed to keep the last sentence of the book — the one people remember most — tried to keep it and make it valid in the new context. I like the screenplay now; I think I've done a good job with it. It took nine months and I'm still working on it. But I learned a lot from that work. In many ways, it's better than the book, swifter, more uni-fied and cohesive, fairer.

Q: *When the producer says that, it sounds marvelous. Another question: Will you be shooting in color?*
EK: I've always had a belief that color can be handled, but I'm not sure I'm right. I've worked in color several times and have always been very careful to talk things out with the cameraman. In the color films I've done, I've liked parts of them very much, others not. I thought the end of *East of Eden* was beautiful, and I thought the outdoor stuff in *Wild River*, especially at the end, was beautiful. And I thought that some of *Splendor in the Grass* was excellent. But the best camera work I think I've ever had was the black-and-white work that Boris Kaufman did in *Baby Doll* and *On the Waterfront*. Both of those films are photographically so subtle and so poetic.

Q: *I think the love scene in* On the Waterfront *is one of the most poetic love scenes I've ever seen.*
EK: I do believe, however, that one of the problems with color is that it was invented and set up labwise to be candy. The color itself was a form of entertainment, a novelty. "Look how colorful this is! Look how pretty and juicy this is!" The color that we use in films and the labs, and the stock itself were devised, not haphazardly or accidentally, but quite consciously and scientifically to be as "colorful" and un-lifelike as possible. All of us have fought against it, have said, "Well, we're going to underexpose and force in the lab. We're going to double-print with a gray negative added." And so on. We've done all kinds of things to deal with this problem, always with the hope of getting color that is an emphasis factor, the way color is in life, and to catch the poetry of the essential gray in life.

Q: *Which film-makers do you admire today, and why?*
EK: I admire the film-makers I admire for the same reason I admire other artists—not essentially because their techniques are new or their techniques are like the ones I happen to have used, but because of the degree of humanity, the amount of human feeling they have. For example, one of the film-makers I admire most is a very conventional stylist, but a most unusual man. His name is Jean Renoir, and he is one of the great film-makers of the world. I always see Hitchcock's films and they always entertain me, but I don't think there's much in them. The films of Jean Renoir seem clumsier but they enlist me, and finally I have an experience

with them. The same with Ray, some of his films are so slow and seem almost pointless. But by the time you are through with them, you have lived through something with their maker. Of the American film-makers, I like John Ford in his prime. I think some of the younger men are fine technicians, but today's new technique is tomorrow's TV cliché. Whether there's jump-cutting or not, whether the screen is full of six images or sixty, I don't think means a damn thing. It's what's done with it. John Ford had soul.

Q : *People say that films are an art form but don't have any great ability to change society or a way of living. How do you feel about that?*

E K : Any good art changes the way life is being lived but not in a mechanical, directly visible way. Certainly the great Russian films of the twenties, when the spirit of that revolution was being celebrated, must have made people feel that their lives had been worth living and the sacrifices they were making were worth making. I think some of our films of the forties and fifties changed human life in the sense that they deepened people's feeling of compassion for each other and their understanding of each other. That is what a great poet, whether he works in prose, in poetry, in paint or in stone, in images, or in the theater does. He makes you feel the humanity of other people. And of yourself—often to your surprise. That's no small achievement. It makes you able to live with people better, with more understanding, with more of what's called tolerance and with more joy too.

Q : *Do you think that because we've been bombarded with so many images that film—although it's very much in vogue now as art form—will lose its effectiveness just because we have too much going on around us?*

E K : Nonsense! People also say the novel is dying! Nonsense! I look forward to reading quite a few books. Things go up and then things come down, and then back up again. It has very little to do with whether the form is worn out. When someone has something to say, a passion about life, when that feeling inhabits any form, it's worth listening to. Music. "Christ," you say, "who wants to hear the same old symphonies?" It depends who wrote them.

Q : *Talking about music, when you prepare the night before, do you have—as some people have—a musical pattern in mind, a rhythmic cutting pattern?*

ᴇᴋ: No. Naturally, I try to have some idea about the first shot. But the thing I try to get hold of most securely is what the essential moment, the climax of the scene I'm to do that day, is and how it should look. If I can, I try to find some way in my mind of expressing that climax so that it is as exact and as revealing as I can make it. I say, "Well, what's the essence of that scene? The high point? How am I going to convey that?" Then I'll know what I am building toward. If I know where I'm going, I can get there. That's the thing I try to work out the night before. I think about it when I'm lying in bed in the morning. I try to think, "Now, what's the instant that tells everything about that scene?" It may be nothing more than a look on someone's face. But it will be the goal I'm aiming for that day.

ǫ: *Let me ask you a specific question about one scene, the scene in* Viva Zapata! *in the church. When I felt the love so strongly between the couple, was this something that just happened, or that you thought about ahead of time?*
ᴇᴋ: The main thing I thought of was—that the love scene would play, that Brando would do it well, and Jean would too—Jean Peters—but the thing I thought of that brought the scene to life was the fact that Zapata's brother was there in the church. The sense of danger and poignancy was due to his anxious presence in that scene. And when I thought of that, I had the scene.

ǫ: *What about the scene in the cab in* On the Waterfront?
ᴇᴋ: That scene was Brando's doing. I don't think I contributed much. The really touching thing was something Brando put in—he just said, "Oh, Charlie," in a certain way. Remember? I don't think he knew he was going to do it or how, but he was so much in the scene it just came out. The tone of his voice at that instant was what made that scene. And what was on his face. No director could have told an actor to do that. At his best, Brando was the best actor we've had in this country in my time. There's been no one like him. I mean, I get a lot of credit for that scene, but I don't deserve it. All I did was put the camera on the two fellows, and they're both good actors, Steiger too, but Brando had this very special genius in those days.

ǫ: *It seems that Marlon Brando has never done work as good as the work he did with you.*

E K : Well, he did trust me and that makes a difference. We understood each other and—well, he was very trusting of me, and therefore relaxed, not on guard, you know?

Q : *This seems to be true when I think back on a great many performances. People like Lee Remick, whom I think is very talented, or Carroll Baker, whom I have never seen as good since* Baby Doll. *There seems to be a whole group of people. You must do something with your actors that somebody else doesn't do. And I would like to know what it is, if you know what it is.*
E K : I don't know.

Q : *Do you rehearse a lot? Do you spend a lot of time with them beforehand?*
E K : Sometimes I do. I don't know. I talk to them . . .

Q : *You mean you talk to them as people, not just as actors then?*
E K : Any simplification is dangerous, but I guess I try to relate the moment of the scene they are about to play to something in their own lives so they understand it experientially, not only intellectually.

Q : *Do you do the same kind of thing, for example, with people who haven't done films before? It's a pretty difficult thing to have them hit that mark on the stage floor and still have the emotion going.*
E K : You can always make them hit the mark. That's not the problem. The problem is to make them move unmechanically. Sometimes you succeed in that and sometimes you don't.

Q : *Well, what about working with professional actors versus the non-actors you used so much in your* Face in the Crowd?
E K : Non-actors are awfully willing, you know. If you show some confidence in them, they're thrilled. So you just get them going, laugh and kid with them, become one of them, and before you know it, they've forgotten all about the camera. Also you minimize the mechanics. You don't say, "You have to hit this mark." You put a table there or a chair or a stick on the floor so they can't go any farther. And so on. As a matter of fact you don't do differently with professionals.

Q : *Do you think that the creative artist tends toward the liberal in politics? Or should?*

EK: I should think so, yes. They're generally full of hopes for man's improving himself; they wish something for man. If they're artists, they have a vision larger than the immediate, and they have a purpose which is unarticulated often, but it's a human purpose, and not a profit purpose. I don't like businessmen in the arts much. I get along with them, I suppose, because I have to. But the whole thing about art is that it's much greater than any business and much greater than anything. It's the highest religion because it deals only with man's spirit, and when you deal with that, you're dealing with what's holy. Sometimes you see a home movie, an amateur film, a student film, a documentary, a newsreel, and you see an instant of sudden light, insight—the fellow who held the camera on his shoulder photographed something that no one else saw or could have seen, only *he* could have put it on the film. That's beautiful—when it's unique and personal and unexpected.

Q: *Don't you also think part of it is what the audience brings to the theaters? You have to have enough people that bring something of themselves in to watch whatever you are putting up there?*
EK: Well, yes, God bless 'em, they're getting more numerous, they're getting quicker, and they love films. I went to that *2001*—

Q: *How did you like it?*
EK: I liked it. It had some kind of poetry. I admire the man for making it. Anyway, that big barn of a Century Theatre was full of young people, and they were so intrigued with *2001*, so enlisted, that you felt it was *their* film. If an artist gives you something that speaks for you as well as *to* you— expresses what you feel that you can't express yourself—well, you should be very grateful to him.

Q: *What about the fact that we still don't have any government subsidy for film-makers. How would you feel about government subsidy?*
EK: I think there should be all kinds of subsidies. That doesn't mean that all films or all theater productions should be subsidized. There's a danger I've always felt that an outfit like George Stevens, Jr.'s outfit, the government agency that put up the funds for the American Film Institute—well, I was speaking to Stevens the other day and he said, "I watch over the film institute people so they don't get too starchy." The thing is you have to

allow things, even encourage things you don't like yourself, because if they're someone's true feeling, well, let's help them speak out!

Q: *What do you think about the so-called revolution in thinking and morals that's going on?*
EK: About time! I mean, I'm all for it. I think our morals are worn out, mostly hypocritical and rarely given more than lip-service. I think marriage—I said it in my book—marriage is in so many cases hypocritical, and—

Q: *It's almost an economic institution, isn't it?*
EK: There's a growing gap between the way people live and the way they pretend to live. There's a profound and swelling hypocrisy in our society, and that's now being shown up by young people. They're saying, "Let's talk about the way it really is, let's talk about facts, and not the way you want to pretend to each other that you live." And the whole middle-class set of values is being re-scrutinized, and they ask, "Is that way of living or pretending to live really worth anything? You guys have mucked up the world, and hundreds of kids a week are being killed in Vietnam. For what? For this? The hell with it! We won't go."

Q: *Do you think that shows the evidence of theater, with things like* Hair, *for example, and...*
EK: I like *Hair*, but I think it's going to be much better than that in time and very soon, too. I think the new ones in the theater are going to be speaking very seriously. I think *Hair* is good and fresh and sometimes beautiful, but there's better and tougher coming.

Q: *Which brings me around to another question: What about censorship of any kind?*
EK: I'm against censorship of any kind. I think everything should be thrown into the light and let people see what they want to see. But there is one contradiction in my feelings. I always feel nervous when I see young children watching sadism on the screen. I wish it wasn't there. I wish they weren't watching it because there *is* something beguiling about it. Everyone's full of antagonisms, and there is something beguiling about Jimmy Cagney, say, punching somebody, and so maybe children are think-

ing, "Well, it's fun. I'd like to push a grapefruit in someone's face." But still, I feel censorship is wrong. One thing I like about what John Lindsay is doing here in the city now is that we have these dirty movies. Not many people go to them, mostly old codgers that don't get a charge out of life any other way. But they're there, so no one can say, "They won't let us show this or that or the other." What the hell? I mean, you have movies that show the sex act. So what? But they're not censored and that fact alone, I think, is important.

Q: *What about the stuff they see on television? You know, Vietnam? I mean, this seems to some people almost the worst kind of immorality.*
EK: I think the news programs on television are tremendous. The coverage of the war in Vietnam has been one of the things that has caused the great feeling against the war. When you see our best fellows being killed and maimed and carried away, when you see the Vietnamese people, south and north, but particularly who the enemy is, the North Vietnamese, slim beautiful young men and women, killed, captured, terrified, you must say, "This is wrong, what the hell, I don't want to be their terrifier. I don't want to be their killer. I don't want to be their capturer." That's basic. Beyond any politics. Everybody who's seen those scenes on TV must feel that. That's why I think the whole TV coverage is one of the best things that has been happening.

Q: *Well, one last question, about critics. Do critics influence you or bother you? Let's take theater, films, and the book?*
EK: Sometimes I've gotten stimulus from critics. They've said things I've valued. A lot of the criticism about me as co-director of the Lincoln Center Repertory Company was valid. I didn't enjoy it when it was being shot at me, but the fact is I wasn't suited to that job, and I finally thought the fellows who said that were accurate. Their hostile criticism of me made me reexamine myself and my work there, and say to myself, "You honestly don't want to do that."

The great thing criticism can do is illuminate. There's one great theater critic in this country, his name's Harold Clurman, and every time I read one of his articles, I see more in the plays than I would have otherwise. After you've read good criticism, you see more. It enriches your experience, and I think there's a great function. I'm not against it by any means.

Of course, there are guys who are trying to get up quick by knocking down everybody.

Q: *But don't you think sometimes, in your case, they have been criticizing you and not necessarily the piece of work?*

EK: I'd say when you criticize a man's work, you are certainly criticizing him. And vice versa. And why not?

Elia Kazan Interview

STUART BYRON AND
MARTIN L. RUBIN/1971

Early Work

I started out as a documentary cameraman. I worked with a guy named
Ralph Steiner when I was an actor in the Group Theatre. In the summer,
Ralph used to say, 'Well, let's go make some films.' I was a Communist in
those days, and we were connected with an outfit called Frontier Films. We
made a film called *The People of the Cumberlands,* a two-reeler about the
strip-miners in Tennessee. We photographed them at work, and we photographed them dancing and at leisure and in their quiet moments, in
their homes. The residents of that community resented our photographing
them because they thought we were New York Jews making fun of them,
and they ran us out of town. That was my first experience photographing
on location.

Ralph and I directed another film out here in New York at the city dump.
It was just a two-reel comedy called *Pie in the Sky.* In those days, these
things were shown at fund-raising meetings. I used to go to them and do
comedy skits that didn't have much social point but were amusing. And
this film was just more of that.

Anyway, my first experience with films was not in the studio, not in
sets, but out in the streets using regular people. So when I got around to
making *Boomerang* and *Panic in the Streets,* it was second nature to me. I
started out in the field where you lug the tripod around, and you set it

From *Movie,* Winter 1971/72. Reprinted by permission.

down, and you do everything. It's all part of, say, film-making, rather than being the Boss-Man Director.

Then I got into the theatre, but the first thing I ever wanted in my life was to make films. When I was in college I saw *Potemkin,* and a few years later I saw Dovzhenko's *Aerograd*—two films that made a terrific impression on me. As a matter of fact, both of them were almost obsessive with me—I saw them again and again. They made me feel how important films were, how much they could say with both thematic relevance and beauty. Then I had a chance to go with the Group Theatre, and I became an actor, and finally I directed a couple of hits.

What about It's Up to You, *which you made for the Department of Agriculture in 1941?*
That was a stage play that had a little film in it. I mixed media—a woman on the stage talked to her image on the screen, and it made a point about rationing.

You also acted in two films in the early 'forties, City for Conquest *and* Blues in the Night, *both by Anatole Litvak. Do you feel you learned something from that, so when you got on the set of* A Tree Grows in Brooklyn *you weren't completely unfamiliar with the surroundings?*
A little bit, yes. Quite right. Also, I learned something from Jimmy Cagney—he taught me quite a lot about acting. Jimmy taught me some things about being honest and not overdoing it. He even affected my work with Brando a little bit. I mean—'Don't show it, just do it.'

A Tree Grows in Brooklyn (1945)

I was offered a script to do, called *A Tree Grows in Brooklyn.* The producer was a very right-wing guy named Bud Lighton. Working with him was one of the important things of my life because I was very sectarian then. I thought that anyone with political ideas different than mine was *ipso facto* N.G. So that was an opening up, it liberalized me. Not that he affected my ideas, but I saw that there were deeper values.

I didn't know a damn thing about shooting in studios at that time. I relied a great deal on Leon Shamroy, the cameraman. That is, I would direct the scenes just like I would on stage, as truthfully as I could, and Leon would make suggestions as to how to photograph them. And really the film is something like a photographed stage play, even the parts that were photographed outside. You're in medium-distance at all times, and the extent of the movement is just two lips going. I didn't have any appreciation of the specific visual elements in filmmaking that make film different from theatre.

Because of your stage background, it seems as if you were very concerned with the pacing in the film. It starts out very fast, with a lot of short scenes played very quickly, and then it gets more and more slowly paced.
That's true. In the first part, there's what would seem to a stage director to be a lack of conflict, a lack of clash, a lack of storytelling as I was accustomed to it in the theatre. Therefore I tried to get a sense of just life flowing by, without stress, without emphasis, just the flow of life through the environment. But then as we got to the dramatic scenes, where the tensions were, and where the meat of the story and the relationships came out, I had to slow down to bring this out.

Did you enter the scriptwriting stage at any point?
No, not at all. Oh, I discussed it with them. I made what observations I had to make. But Lighton wrote the screenplay himself, along with the credited scriptwriters, Slesinger and Davis.

What about the grandmother's speech on America being the only place where you can rise above your station? That sounds like the same man who wrote America, America.
Yeah, that's partly me. That is, there was a little about it in the script, and I said, 'Why don't you say more, because it means so much to me.' And I told them what I felt as an immigrant, as a guy who was born on the other side and came over here. I influenced an *emphasis* there rather than initiating the idea.

The mother, played by Dorothy McGuire, seems the first entry of one of your prototypical characters—the person who has one idea he must follow.
What I stressed in that—although I didn't like the way it came out—was the puritanical quality, the person who's obsessively puritanical. And that's something that's thematic all through my films. In my past, I've had a lot of contact with things that deal with puritanism—the rigid side of moral-

ity, the morality that things have to be a certain way. I mean, she never learned to bend. But I thought that character was cleaned up. I think there's more bitterness in it than came out. I felt all through that film there was a patina of conventionalism—the costumes were all too clean, and the people were all too goddam nice. It isn't that I have anything against it—hell, it was a first job. And if you look at it in the period, it does have beauty in it. But there's a surface conventionalism about the film, and whatever values are in it come up through that. I think the best thing in the film is the face of the little girl—the lyricism in the character. I liked Jimmy Dunn in it, too—he had the perspiration of anxiety about him.

When Dorothy McGuire and Peggy Ann Garner are returning from the father's funeral, you include them both in an extended two-shot even though they have different reactions to the event—a technique you seem to prefer in your later films.
That's very accurate. I do that constantly now. I never liked singles, except if they point up something a hell of a lot, or if the person's in a mood by himself. But I do that a lot, because it's interesting to look at two people in different conditions with different attitudes at the same time. There's a tension in the fact that they're both appearing together that you don't always get if you cut.

McGuire's speech when she's in labor also anticipates a device you use in later years—somebody getting to a highly emotional state for one reason and, because of it, revealing separate things that they were afraid to say in a calm state.
Yes, I do that a lot. I feel that happens a lot in life. I feel one thing triggers another, unexpectedly. I think because of a condition we get in for one reason, we release something. That's just something I feel about the experiences of people in general. But I didn't realize I did it there.

This might surprise you, but it seems to us that A Tree Grows in Brooklyn *is the one of your early films that really looks forward to your mature period.*
I'll tell you what I think is basic to that: ambivalence in the characters. That relates to a hell of a lot of the work that starts with *Zapata* and *East of Eden*. Because there's no good or bad in the film. The mother is 'good' socially, but she's really the heavy. Just as Jimmy Dean in *East of Eden* is

'bad' socially, but he's really good. That kind of ambivalence starts quite consciously with *East of Eden* because that's when I thought, 'Fuck this puritanism—I want to say something.' Anyway, that's basically why the film points ahead.

The Sea of Grass (1947)

Then you went to M-G-M for one film . . .

Don't mention it. There's one story about that film that tells it all to me. I wanted to make a picture about the West because I feel that there's something glorious that died there. And I love country—I live in the country now. I had a great feeling for that subject. So here's what happened—I went to see Pandro Berman, the producer, and the first thing he said was 'I've got 10,000 feet of the most beautiful background footage you've ever seen in your life.' I should have got up, said, 'Thank you very much, Pandro,' and walked out. But I was too dumb to quit. I was in a mechanism called Metro-Goldwyn-Mayer, which was run not by Pandro Berman, and not, oddly enough, by L. B. Mayer, but by the head of the Art Department, Cedric Gibbons. He ran that damn studio. There was a rigid plan about how every film was going to be made, and this film was going to be made in front of a rear-projection screen. So what it ended up, to my vast humiliation, was that I never saw a blade of grass throughout that picture! Or there'd be two or three live horses, and behind them a rear-projection screen with other horses standing there. It really got so embarrassing, I was ashamed of myself all through it. I thought, 'What the hell have I gotten into?' But by that time I couldn't get out of the film.

Another thing that happened was I was very proud I got Katharine Hepburn to cry because I thought she was a cool person. Not at all—if she wants to cry she turns it on. But I was very pleased with the rushes, and I said to Pandro Berman, 'Gee, Pandro, did you see the stuff? I think she gave a terrific performance.' He said, 'Well, Mr. Mayer doesn't think so.' So I went to see Mr. Mayer. I said, 'What are you talking about, Mr. Mayer? She's terrific in that scene—she cries all through it.' He said, 'The channel of the tears is wrong.' I said, 'What do you mean?' He said, 'They go too near the nostrils.' I said, 'But, Mr. Mayer, Mr. Mayer, that's the way the girl's face is made!' He said, 'There's another thing—some people cry with their voice, some with their throat, some with their nose, some with their eyes. But she cries with everything! And this is excessive.' I said, 'God, I still won't shoot that over, Mr. Mayer.' And he said, 'Listen.' Then he got tough with me. He said, 'We're in the business of making beautiful pictures about beautiful people, and anybody who doesn't think so has no place in the industry.' I finally didn't reshoot it, but again I had my cue. I should have said, 'Well, I don't want to be in your fucking industry!' And I should have walked out then. It's funny because it wasn't anyone's fault but my own. It wasn't that anyone bossed something on me—I just got repeatedly deceived by myself. But I was in a machine—put it that way. I was a cog, a useful little cog in a machine that overwhelmed me.

Boomerang (1947)

Boomerang was a reaction to *Sea of Grass*. That is, I read the script, and I said, 'Jesus, this is where I should be at!' We shot that *entirely* on location—not a set in the picture. We used only a few actors, and the rest were all people from Stamford, Connecticut—members of the police force, for example. Cops act good, by the way. I don't know why it is, but something about that profession makes them all good actors. We shot on the streets at night with as many as 5,000 people watching. The picture was a terrific thrill that way—it made me see my identity. I really enjoyed that life, whereas I was miserable on the M-G-M set. For one thing, I was miserable living in Hollywood—I never liked the place. I never unpacked my bags.

Another thing I learned from *Boomerang* was that it cut through a lot of bullshit about photography—'beauty' photography. On *Sea of Grass* I was initiated into all that careful back-lighting and halo-lighting and line-lighting and so on. But the cameraman on *Boomerang* was an old guy who just put the camera down and turned the box on. And it looked better to me than the other! It was so simple, really—so much simpler than that enormous mechanism of making 'beautiful pictures about beautiful people.' That was a big thing I realized. Not that I did too much about it for a while.

When the district attorney is trying to save the life of this man who's been wrongly accused, it's brought up that his action could endanger the town's entire reform administration, and a politician asks him, 'Is the life of one man more important than the good of the whole community?' This problem is somewhat dropped in Boomerang, *but it comes up again later in your career—in* A Face in the Crowd *and* Wild River, *for example.*

Well, I think it's much more black and white in *Boomerang*. I wasn't dealing in ambivalences then—I was avoiding them. My whole thing around that time was clarity, thematic clarity. And I think that the character of the politician, Ed Begley, was too much of a heavy and therefore less interesting. In that sense, I think the film is thin. I think it's a good film. I thought everything *worked*. It was a piece of mechanism, a fairly effective piece of storytelling mechanism. But I wouldn't do that now. Not a goddamned thing in it would I do now.

The Begley character marks the first appearance of the idea, later elaborated in
East of Eden, *that one can be on the right side politically and on the wrong side in moral and personal relations.*
Yeah, but the stone is turned over and he turns out to be an awful shit—a sweaty, terrible little villain and all that. It's just flipped over at one moment. I wouldn't do it that way now because my feeling is that the whole community is involved in that. The corruption is so twined through everything now—it's not just one person who's the heavy. It's so deep in this society that people don't know any more. It's deep in the police force. It's deep in the heroes. Christ, the goddamned district attorney would be in it! I think if I were making the picture now, I'd have the district attorney do something terrible!

Would you have preferred to keep the case unresolved—that we never found who the real killer was?
No, I would have resolved it, and then had an irony. I mean, I'm more on the irony thing now. Or I would have had them find it, but then they would have found other things, and somebody would have silenced it, which is what I believe now.

Gentelman's Agreement (1947)

No matter what I think of it today, what I remember most about *Gentleman's Agreement* is that at the time no one said 'Jew.' When it was being made, all the rich Jews in California were against it. And the Catholic Church was against it because they didn't want the heroine to be a divorcee. There were a hell of lot of people who said to Zanuck, 'We're getting along all right. Why bring this up'? And, in that sense, it was a step forward at the time. On the other hand, it was, as far as it went, essentially a 'Cosmopolitan' story, wasn't it? It was dressed up with these overtones, but essentially is was a very familiar, easily digestible story with conventional figures going through it. There isn't anything unpleasant in that picture. It was kept on a level of acceptability. It surprised people, but it didn't shock them.

There's one part of it I like, when I look back on it, which is where Dorothy McGuire is telling Garfield how she couldn't stand all this bigotry she overheard. And Garfield says, 'What did you *do* about it?' That's a scene I liked. The rest of it just looks Hollywood to me. They're all dressed-up, and they're all going through these well-bred manoeuvres of social behaviour. Whenever I see it, it reminds me of the illustrations in 'Redbook' and 'Cosmopolitan' in those days. I mean, those people don't shit. They don't do any of the natural functions. They'd walk through, and their dress was always perfect. That was just before I began kicking the hairdresser and the wardrobe people off the set. I wasn't doing that then. But I think that film is directed, again, like a stage play, and it's rather well directed. I think the movement in the scenes, and the way the scenes are paced and staged and so on—it's good stage direction. I'm not particularly fond of it, and I was awful glad when it got over.

Pinky (1949)

A continuing question—and there are about four different answers on record—is how much of what Ford shot remains in Pinky.

Nothing. The story is that Ford had the shingles. Now I think he didn't have the shingles! What happened was that Ethel Waters hated him, and he hated her. So, Ford 'got the shingles.' What he did was he just got in bed and said, 'I can't get out of bed.' Zanuck asked me to come out there and finish it, and I said, 'O.K.' I didn't even read the goddamn script until I got off the plane. Darryl showed me what Ford had shot, and I said I'd like to start from scratch, because actually Ford's stuff was N.G. I think he's a terrific director, maybe the best we ever had. But the stuff he shot for this was no good at all; it was terrible. I guess he just got into a set-up where he was disgruntled, and he rebelled against it. So I got things going again. I calmed Miss Waters down, and I calmed Jeanne Crain down, who was sort of terrified by him too. I shot it in seven weeks. I didn't stay for the editing. I didn't do a damn thing on it; I just did a job. I did my best with it, and I guess it has certain values, but it's not one of my favourite films. I also felt there was some essential cop-out in casting a white girl in the lead.

Do you think the experience of making Pinky *helped trigger your interest in the South?*
No. When I was in the Movement, I used to go to the South a lot. I had a lot of friends in Tennessee; I knew a lot of lefties there—I told you I made a picture about strip-mining. I even wrote a play about a strike down there. So I was always interested in it. But, again, we shot outdoor scenes in the studio and so on. By the time I got through with it, I was so sick of false horizons and painted backdrops. I probably should have taken charge of the picture more and said, 'Look, I want to do this. Let me have it.' But I just did it and got back to New York.

What would you have changed the most?
I guess I would have done something about the blandness of the leading lady. There's something bland about that film. Jeez, it seems like so far I don't like any of the pictures I made!

Panic in the Streets (1950)

Panic in the Streets *is by far your most fluid film to that date.*
Well, by the time I got through with *Pinky* and *Gentleman's Agreement*, I said to myself, 'Look, I'm not making films, I'm photographing plays.' I began to study films again, especially Jack Ford. And I said, 'I'm going to make a film that's all action, and I'm going to start using the camera to tell the story. I want to make a film like a silent, as close to a silent as I can. I'm going to try to make something that is specifically filmic.' Then I read this script. It wasn't much, but we rewrote it every day on location. That was the fun part of it. We were shooting in New Orleans, and we had a hell of a time. I hung around the harbor, and I felt the wind on my face, and I thought, 'I've been indoors all my life! I've got to get out of the theatre and into film!' It just freed me of all that inside-a-set tension and just directing miniscule little bits of acting. And it's funny, because I got into film because of outdoor films—*Potemkin* and *Aerograd*. *Aerograd* particularly has this terrific air of the forest and the cold and the leaves.

Yet in a way Panic in the Streets *seems you declaration of independence from some Russian principles. For example, this is your first film which really uses long takes.*
Well, I studied *Young Mr Lincoln,* for example. As I say, Jack Ford had a big influence on me. He had a scene where someone is shot in a grove. Well,

he didn't go up and shoot that like I would have. He had a little puff of smoke in a grove, and the puff of smoke rose up through the night and through the trees. And I thought, 'Jesus, what I would have done is to go up there and take a shot of the pistol and a shot of the guy's face and all that shit.' And it would have been just another scene. But Jack's a *poet*. He just sat back there and looked and said, 'What the hell, that's all right, it'll get over.' He let it go! It made me feel, 'Christ, I can go much further in this direction! And use long shots!'

What do you like about using long takes?
It arouses empathy from the audience. It lets them sit there and start to come out to it. You're not shoving it at them; you're letting them work, letting their imagination work. You're not saying, 'Look at this closeup! Look at his reaction to that! Look, he's getting angry! Wham! Wham! Wham!' I say, 'Well, that's all right when it's important, but let 'em work, let 'em work.'

Another thing I learned from Ford: he's a great guy for foreground objects. He puts an object in the foreground that's critical at some point in the latter half of the scene, and he moves the people up to that object. It breaks up the foreground spatially, so that the shot has quality, not abstractness. I used that a lot in *Panic in the Streets*.

Although both this film and A Streetcar Named Desire *take place in New Orleans, in* Panic in the Streets *it's anonymous, it could be any city, whereas* Streetcar *has a New Orleans feel.*
That's another thing I learned in that picture—the lab killed me. I had scenes in it where the walls were actually perspiring. There's so much wet corrosion in New Orleans, which is where we went on location. But when you look at it on film, you wouldn't know. On *Streetcar* I had a terrific art director, and I said to him, 'I want these walls to perspire!' So we put a little water pipe down in those walls, and you could see the moisture coming through the plaster. I mean, he worked *hard* to create that feeling. And that was in a *set*. When I photographed it actually in life, it didn't come over.

Do you think you brought any of your experience from Panic in the Streets *over to* On the Waterfront.

Oh, a lot, I don't think I could have made *On the Waterfront* like I did if I hadn't done *Panic in the Streets*. For one thing, I got to love the waterfront. I still love it. I'd love to make another picture about it. I love water. I really have a thing about that. I love harbors. My favorite shot in all my pictures is the shot of Ellis Island in *America, America*. I love that shot—when they're all laying around with the American flag up there. I learned a lot about that in *Panic in the Streets*. That film might seem conventional to critics, but it was a big change for me, for my attitude toward everything. It was a liberation for me. I also think it's the only perfect film I made, because it's essentially a piece of mechanism, and it doesn't deal in any ambivalences at all, really. It just fits together in the sequence of story-telling rather perfectly. But that's really why I did it, and I got a *hell* of a lot out of it for future films. My other critical film for big change is *Zapata*. That changed everything.

A Streetcar Named Desire (1951)

Then would you view A Streetcar Named Desire *as just a kind of parenthesis in your career?*
Yeah, something like that. I have affection for a hell of a lot of people, but I don't have affection for anybody as much as I do for Tennessee Williams. Having directed the play, I didn't want to do the film—I hate to do things twice. It's unbearable to me, impossible—I haven't done any other movies out of plays. But Williams asked me to do it, and after a while I just did it. Then I said, 'Well, I have to make a movie script out of it.' So we worked on it three or four months, and we 'opened it up.' I read it, and I felt, 'Gee, this is pretty good.' Then I put it away for a week and went somewhere. When I came back, I read it again, and I said, 'This fucking thing stinks.' I turned against it, and I took the script of the play, and I just made the play. And that's all I did.

My main concern was working on the performances. I was good at that kind of thing then—I don't think I'm so good at it anymore. I was much more meticulous then about directing acting. My only problem in that film was that Vivien Leigh had played *Streetcar* in London, directed by Larry Olivier. So when she came over here, she had the whole performance worked out, and it wasn't anything like what I like. Larry's direction was an Englishman's idea of the American South—seen from a distance—and Vivien's conception of the role was a bit of a stereotype, just as my direction of a British character might be. So for the first couple of weeks I had a lot of problems. Then gradually I won her over, and she began to cook. And I think that in the last half of the picture she's a hell of a lot better than she is in the first half.

I thought that was deliberate, though. I thought in the beginning we're supposed to be on Brando's side and against her, and then the tables turn.
Now this is another place where I did ambivalence. And I've been criticized for this a lot. Some people say I made Brando the hero. I didn't mean to make Brando the hero. But I wanted to show exactly what Williams meant, which is that he, as a homosexual, is attracted to the person he thinks is going to destroy him—the attraction you have for someone who's on the other side, supposedly dead against you, but whose violence and force attract you. Now, that's the essence of ambivalence. And that's what I tried to do, so that you felt sorry for her but could see, however, that his force was healthier. That's why I made Brando attractive.

One of the striking things in Streetcar, *something that now we would call Brechtian, is that there's such disparity in the dialects—Brando has a Brooklyn accent, Kim Hunter has a Midwestern accent, Vivien Leigh has a Southern accent, and so on. It's as if there were a deliberate attempt not to make it a regional, naturalistic drama.*
That's the way I think of Williams—in all the things we did together, although I kept a regional flavor, I tried to take out the little miniscule bits of local color. For instance, I cast Barbara Bel Geddes in *Cat on a Hot Tin Roof.* He finally approved of it, but he kept saying, 'Barbara! More melody! More melody!' I said, 'For Christ's sake, I'm going to walk out of this theatre if you talk to my actress once more.' He said, 'Yes, yes, I won't say another word, but she should have more *lilt*, more Southern *lilt!*' And I tried to make *Cat on a Hot Tin Roof* very abstract. It was staged on a triangle protruding into the audience, and the actors would talk into the audience all through it—it wasn't realistic at all. Well, I did things more and more that way, didn't I? I got less and less interested in naturalism.

Viva Zapata! (1952)

Do you think this is the first film where you learned to show parts of actions rather than whole actions?

Yes, I do. Well, everybody influences everybody, but the film that made a big impression on me was *Paisan,* particularly the last episode. Rossellini does a marvellous thing there when he gets to his climax—he leaps, he doesn't walk to the climax. He jumps to something and then he jumps over something, he jumps to something else and then he jumps over something.... It's a fantastic thing. I learned to try to jump crag to crag, rather than going all through the valleys.

I love *Viva Zapata!,* by the way. This is the first film we've come to that I could say I really love. The visual style of the film was taken from five books by two Mexican still cameramen, the Casasola photographs—this was the most photographed war up to that time, I guess. And they're absolutely brilliant. Some of those photographs I imitated pretty exactly. When Zapata and Pancho Villa meet, and their staffs gather around them—that's an exact reproduction right down to the casting.

Do you often use photographic material for an inspiration? Parts of Wild River *look based on Depression photography.*
That's right. A lot of the photographs I used in *Wild River* were taken by Marian Post, who worked for various government New Deal agencies. They meant a lot to me. They're very... well, 'inspiring' isn't the word. Photographs are a *challenge* to you. You look at them—there's the real thing, and there's also poetry in them. And the challenge is how to get both the reality and the poetry at the same time, because one without the other is not what I'm interested in. I use real photographs of real events as a source much more than paintings, although I admire Goya and Daumier particularly. In *East of Eden,* I again imitated a lot of photographs—the 'Kill the Kaiser' march was taken from photographs.

What was your attitude to the dogmatic intellectual played by Joseph Wiseman?
I felt that character came out a little strained, a little dehumanized. Now, a *little.* Listen. I was in the Movement, and I saw guys like that. V. J. Jerome was not a hell of a lot different. You don't know who V. J. Jerome was? A Party hack.

The execution of Madero is done with sirens in the background, which is an effect you pick up in On the Waterfront. *Why did you use it here?*
I guess I got it from when I was in Manila during the war. I was in Manila right after it was recaptured—there was shooting all over the city, and the

sirens were constantly going. And I always had the feeling that this one large sound was covering a deadly small sound. Also, there's terror in it, because it makes a mystery of what's really happening.

Is that why you used it in On the Waterfront *during Terry's confession?*
No. In *On the Waterfront* the scene was just so lousy, because it was saying something that the audience already knew, so why say it again? All that was important was the emotional effect on the girl.

The idea that the people must be their own leaders is also something that comes up again in On the Waterfront.
Well, I believe in democracy. I believe that democracy progresses through internecine warfare, through constant tension—we grow only through conflict. And that's what a democracy is. In that sense, people have to be vigilant, and the vigilance is effective. I truly believe all power corrupts, I really believe that—and I've seen it on the left, on the right, in the theatre, in films, everywhere. I think success is a much greater problem than failure.

Man on a Tightrope (1953)

I enjoyed making *Man on a Tightrope.* I enjoyed the German crew, I enjoyed the Bavarian Alps, and I enjoyed the little circus we worked with. I think it has some merits; I don't feel ashamed of it. But I don't think it's a very good film, and parts of it—like the romance between Gloria Grahame and Freddy March—are ridiculous, preposterous.

I was in Germany for five months, and when I got back to the United States I called up Zanuck and said, 'Look, I haven't seen my family for so long, I'd like to stay with them for a while.' He said, 'Oh, sure, sure!' I was surprised at how agreeable he was about it. Then I came back to the studio—I'd had a big tiled office in the white building—and someone else was in the office. I said, 'Where am I supposed to go?' He showed me—it was a little tiny office with one secretary for two people in the old writers' building. I thought, 'Shit! I'm dead.' The whole thing was a tip-off for what had happened: on the desk was a letter from Zanuck saying, 'I've cut twenty minutes from *Man on a Tightrope*—and I know you'll like it.' Well, the preface to that is, 'If you don't like it, fuck you.' That was the last time I let myself get into a situation like that, and it was the last time I worked for an all-powerful studio boss. Cutting is at least a third of a picture—if you don't have the right to do this, then don't make it.

On the Waterfront (1954)

On the Waterfront *caused a controversy in Britain. Were you aware of Lindsay Anderson's article attacking the ending as a fascist cop-out?*
Yes, I was. I thought it was an interesting and well-written article, and I disagreed totally with it. I thought I knew more about the waterfront than anyone except Budd Schulberg. It wasn't a careless job of research; I was living there, and I learned a lot about the waterfront—and also about the politics and elections, which Lindsay Anderson didn't know a goddamned thing about. All he had was this schematic left-wing idea about the ending. There's nothing fascist about the end of the picture.

I have another feeling that fits into what Anderson said, which is that I believe heroes play a role in society. They may be a hero for an hour or a day, but there are men who make a difference. Many abrupt social changes in the history of the labor movement have come over the body of a martyr. The high point of the San Francisco general strike of 1934, which made a big impression on me at the time, came when the bodies of two dockworkers who had been killed were laid out in the middle of the square. It started out as a funeral march, and it ended up as a general strike.

Now, I don't say the waterfront has changed—it hasn't. But it came goddamned close to changing. A vote was taken in that union after the picture was made, and it came within just over 100 votes of changing the leadership. I don't even say that if the leadership had been changed, it would have been a permanent change for the good. But it would have been a temporary change for the good. I think democracy progresses, as the French say, *reculer pour mieux sauter*: you go back, you go a little more forward. We're in a constant state of tension. I believe in Marxism, you know—I believe that one thing affects the other, I believe in interplay, in the dialectic. But I never meant that when they go back to work at the end of the film, there isn't going to be that same corruption starting up a month later.

Several critics—including Roger Tailleur, who wrote a book on you—interpret On the Waterfront *as a defence of the giving of testimony by you and Schulberg before the HUAC committee. Do you agree?*

Well, I think it's partly affected by that, naturally. I went through that
thing, and it was painful and difficult and not the thing I'm proudest of in
my life, but it's also not something I'm ashamed of. I was affected by that,
but it's not the main thing in the film. To say that we made the film as a
defence of that just isn't so. Because that's exactly what happened on the
waterfront. The story is based on the experiences of a real person: I used to
have dinner with him all the time. Schulberg and I went over there while
the inquest was going on. And it happens again and again. It happens at
all these Mafia trials. Silence, silence, silence. It's happening in the My Lai
investigations. Silence, silence. People don't say anything. Don't snitch,
don't say it. That's a very characteristic and very genuine inner conflict of
a man. So, to say that I'm not affected by what I went through in my life is
not true. But it's not the main subject of the film. Nor was it the original
reason why I did it. As a matter of fact, *On the Waterfront* did not start with
Budd Schulberg, it started with Arthur Miller. Long before I knew Budd
Schulberg, and long before my testimony, I went to Arthur Miller and said,
'Let's do a story about the waterfront.' So it was my intention to make a
picture about the struggles on the waterfront long before that.

Do you agree with Tailleur that A View from the Bridge *is Miller's answer to*
On the Waterfront?
I don't think Arthur Miller is that small a guy. He meant to write a play
about the waterfront many times before — he worked on the waterfront
during the war. But to say that he wasn't affected somewhat by one of his
best friends doing something he disagreed with is bullshit, too, isn't it? It's
a coloration, a degree, rather than the whole thing.

This was the third and last film you did with Brando. Does he like to underact?
He doesn't underact inside.

*I meant that one gets from Brando a feeling of great force restrained, which is
what gives his performances a lot of their excitement.*
I think that's what I feel in life. If I were to get mad at you, I would never
show it. You'd only notice it if the camera were sharp, and I were the sort
of person an actor is. But in life — for instance, if you're in love with someone, you don't know it, and it comes as a heavy shock to realize it. Or
anger, especially — anger is always held back, restrained; direct confronta-

tion is concealed. That's my own taste, and that's why I like Brando, and that's why I understood him. He's like that—he's full of deep hostilities, longings, feelings of distrust, but his outer front is gentle and nice. That's him. Brando is, in my opinion, the only genius I've ever met in the field of acting. He would constantly come up with ideas that were better than the ones I had. All he'd do was nod. I'd tell him what I wanted, he'd nod, and then he'd go out and do it better than I could have hoped it would be. To my way of thinking, his performance in *On the Waterfront* is the best male performance I've ever seen in my life.

We shot *On the Waterfront* surrounded by people, by spectators. It was great; it was like a public trial. We photographed scenes in front of a line of longshoremen who were watching their lives being filmed. Once I was grabbed by the neck, thrown up against a wall, and the guy was going to beat me up. This was just outside a bar, and a little longshoreman inside saw it and came out. He got a hold of the guy who was going to hit me, and he murdered him, he beat the shit out of him. The atmosphere was that violent. There were things I can't tell about corruption, about our paying off people—little black sacks, things like that. We were right in the midst of life on that picture, and it shows, doesn't it?

East of Eden (1955)

East of Eden *and* On the Waterfront *share a sense that the only time any real communication can take place is when two people are alone. Whenever a third person—even someone sympathetic—is around, nothing happens. In fact, a great deal of* East of Eden's *visual style is built on two-shots being invaded by a third party.*
It's true, I feel that. I used to be that way—I was terribly inhibited and shy, I couldn't even communicate. I had trouble talking to my father, I had trouble talking to my mother, and I had hardly any friends to talk to. And all my films bear that stain on them.

There's an associated theme in your films of a person not being able to communicate the seriousness *of a situation.*
Yes, I have often been unable to communicate the most serious things. For example, I can't fight with people. What I'll do is I'll just walk away and not see them. It's harder to say important things to people than unimportant things. I think the relations between the sexes are like that—the most important things are not said.

What was it like to work in color and 'scope for the first time?
George Stevens said a very smart thing when he saw CinemaScope. He said, 'They've finally found a way to photograph a snake.' I felt that way—it was a ridiculous form. I didn't choose it, but at that time everything was being made in it. So I thought I'd try it. I went out to do some tests the first day, and they said the object you were photographing had to be six feet away from the camera. I had a wonderful old guy named Ted McCord as the cameraman, and I told him, 'Now, push it! Push it in!' He said, 'Six feet!' I said, 'Fuck six feet!' We broke all the rules, and that six-feet rule was bullshit. That was just a desire to get everything as 'nice-looking' as possible. Then I was able to do this foreground-object stuff I mentioned; I made all the frames different—the film is all busted up that way. In that sense, using 'scope was a good experience.

How do you feel now about the use of the tilted-angle shots in the scene at the table between Dean and Massey?
I thought they were sort of good there, because they gave you a sense of rigidity—'That's the way it is whether you like it or not.'

Would you have done that if the film were not in 'scope?
I don't think so. I had trouble with it at that point. Because that would have been terrible—two single-shots, and cutting back and forth between them in that enormous space. I just didn't know what to fill the frame with that day. It was not my idea, by the way—it was Ted McCord's. I said to him, 'This is awful. What are we going to do?' He said, 'Why not tilt it?'

East of Eden *is the first of the big father-son confrontations in your films...*
A few of those, aren't there?

Did you see it as very personal when you read the Steinbeck book?
No, not when I read the book, but when I was working on the script. I saw the Dean character as similar to myself. I loved my brother, but my father always preferred him. He called him 'Sweet Avie'—my brother's name was Avraam in Greek. I always thought, well, he's a nice guy, but he's just as human as I am!

After Massey reprimands Dean for stealing the coal chute, they're reconciled at the end of the scene, but you dissolve out as it happens, we barely see it. Did you

do that intentionally to express Dean's point of view—that he would be more conscious of his father's reprimand than his reconciliation?
Yes, I did. I wanted all of Dean's things to be fleeting. I wanted to make it so you only got a glimpse of what he felt. The opposite of rigid, the opposite of ritualistic or schematic.

Even though East of Eden *is very much a character study, and even beyond the exigencies of 'scope, you use an unusually small number of close-ups in the film.*
Well, I felt that Dean's body was very graphic; it was almost writhing in pain sometimes. He was very twisted, almost like a cripple or a spastic of some kind. He couldn't do anything straight. He even walked like a crab, as if he were cringing all the time. I felt that, and that doesn't come across in close-up. Dean *was* a cripple, anyway, inside—he was not like Brando. People compared them, but there was no similarity. He was a far, far sicker kid, and Brando's not sick, he's just troubled. But I also think there was a value in Dean's face. His face is so desolate and lonely and strange. And there are moments in it when you say, 'Oh, God, he's handsome—what's being lost here! What goodness is being lost here!'

Also, he's not really a close-up actor; his face is expressive from a farther distance back. One feels that he had to try harder to pump his feelings across this little extra distance, that there was a greater strain of expressing himself.
I think that's true. Very often, on the set, he was terribly tense and pent-up. And then when he got loose, you felt that some little string had been tugged, and he went into this jiggle. When he dropped the money from behind his father's back, he went 'Ahhhhhhhhh,' and spun around with his arms outstretched—like a weird puppet. Now, if I had been in close-up, I wouldn't have seen any of that. I also think that was effective against Raymond Massey's absolute rigidity. By the way, the great one in that picture, the one who helped it come through behind the scenes, was Julie Harris, because she was so kind and so tolerant to Dean. He was difficult, and I had to be rough with him several times. But she was very kind to him, and she supported him.

Baby Doll (1956)

A big change that happened to me around this time was I started to wonder if I could write my own scripts because I put together the script of *Baby*

Doll, which Williams then worked over. Then, during the shooting, he used to send me bits that said, 'Insert somewhere.' So I was pretty free—I was making up my mind every night what we were going to do the next day. That got me interested in writing for the screen. In my opinion, that film's better than *Streetcar* or any other film made from Williams' work. That's another film I like. I don't think it's a big film—it's not a heavy, pompous film pregnant with meaning. But as a light, black comedy, I think it's beautiful. I made up my mind to make the whole thing a sort of macabre lark.

In later years, starting really with Splendor in the Grass, *it seems that you developed a style in which the film is both a drama and a comedy at the same time. But in* Baby Doll, *it's as if you hadn't yet worked this out, so that it alternates between dramatic and comic scenes.*
That's right. I didn't quite blend it together. I had that stylistic thing in mind, it was an attempt to do that, but I don't think I did it. Some of the farce element was a little too over-farcical. I think the serious stuff was pretty well done, but when they're running around upstairs, even though it was funny, I went a little too far. I should have mixed it up more.

This is the first of your films in which blacks from time to time act as a chorus, commenting on the whites' behavior—a device you use later in A Face in the Crowd, Wild River, *and* Splendor in the Grass.
I didn't realise that, but it's true. I did it *here* consciously. I thought, 'The blacks are sitting down there, and they're laughing at these fucking whites.' And they do. They tell stories about whites just as the whites tell stories about darkies. If you go to a black home, they'll tell you stories about the boss, and how silly he is, and how he got drunk, and who he's fucking, and everything else.

In Baby Doll, *there's even an extension of this—there's often an audience for the ridiculous antics of the main characters, like the group of Chinese watching Archie and Baby Doll when they first come into town.*
Yes, that's absolutely true. And they *are* ridiculous. But I'll tell you something that starts in *Baby Doll* which I think is more mature—when I'm against somebody, I still maintain a certain degree of affection toward them. Whereas in *East of Eden* I did not—I wanted to kill Massey, I really

was against him. In this film, these Southerners are bigots and everything else, but there's a certain affection in it which I believe is more mature and complicated.

But, of course, one way of looking at East of Eden *is as the playing out of an Oedipal dream—you kill the father, and yet you reconcile with him.*
It's a dream, a wish-dream—that my daddy will love me, but that he'll also get the hell off my back. Don't we all feel that?

The photography in Baby Doll *is striking—it's all so white and gauzy.*
The whole idea was white on white. Bleached out, bleached out—the end of the South. The white man's bleached out—his home, the paint, is bleached out. White on white, white on white, white on white. Wherever I could, white on white. That's why she's always in white—bleached out, no make-up on her face. Contrast to the Italian, who's got a black hat, black shoes, black shirt. He's strong—newcomers, the new people in the South, fucking up the Old South, rejuvenating it through new blood. And the blacks, above all. So it's a contrast between white-on-white and black—the death of the South.

I think people expect the film to end in a Buñuelian way. They expect an arrange-ment—that Archie will accept Baby Doll's being serviced by Vacarro in exchange for his business at the cotton gin. But the end seems to imply that he puts ego and sexual pride above the economic factor.
No, I didn't mean that. What I meant was that Vacarro had her, like a good wop, a good Greek, fell asleep, looked at her—and there are other girls in the world. He didn't want to get tangled up with a piece of baggage like her. He might even sue the husband the next day; he wouldn't give a shit. It wouldn't mean that much to him—it only means that much to Americans. I don't even know if it means that much to Americans, actu-ally—we just make a lot of it in our films. But actually it's just an act that we pass on. That's why I think Williams' last line is perfect—'We have to wait and see if we've forgotten to remember.'
    Were you around during the Catholic controversy about the film? When Cardinal Spellman condemned it? He made statements that were front page in the New York Post—he said, 'I spent Christmas with our

boys in Korea. I felt their sacrifices, and what they are doing for this country. And what do I find when I come back to America? *Baby Doll.*' He
actually said that, in the pulpit of St. Pats! I said, 'Well, I'm flattered very
much that you think we're that important.' Did you ever hear how I found
out he hadn't seen the picture? I guessed it! I had a reporter I knew on the
Herald Tribune call him up. Spellman's secretary said, 'Wait a minute.'
Then she came back and said, 'He's not available to talk about it.' So this
reporter said in the Herald Tribune that he couldn't get an answer to that
question. The Post then picked it up and said he didn't even see the picture. Then they had an editorial saying it was un-American that he didn't
see the picture!

A Face in the Crowd (1957)

If you were making the film today, is there anything you would change to update
it, or do you feel it's still pretty accurate?
Well, it's not intended to be accurate in a literal way. There was an intention to make that picture larger than life. Budd Schulberg always talked
about a picture his father [B. P. Schulberg] made years ago in which a
German actor screamed at the end, 'Nobody loves me!' We *did* try to make
the picture on a heightened level like that. And I'm criticized often for it.
But it's my taste. I don't deal in naturalism anymore; it doesn't interest me
much.

One thing I would do differently today: I feel the picture is at several
points over-explicit. I'm not sure I like all of Matthau's speech at the end,
when he says to Griffith, 'I know what will happen to you. Someone else
will take you place,' and all that. I think telling the audience, 'This is what
the picture means,' instead of letting them find out what it means, is of
that time, not of *our* time. Another thing I would change is I would try to
make the audience like Lonesome Rhodes more in the middle area of the
film and even at the end, so that you are still being seduced by him. As
it stands, the picture allows you to take a comfortable position and say,
'He's obviously a danger.' Actually, he's *not* obviously a danger—we're still
being caught up in that kind of influence. I'd mix things up more, so that
the audience is implicated and doesn't stand on that safe platform of re-
moval. I think the worst thing that can happen in a film is when you say,
'Oh that's about *him*! that's about that shitheel! That's about that villain

over there! It's not about me.' That's what I would do differently, and that's what I tried to do with *America, America* and my other recent films. I try to be merciless and therefore more genuinely sympathetic to everyone.

The intellectual figure played by Walter Matthau comes out like Wiseman in
Viva Zapata! *— ineffectual, a little sour.*
Well, I certainly didn't regard him as a *raisonneur,* the figure in a French play who says everything right. I thought of him as someone weak and vengeful. When he slams the book down on the bar and says, 'I'll get back at him through this book!' — it's a gesture that's semi-impotent. Why did-n't he ever confront Rhodes directly? He only does it at the end, when Rhodes is down.

The common critical wisdom about A Face in the Crowd *is that something goes wrong around the middle, and the film is derailed. In previous interviews, you've agreed with that.*
I think that less now than I did then. When I saw the film again recently, I thought it was better. The whole problem was the mixture of styles — to try to get both a tragic ending and a satirical first half is an awfully hard tightrope to walk. At the time, I didn't think I had walked it successfully. But seeing the film now, it seems less real and more real. It seems less real realistically and much more real symbolically, on an ultra-realistic level.

I think a problem people have with the film is that there are two extremes. On the one hand, there's the non-naturalism, but at the same time there's a fantastic amount of versimilitude, little sociological details like the fact Griffith wears an undershirt instead of a T-shirt.
That's good for them — it's good for them to be shaken up. For example — the undershirt thing. I wanted to suggest that there was a slightly stale odour about him — that he slept in that undershirt, and he never took it off, and he even fucked with it on. Well, that to me is *both* a naturalistic element and it's *supranaturalism,* because it has overtones that go deeper than just the fact. And that's what you see in life when you walk down the street, if you notice people. Have you ever noticed how many people talk to themselves walking down the street? Is that naturalism? When you show a street scene in a film, you don't see people talking to themselves. But it's endemic, it's everywhere. My idea is that if you notice how people

actually live, think, feel, exist, and you *show* it — very soon, by piling up incidents, you get something that is at once naturalistically true but also has overtones that are more meaningful.

Wild River (1960)

After *A Face in the Crowd,* I began to feel that I should write my own scripts, and I tried, I tried hard, but it wasn't a success. I wrote four drafts of *Wild River;* then I went to Paul Osborn and asked him to do it. Some of my original stuff is still in the picture. But I didn't know enough to do what I think I can do now; I'm a better constructionist now. Paul is an excellent constructionist. He has an innate, simple sense of structure.

I was anxious to make something about the TVA because I was in and around the South during those years. One of the things I tried consciously to do was to capture the beauty of simple lives — the music, the corn, the autumn, the winter, the water, the faces of that part of the country. As I said, I used to go there a lot; I had a kind of romance with it. It dawned on me there how beautiful it is — how beautiful dry corn is, how beautiful the music there is. I love *Wild River* — just the ease of it, the simplicity. I tried to deal more with my own sense of beauty, rather than what I did in *Baby Doll,* where I made things a bit grotesque. I tried not to do that here; it's purer, one of the two purest films I've made.

One painful memory I have about that picture is the way it was sold. Or not sold. It was just put on, taken off, never shown, nobody saw it. I had to bully Skouras into showing it in Paris, where it was acclaimed immediately. But here it was nothing. It was so insulting; I've never gotten over it.

One indication of the more restrained tone of Wild River *is that you don't show Chuck being beaten by Bailey, in contrast to the violence in your earlier films.*
That's true. I wrote that scene; that's one of the few things in the film that I wrote myself. And also it's semi-affectionate, and I guess one reason for that was I had an awful lot of affection for all the people in that area. I knew a lot of toughs like that; I was run off a lot of places when I was in documentary films. I also knew a lot of guys like the three sons of the old lady. And they throw Clift in the lake, but they don't beat him up or kill him.

Wild River *is probably your most Fordian film, but if Ford had made it he probably would have seen only the side of the old lady.*

Yes, I think the film shows a fair view of things, because I do try to stay...
on both sides. I was going to say that I stay in the middle, but that's not
exactly it: I show both sides.

*The film does finally seem to say that socialistic planning was what had to be
done.*
No, I say it's what *happened.* I say there's something good going down,
something dear and valuable. I say something was lost. I believe there's
something lost in our society now.

As opposed to Viva Zapata! *or* A Face in The Crowd, *here the intellectual figure, played by Montgomery Clift, is the hero. You also seem more positive about
his ineffectuality.*
I think that figure realizes his mannerisms. It's a romantic idea of mine. I
feel that by the end of the New Deal that figure had played himself out. By
the time of the war, many figures like that were getting into what the kids
are into now—the values of the simple life. And I let Clift do that. In
other words, I let him get "engaged" to a family, fall in love with the girl
but also fall in love with the old lady. A scene I like a lot is where Clift falls
down drunk in front of the old lady's porch. He's reduced from being a
Washington bureaucrat, and she looks at him, she's victorious. At the same
time she gets to appreciate him.

*The theme of the single-minded character is continued here—obviously it's the
old lady, but also Remick.*
Yes, she's completely non-intellectual, she doesn't think. And because she
doesn't think rationally or intellectually, she often catches him off guard,
says things he's not prepared for.

*And she anticipates Clift's arguments. She says, 'I know what you're going to
say. You're going to say you're not ready for marriage yet.'*
That's right. Because it's finally her *will*—it's firmer, more direct. He sees
all the answers—he's like us intellectuals, so he calls her up, and then he
waits two days, he goes back and forth. But she finally gets him, because
her will is clearer. She says, 'You're gonna marry me.'

*And he changes. In your later films especially you seem to be almost a messiah
on the possibility of change.*

That's true, absolutely true. I had a big argument once with Tennessee Williams about that. He said, 'You're all wrong. People don't change. They stay the same.' Yet I want to repeat that I also like people who don't change. I love Mrs. Garth, the old lady. She was wrong in terms of progress, the way the world had to move. Absolutely wrong, intolerable, ornery, unbending. But a kind of person I like. I like obdurate people—what's called inner-directed. The kind who will stand up and say, 'I'm not gonna change.'

Splendor in the Grass (1961)

One assumes that Splendor in the Grass *began with your association with William Inge on the Broadway production of* The Dark at the Top of the Stairs.
Right. He told me a story idea that he had. He wrote it up, and it was like a long novel. Then I worked on it, pared it down, and made a screenplay out of it. Then he worked over it. It went back and forth between us constantly.

Now here's an odd thing: *that* is the picture some French critics say is the best one I've made. Hard for me to understand that. I like the picture, but I don't think it's particularly filmic.

One reason they like the film might be that there's a great effort now to merge Marx and Freud in French thinking. There's a phrase in Godard's British Sounds: *'We have to study Freudian economics and Marxian sexuality.' And* Splendor in the Grass *seems to say that Victorian repression was still in America in the 'twenties, and people compensated for their sexual frustrations in the stock market.*
By God, I think you've got it! I think that's it.

For example, when Natalie Wood's mother says, 'US Steel went up fourteen points today,' she's having an orgasm, the only one available.
Right, and Beatty's mother is brutalized by her husband, who doesn't get his sex at home but runs to New York, gets laid, and plays the market.

There's another example: during the first kiss between Wood and Beatty in the store, you hear someone saying in the background, 'Ten pound sack of grain!'
Right! that's it! It never occurred to me. I was just trying to put on the screen what I saw, but I remember putting that line in there behind the

kiss. I never thought of that, but it's true. That must be what the French like — that the two blend, the two become one.

When the film came out, Stanley Kauffmann criticised it because he thought the idea that you can go mad from not having sex is as false as the Victorian notion that you can go mad from too much sex.
Chacun á son gout. What can I say about Stanley Kauffmann? That's not really why she went mad. She went mad because she wanted to fulfill her meaning as a person in a physical way. But she had within her things which inhibited her, so she always felt guilty about it. That's the inner conflict of the girl. But when you simplify it down to what Kauffmann says — that's not what happens. What is madness? Madness is often precipitated, is it not, by two equally strong opposing feelings which result in a clash that the person cannot resolve. The person cannot deal with it, and so it blows his mind. That's why 'blows his mind' is an apt expression; it's like a short circuit. And this girl's a frail vessel.

I want to add another thing: the leading institution for taking care of people who crack up is located in Kansas. The Menninger Clinic. And it's right in Middle America. Isn't it odd and interesting and necessarily significant that the place is there? I visited the place often, and a lot of the patients are women. There's a price, in other words, for their morality.

Splendor in the Grass, *like* The Arrangement, *deals heavily in psychiatry...*
How do I feel about it? Well, I was helped a lot. I went to two psychoanalysts in my lifetime. The first one didn't help me. As a matter of fact, his policy was one of accommodation — in other words, allowing me to get through the day. The second one, at my wish and instructions, was much tougher because I was 55 at that time, pretty late to start writing your first novel. So I was determined not to waste any time. And he made me face a lot of the problems why I couldn't write a novel, and I was able to start writing. It made a big difference in my life. I felt then that psychiatrists could be very helpful, more so than I do now. I now think that they can be very dangerous. But in *Splendor in the Grass,* I had a sense of the necessity of accepting limited objectives. Limited objectives — those were words I used a lot.

You reject that in The Arrangement.
Yes, I do. I don't feel that way now at all. In *The Arrangement* I tried to say that the traditional society analyst is *there*, and his function is to stroke a

person and somehow make him get through the day. Also, I think *The Arrangement,* especially the book, is inhabited by a sense of the divided self, and that we've become less confident that one side can survive the other. I read Laing's *The Divided Self* at the time I was writing the novel.

In both films, the mental institution is flooded with sunlight, almost as if it were a religious experience.
Much more so in *Splendor in the Grass* than in *The Arrangement.* In *Splendor in the Grass,* the white suggests a resolution to her problems. I think that's also indicated by the way she responds to her boyfriend's marriage at the end. That last episode is the part I like best in the film—where she goes to visit her old lover and his wife, and then she drives away.

And it's very dry weather in that scene, in contrast to the water imagery in the rest of the film, as if to suggest real maturity.
Well, again, accepting limited objectives. That's a thing the other analyst tried to impress on me: realize what you are and work within your limitations. That was in the air in the United States at that time. I rejected that later—my life style completely changed.

America, America (1963)

Concurrent with your decision to write your own screenplays, beginning with America, America, there's also a major change in your visual style—your films are constructed much more in terms of shots than in terms of scenes.
Yes, that's true. I did get more interested in that, and partly because I was freer of someone else's script; I didn't have to respect every word. I felt that, having come out of the theatre, I was medium-shot prone, dialogue-obsessed. Also, when I went to Greece and Turkey to shoot the film, I got a tremendous exhilaration from the surroundings. They were very romantic environments for me, so they aroused this change, too. But actually this tendency started before, back in *Viva Zapata!,* although it did come out much more when I was on my own.

It seems that your style of directing actors also changed to accommodate this.
Yes, that's absolutely correct. I became less psychological, and less interested in the little turns and changes of inner feeling. I think it's somewhat more epic in its style—the feelings are simpler and bigger. I do think that's an accurate observation, although *Wild River* was this way, too.

Yes, one thing that starts with Wild River *is that you don't have the kind of big powerhouse performances you used to—the performances are meshed much more into the film.*
Correct. In this film, I just finished making, *Home Free,* you're not aware of anybody standing out. You see, even in a film like *East of Eden,* I was influenced by the theatre, where it's carried along by a scene of conflict expressed by dialogue conflict; there's an interchange of positions with one person having an objective in relation to another person, then the response, and all that interplay. I became less interested in that. But as I say, that started back in *Zapata,* which is all in shots—the two things are concurrent. Brando's character is not elaborated, and it's not interesting qua psychology. My interest in that picture was in the *sweep* of the events. And the characters are introduced at the top of their crises, and then dropped and changed. This is a result of handling time in a much swifter way, the way it is in life—it seems to go along smoothly, but violent and quick changes are happening underneath the surface, and suddenly you realize, 'Christ, I'm not where I was two weeks ago!'

That style leads to a common criticism of America, America: *that Stavros doesn't basically increase in self-awareness—he just has this one static goal, to get to America—and this single-minded character doesn't permit great psychological change.*
I don't agree with that. The nicest thing he does in the picture, to me, is when he says to the girl he's about to marry, 'Don't trust me.' And when a man is self-aware to that point, where he knows that in a crisis he's not to be trusted in regard to his main goal, I think that's a terrific piece of psychology. Actually, I would be false to elaborate on his character, because my feeling is that you watch this fellow grow slowly ready to sacrifice more and more of himself, to do anything. That is, he starts out as a very 'pure' and father-morality-ridden boy, and gradually he gets clipped of all his sense of worth. So he's left with his obsession, but without his character. In other words, the film is about what it *costs* to become an American.

How much relooping did you do on America, America?
Well, that was criticized by Walter Kerr. He was wrong about that. He had a valid point, which was that very often you couldn't understand Stathis Giallelis. But that wasn't as a result of relooping. He just didn't know what

our problems were there. One day on the waterfront in Istanbul, we had 5,000 spectators. They always numbered in the thousands. They were mostly hostile because the newspapers were printing headlines saying I was making fun of the Turks. So they were noisy, and you couldn't keep them quiet. Therefore, the level of the sound had to be kept down, and Stathis didn't make a good track. I should have looped *more*—ironically, Walter said the exact opposite of what I should have done. I should have looped the whole picture the way Fellini does. Except that my background soundtracks were so excellent I didn't want to lose them.

The fact that Stavros first sees America from Katherine Balfour's porthole conveys that that's how he got his passage, as a gigolo . . .
Yes, but it also keeps the mixture going of sinfulness, which he would feel a lot. He feels all the time that he's betraying his father's standards. So when he looks out the window, there's shame in it, and he feels his father slapping him across the face and then offering his hand to kiss. That's strictly minority psychology, what a father means to a Near Eastern kid— the role of the father in your soul, his presence and his strength. I was one of four brothers. One was born in Germany, and I was born in Turkey. The other two were born in America, and they enjoyed my father, they had no problems with him. But my older brother and I were obsessed with the problem of my father. I never stopped writing about that guy, or making films about him. *East of Eden* is about my father. But I think it's much deeper in *America, America* than it is in *East of Eden,* where it's mechanical: the good boy and the bad boy. The interesting thing is when the good boy and the bad boy are in one person; in *America, America,* I put Cal and Aaron into one body shell, and they fought it out inside. When the father slaps Stavros, he doesn't rebel—he kisses the hand worshipfully. So he's got both in him.

The Arrangement (1969)

Then you wrote a novel . . .
Then I wrote a novel, yeah. I was really at a bad time in my life when I started that book. My wife had just died, and I was fed up with the theatre, and I hated Lincoln Center. And I didn't like New York, and the whole goddamn thing. So I suddenly said, 'I'm gonna quit. I've got some money saved up. I'm just gonna leave.' I went on a trip around the world, and I

did just what I wanted—I lived in Paris for three weeks, and I lived in London for a while, and so on. I did what we all want to do some day—just to go and live in different places.

As Eddie says in The Arrangement, *'I'm going away . . . into myself.'*
Yes, that's right. Exactly what I did. And in the mornings, I began writing letters to myself, and I began to think about things that had happened to me. Slowly, it began to take another form, and it developed into a novel. Then I disguised it more and more, and I got farther and farther away from myself. But two things always remained very accurate in that book: my mother and my father.

Do you think the casting of Kirk Douglas rather than Brando affected the way you made the film?
Yes, I do. I think I gained by it, and I think I lost by it. The thing I think I lost was this inner-contradictoriness that Brando has, this terrible ambivalence.

If you had used Brando, would you still have externalized that aspect in the form of his alter-ego?
Yes, I think Brando could have done that brilliantly. He's awfully good at physical characterisations. I probably would have still done that, although I did elaborate it with Douglas. But there's a viability with Douglas—that he fits into being an advertising man and a driving, ruthless person better than Brando could have. You would always suspect Brando. In that sense, I think he gave a truer performance than Brando would have. Kirk's awfully bright. He's as bright a person as I've met in the acting profession. And I can't understand it when people knock his performance because I think he's terrific in the picture.

Of course, you would always suspect Brando, which would suggest more the intellectual man of integrity who has gone astray. What was hard to imagine in Douglas was that the character at one time could have been something else.
Yes, correct. Or that he could have been a writer. There's a basic ambivalence about Brando that is more like what I do, more like my own work: I'm involved in a lot of pieces that are at war inside myself. I also think something about the part was very close to Brando. He made it impossible

for me to use him — I guess that's the accurate way of putting it — for various reasons, but among them was that something about the part made him uncomfortable. It was very, very close to something basic in him.

Some people consider the animated snapshots and Eddie talking to his alter ego to be crude devices in relation to the rest of the film. How do you feel about them?
I guess they are a little crude. Personally, I like them, because I think they're the nearest I could come to expressing the ambivalence he felt. What I tried to do was to keep two levels of consciousness going at times. For example: the past is alive in the present. It happens to us all the time. He walks out of his father's room in the hospital, and he sees his mother sitting in the waiting room. He looks at her, and she looks so sad and desolate and forlorn. But he remembers that she used to hide him, and make him sneaky, and conceal him from his father so that he could read behind the sofa at night. He remembers that. That's what happens to us all the time, isn't it? You're with somebody, and he's irritating you, and you think, 'Gee, he really said beautiful things once.'

It's a double level, and that's more important than having a straight realistic line — it actually expresses more. Suppose those things are a little crude. So what! So, fuck it, they're a little crude. Sometimes the crude devices are better. Bresson has many crude moments, you know. There are some terribly crude and corny things in *Mouchette*. But he's trying to express something poetic and deep, and you have to respect that. Actually, I think *Last Year at Marienbad,* which is supposed to be so subtle, has many crude devices — boring devices like the statues turning. That's old documentary shit. But I like them because he's trying to say something other films don't say. Everything can't be judged by whether it's smooth or crude. There has to be a higher category of evaluation — that if it succeeds even partly in expressing something difficult and not frequently expressed, it's worth more than something that's smoothed out. Willie Wyler's films are all smoothed out. You're never going to get any crude moments in them. But what's happening to Willie is that they're getting less and less personal.

One of the more remarkable passages in the film is the long scene in the hotel room where they're trying to get Eddie to sign away his property — it's like an avalanche, with all these things happening at once.

Don't you think that's an unusual goddamned scene? I mean, that's worthy of anybody. Where in American films is there a scene like that? Is
there any? I can't understand why they put that picture down!

Well, when Splendor in the Grass *came out, a lot of people said it was hysterical. You go to see it today, and it looks absolutely classical! The same thing
might be true of* The Arrangement—*you're ahead of what may become general
technique.*
Do you think any man who's worth a shit could be *not* hysterical about
the situation in the world today? I think an element of hysteria is a mark
of sanity. I think if you're not still angry at the age of 61, you should be
shoveled under. How can you look at what's happening in this country
without being furious? Wait until you see this film I'm doing now! I don't
know if they'll be able to take it. I mean, it is so mean and so violent and
so full of anger—what other response can you have to Nixon? The whole
world is in such a state of horror that you cannot respond temperately to
it. I don't say I've done everything good in my life, but at least I've done
that much. And so it's hysterical? I stand up for that! I'm proud of it. I'm
glad it is. I wish it were more.

On the other hand, a film like The Damned, *which is just as 'hysterical,' got
very good reviews.*
You want to know what I think? I think my picture is much better. Why?
Not because of the style, or because it's excessive or not excessive, but
because of what it says. I believe a hell of a lot of picture-makers today are
making metaphors. They say, 'This takes place in the Wild West, but it's
really about speaking out.' Or, 'This takes place in the jungle, but it's really
about Vietnam.' My picture says, 'It's about what the fucking thing is
about! Now, come on, look at it! You may not like the son-of-a-bitch who
made it, but he's talking about *you!*' Well, I've got to be excessive because I
want them to look at themselves—and myself, I'm not excepting myself.
So I think that's harder for them to take. They can take a metaphor. *The
Wild Bunch!* Oh, what bullshit! It's not about violence. It's not about the
violence that's out in this street here at night! Show me a picture that's
about American life today. Where is it? Name one, quick. But when they're
shown the thing itself, and it's about suburbia—it's about Judith Crist's
neighbor or Vincent Canby's cousin—they say, 'Oh, it's excessive. We're
not like that.'

When you're dealing with it directly like that, a lot of critics prefer that it be done calmly, like Five Easy Pieces.
Well, isn't the same thing true about *Five Easy Pieces*? 'It's about those lower class people out there.' Or Eric Rohmer. That's another metaphor. It's *out there,* about *those* people. But this is about *you,* ya sonovabitch, in your button-down shirt!

Home Free (1971)

I just finished a film called *Home Free* that my son Chris wrote. It's about two soldiers coming to visit a third soldier whom they'd known in Vietnam, and what happens between them. It's about a lot that's in the air now. And the great experiment with it was to get back to the basics of film-making. *The Arrangement* cost almost $7,000,000, which was a big shock to me—I'd never made a film that cost over a million-and-a-half before. I would say about a million of that budget was operative, and the rest went here, there, and everywhere—to pay for changing the offices at Warner Brothers, and so forth. It's absurd. When we got through with the principal photography of *Home Free,* we had spent a figure of money—$60,000—which was exactly what Faye Dunaway's agent got for his services on *The Arrangement*. That's a pretty cute piece of irony, isn't it? On *Home Free,* I had a crew of four—a cameraman, a lighting man, a sound man, and one guy who did everything else. That's all. And it was suddenly so simple, so pleasurable, so without strain. I got down to what you *really* need to make a film, because that's how I started out—doing documentaries with Ralph Steiner and Frontier Films. In those days, I used to carry a tripod. And this winter, up in the snow where we were shooting, I carried a tripod again.

The Political Issues; The HUAC: *Viva Zapata!* (1951), *Man on a Tightrope* (1952)

MICHEL CIMENT/1974

The HUAC (House Un-American Activities Committee), with which you collabo-
rated by giving names, was not only anti-Communist, it was also against
everything liberal that had been done in America since the New Deal, which you
supported. Furthermore it was doing to you and to other people what you criti-
cised your Communist cell for doing before the war: forcing people to do things
they did not want to do, controlling their thoughts.
Well, I don't think there is anything in my life towards which I have more
ambivalence, because, obviously, there's something disgusting about
giving other people's names. On the other hand, I think that when it's
discussed now, it's discussed without relation to the period during which
it took place. For one thing, at that time I was convinced that the Soviet
empire was monolithic (which proved not to be so). I also felt that their
behaviour over Korea was aggressive and essentially imperialistic. I certainly didn't like the people on the Right, and I made that clear in all my
statements. On the other hand . . . well, as I say, it's ambivalent. Since then,
I've had two feelings: one feeling is that what I did was repulsive, and the
opposite feeling, when I see what the Soviet Union has done to its writers,
and their death camps, and the Nazi pact and the Polish and Czech repression — well, Krushchev says in his book what we all knew at that time was
going on. It revived in me the feeling I had at that time, that it was essentially a symbolic act, not a personal act. I also have to admit, and I've

From *Kazan on Kazan*, Viking, 1974. © 1974 by Michel Ciment. Reprinted by permission of
Sight and Sound and the British Film Institute.

never denied, that there was a personal element in it, which is that I was very angry, humiliated, and disturbed — furious, I guess — at the way they booted me out of the Party. In a sense they made it impossible for me to stay in. I knew, because in a small way I was part of the machinery, that orders were coming from above, which we, I, were supposed to hand out below. I despised the men at the top; I had affection for some members of the Party, but the cultural man, I really disliked his ideas and what he meant. There was no doubt that there was a vast organisation which was making fools of all the liberals in Hollywood, and taking their money, that there was a police state among the Left element in Hollywood and Broadway. It was disgusting to me, what many of them did, crawling in front of the Party. Albert Maltz published something in *The New Masses,* I think, that revolted me: he was made to get on his hands and knees and beg forgiveness for things he'd written and things he'd felt. I felt that essentially I had a choice between two evils, but the one thing I could not see was (by not saying anything) to continue to be a part of the secret manoeuvring and behind-the-scenes planning that was the Communist Party as I knew it. I've often, since then, felt on a personal level that it's a shame that I named people, although they were all known, it's not as if I were turning them over to the police; everybody knew who they were, it was obvious and clear. It was a token act to me, and expressed what I thought at the time. Right or wrong, it wasn't anything I made up, I was convinced of it. I had behaved secretly for a long time. Our behaviour in the Group Theatre was conspiratorial and, I thought, disgusting: our cell would discuss what we were going to do, then we would go to Group Theatre meetings or Actors' Equity meetings and pretend we were there with open minds. The whole thing was a way of taking over power. Solzhenitsyn describes the same thing. It was something, in my small sphere, that was symbolic of what was going on in the world. I preferred at that time doing what I did, to just remaining, by my silence, part of the thing. Defecting — that would really, to me, be defecting and lying — saying, 'Oh, I don't know anything about it, I don't know anyone, it doesn't exist, you're foolish to think anything like that goes on,' and all that. I never told a lie, I never told one lie; I've never done anything for money. I've never even directed a play because I thought it would make money. I've always done everything for my own reasons. They may not be reasons anyone else has, or anyone else would agree with, but that's the other person's problem.

Your next films show that in fact you were nearer to the people on the other side than to the people you co-operated with.

I always said so — I said so in my statement. 'I'm going to make the same kind of films,' I said, 'but I'll make better films.' Anyway, let me just say this: I was given this story about the escape of a circus, *Man on a Tightrope,* and I ran directly into the block I've always had, which is, I mustn't say anything against the Soviet Union — which was automatic. I thought suddenly that I was an automated person, that I didn't have the courage of the truth and of my convictions. I said: if I really believe this — it was a true circus, it really happened — why do I shrink in fear and terror from saying so? What sort of a person am I? I, by my silence, am part of this conspiracy of lying. I believed that many of the Left who testified or refused to testify didn't tell the truth; they told lies. I told the truth. I think it's important that people should know what goes on in their country, behind the scenes, and in this country, particularly, where decisions are made, presumably, and in some cases actually by people knowing what happens. The whole basis of democracy is: tell the people the truth and they'll make up their minds. And I did.

Man on a Tightrope — I didn't think the script was very good. The writer, Robert Sherwood, a brilliant and wonderful man, was exhausted, at the end of his life. But I said to myself, I'll get a real small German circus and go on the spot, and show how it really happened. That way I'll lift the other guilt off me, which was painful to me: I mean, I was really ashamed at being so terrorised, so immured in Stalinism. Many of my friends are still unable to face the truth of that situation. The Stalinists here are so terrorised and so automated that they can no longer take stands. These very, very intelligent and really nice people went right through the whole Czechoslovakian crisis recently and they *still* won't criticise the USSR. I think there are a lot of people here who are still Stalinists. I would fight to the death not to let them control me. I really hate them a lot. What I thought, then, was that there should be a strong, non-communist Left in this country. I don't mean the socialism they have in England, where every Socialist prime minister becomes an earl or a lord right away. Today, in this country, because of the youth, there's a strong non-communist Left. They despise the former Stalinists: they say they're liars and that they're irrelevant.

But don't you think that at that time the danger for America, the threat, came
more from McCarthy and the extreme Right, which was also trying to get control
of the country?
I never felt that. Other people all over the world have felt it, and I've been
criticised on that ground. I never felt that McCarthy was a big threat. In
the first place, the man that put him down was a Republican, Eisenhower—
a very reactionary, very traditional Republican. The judge that exposed
him was also that way. I always had faith in America's process of putting
light on her problems. What killed McCarthy was one moment on television, when the whole world saw him whisper to a lawyer sitting next to
him—and in that instant they recognised he was a bad man. He *was* a bad
man. He was an embarrassment to me and to many of the people on the
same side I was on. What I say now to my critics is: look at the work I've
done since.

At that time, people wrote articles, they humiliated me in the press.
Okay; they were right to fight back for their lives and for what they
believed in. But what they said was that I was finished, corrupt and would
never do anything again. As is obvious—I don't have to point it out—I
began to make good films, really progressive and really deep, only *after*
that period. The first film I made after that was *Zapata*, which I prepared
before, and made during and after. Then *On the Waterfront*. Because of
what I'd done, they said *On the Waterfront* was fascist in its ending. Well, it
was *not* fascist; it was an exact description of what happened. I felt the
workers would be in the same situation again; they had not conquered the
corruption. The last thing Lee J. Cobb says is: 'I'll be back.' And he did
come back. I knew the waterfront in Hoboken intimately. I spent months
there. Schulberg spent a year there. There was an election, after the film
was made, in which the 'good' side, our side, lost by something like a hundred votes, out of two thousand—a very small margin. The waterfront has
never got any better, it's the same now, just the same.

I have never, because of my nature, felt apologetic about anything I did.
I don't say that human beings don't make mistakes; I have often. I don't
say that what I did was entirely a good thing. What's called 'a difficult
decision' is a difficult decision because either way you go, there are penalties, right? What makes some things difficult in life is: if you're marrying
one woman you're not marrying another woman, if you go one course

you're not going another course. But I would rather do what I did than crawl in front of a ritualistic Left and lie the way those other comrades did, and betray my own soul. I didn't betray it, I made a difficult decision. It was—it still is. I've never been at ease about it. I've never said: 'Sure, that was good!' It's not that simple.

You could have made your statement two years before or two years later; but it came at a time when the witch-hunters were trying to control the thought of the American people in a totalitarian way, because it was not only Stalinist commu-nism that they were fighting but any kind of socialism, any kind of intellectual freedom . . .
But I never felt, because of the job I had done, was doing, and planned to do, that I had been silenced in any way. Rather, I have spoken more freely and more boldly since then. I never said I liked McCarthy, I despised him, I really and truly did, I said that publicly all the time. I said: 'I'm embar-rassed at being connected at all with these people.'

In 1953 you wrote in your notes: 'We must protect ourselves from the Communists, but also from the consequences of our rage at them.' You sensed the possible dan-ger of being on the side of the conservatives by sheer anti-Stalinism.
All I can say—I don't say it loud, I can't beg anybody's pardon—when people criticise me, is: look at my pictures. I think I've done social and critical pictures ever since. In *America America*, in *Splendor in the Grass*, in *Wild River*, I think I've made pictures that are *Left*. And *The Arrangement*— the book, too. And I'm still called a communist; my name is still on that list. I'm still attacked as a communist; these people on the Right look at my work and say: 'Well, he's still doing the same stuff.' Wait till they read *The Assassins*. I'm going to change my phone number, because I know I'm going to get all kinds of attacks. I don't want to be terrorised. That's why, now, the Left is suddenly beginning to get favourable to me, saying I did a bad thing but looking at my films. In the last two years they've begun to change and to respect me again.

Do you think that the resentment at what you'd done, at least partly, gave you strength to go on?
I think it made a man of me. Up to then, I was the blue-eyed boy, every-body's darling; I was both very successful and very Left; I was the living

demonstration of how you could be on the Left and still be in the gossip columns and be envied for the money you made. I was essentially an other-directed man; I was really working for the praise of others, for the notices in the papers. This thing made me say: well, not everybody likes me, I've lost many of my best friends (they would pass me in the street and not say anything, not even nod to me). I said, okay, I'm going to satisfy myself now, not the critics, not even my friends. The ironic thing was that I also became vulnerable in the eyes of the movie executives. The first thing they did was to cut my salary down. They said: 'You're damaged goods now, we're not going to pay you that much.' Zanuck or Skouras or somebody actually said to my agent: 'He can take it or leave it, that's all we are going to pay him.' It was less than half what I got before.

You said Zapata *was prepared before the HUAC testimony.*
Yes, various things started *Zapata,* but it was my idea. I went to John Steinbeck and I said that I'd been thinking about this man. And John suddenly took hold of it, very strongly. He said: 'I know about him, I've often thought about him,' and he told me he'd be interested in it. But there was something deeper, which was maybe only partly conscious on our part, and that deeper thing was that we were both reaching for some way to express our feelings of being Left and progressive, but at the same time anti-Stalinist. We lived near each other then, were very close friends.

I think that somewhere in the back of my head I'd always been looking for a subject like the great Soviet films that I liked in the thirties — *Potemkin* and *Aerograd.* I'd had the idea of making a film on Zapata since 1935 when I took a trip to Mexico and heard about him. We were interested in his tragic dilemma: after you get power, after you make a revolution, what do you do with the power and what kind of a structure do you build? John thought that he should do research before we even talked any more about it. He was at a loose end: his second marriage had busted up, and he hadn't yet met the girl he was married to till his death — Elaine. So he went off to Mexico and stayed there a while — a couple of months, I think — got Mexicans to help him with the research, and he did a lot of reading himself as he knew Spanish well.

In some subtle way that I only partly understood, *Zapata* was the first film I made which was autobiographical. I was, during that time, really at the peak of my career position, whatever the hell that means — I was more in demand than any other stage director, and I was also the 'two-coast' sort of 'genius' who was working successfully both places. But I was just beginning to question myself as to what I really wanted to do; I certainly didn't want to continue in the rat-race of trying each year to have another success to stay on top; and I was beginning to wonder—questions which came up again a decade later—what were my own feelings about these things, about all issues, about life itself, and my own life in particular. So that the seed of what was to be a lowering of my own position—what people around New York called my 'confusion' or uncertainty—my self-questioning was beginning. In that sense, the figure of Zapata was particularly attractive to me, because after he got all the power that comes with triumph, he didn't know what to do with it or where to put it or where to exert it. He felt about things as I was beginning to feel about my own situation. So all these three things—the fact that he was externally colorful and interesting, the fact that he represented a Left position that was anti-authoritarian, and the fact that in some way he was related to my life story, at that point in my life—were reasons why I became so interested in the subject.

He had also an ambivalent relationship to women. He wanted both a peasant woman and a woman of a higher social level, with more education and greater refinement. What he did was to go outside his class. He moved up into the middle-class, and he had to court her in the old-fashioned ways; he got dressed as a middle-class landowner. And in a way it was his first betrayal of himself, to court a woman that way and to marry that type of person. Later in his life, when she disappears temporarily, he's seen fleetingly with peasant women, following him or looking after him; but this was a move in a direction opposite to the one he stood for publicly. That's the way I looked at it, that's what I had in mind. That's partly why we cast Jean Peters, because I wanted someone brought up as an elite person in a small town.

Anyway, John worked terribly hard and, I think, very conscientiously—he got Mexicans to go into the back-country and find Zapata's remaining relatives, or people who'd known him, seen him. He wrote all the research out in a form which whatever actor played Zapata could understand. I think with any hero who's dead five minutes, different people viewing his career would have different thoughts about him, pointing to different significances. Well, it was the same here, except that there was one subtle difference. I felt that the communists of Mexico were beginning to think of Zapata as useful, a figure they could glamorise in anti-gringo, pro-Mexican nationalist struggles. They thought, especially since he was dead and it was long ago, he could become a useful idol or god to call on. They didn't like our film because it showed him as being unclear. Obviously he *was* unclear, because he hesitated, and didn't know what he was doing; he was trying to find a new path for himself.

I wanted to make this in Mexico very much, and I submitted the picture to the head of the syndicate of film technicians—a cameraman named Gaby Figueroa. I wasn't very keen on having him photograph the picture; he made all women look like madonnas, and he loved very corny effects like large crowds carrying candles. But when we first met I found him intelligent and agreeable, and we had some good conversations. Then he read the script and his whole face changed. He demanded certain changes; he said he couldn't work on the picture unless certain things were different. Furthermore, he would oppose its being made in Mexico unless we made those changes, and we told him to go to hell. The conversations ended abruptly, and we said we were going to shoot it somewhere else. He said an amusing thing: 'Suppose a Mexican company came up to Illinois to make a picture about Abraham Lincoln's life with a Mexican actor playing the lead, what would you think of that?' And I said to him: 'I think it would be great, I'd love to see that.' We left Mexico the next morning. I decided to make the picture in Texas, as close to Mexico as I could, on the Mexican border.

Obviously Zapata *avoids both the very faithful biography of the man, step by step, and also the political story of the country. You chose to make sketches, to show various aspects . . .*
When John came back with his research, it was overwhelming; even if it had been shorter, we would still have had to decide on the form of the picture—which story to tell. You could tell a hundred different stories with that material. The story we wanted to tell was of a man who organised himself and his comrades, the people around him in his province, because of cruel and terrible injustices; he organised them to revolt, and the revolt spread because of the repression that it faced, and because its causes were just. And the revolt resulted in a successful revolution. That's the first act.

We then told the second act, which was that once he got power, he didn't know how he wanted to exercise it. He was bewildered; and he began to find that power not only corrupted those around him, like his brother, but he had also begun to be corrupted by it himself. The third act was that he walked away from it; he walked away from the seat of power and so made himself vulnerable. He lost the soldiers who were protecting him, and the prestige that protected him; he became an easy target for destruction. So we organised John's material around these three movements. Once we did that, we knew what part of the material we wanted to use, where it would fit in and how it would work. I also found a technique of jumping from crag to crag of the story, of preparing an incident carefully but not playing it out in length. I think it was the first film I made that was structurally cinematic, where just a suggestion of an incident tells you more than the full playing out of it; the first picture I did that just jumps like that, where it's a lot of short incidents, held together by a frame that is essentially cinematic.

Then the other thing was to find an external style for this, and I found a book down in Mexico, *Historia Gráfica de la Revolución*—from 1900 to 1940—Archiva Casa Sola. It contained the most complete record of a war I'd ever seen, the detailed story in photographs. The men who had taken the pictures were excellent photographers, and knew how to capture what Cartier-Bresson calls 'the decisive moment,' the exact moment when something is at its most significant. Some of those photographs are arche-typal. They had a great quality of underplaying horror, that is, there'd be horrors and drama and death there, but it was taken as a matter of course. It was the nature of a revolution to show that and to deal with it. These photographs were of great use to me, and I went so far as to imitate them, in some cases exactly. There's one scene in particular where Pancho Villa and Zapata meet in Mexico City, when they come into a room to be pho-tographed, surrounded by their subordinates and henchmen. I reproduced that scene exactly. I got extras to be made up exactly like the ones in the picture, and I placed everybody in exactly the same position. I rehearsed it many times with the pictures in hand; just as a stunt, I tried to re-create that moment in history so it would be authentic.

I also did something that I was going to do later on other pictures: I went into a small Mexican town named Roma where I was meaning to shoot the picture, and presented myself to the people and to what authorities they had. It was a very sleepy, debilitated town, not prospering at all. Anyway, we said we were going to stay there, and of course they were delighted to have us, because we brought employment with us. I said I would like to make a band of whoever played music, especially people who had been in Mexico twenty, thirty, forty years ago — all the old-time musicians. They all came around with their marvellous old instruments. I chose about a dozen of them and without much rehearsal I had them play for me in unison, not in parts but in unison, the old songs of the revolution and the old, classic songs of Mexico that they remembered. In this way I got the basis of the score. The only mistake I made was that I should have somehow used them to make the actual score. But I gave the tape to Alex North who used it very well, I think. I found that it's a good way to work, because it's using the background to provide the music for you, and it's as authentic as the scenery. We got some terrific musical effects just by doing that. I was thinking at one time of having a 'corrida' — a kind of running song-commentary. It's something that appealed to John and we worked on that, but though the idea sounds good, when you use it repeatedly you can't find a way to make it progress. It started out effectively, but then it got slower, and heavier, and then interrupted the narrative. I never was able to solve it, and finally let it go.

There's a danger in this type of film that says that every revolution at one moment becomes perverted: it can be seen either as revolutionary, 'Trotskyist,' saying that the revolution is permanent, or as very reactionary, i.e. every change brings a new kind of oppression, then why try to change anything?
We were very conscious that it could be taken to be saying that the revolution was futile. But we tried very definitely to avoid that by saying, at the end, 'The people still think of him, he's still alive,' that at the end he was trying to create the revolution again, that he did educate himself to a point — in other words, we tried to say that there *is* a next step, that he was beginning to find it, and that he didn't. We had that in mind, anyway. And, at the end, the ritualistic Leftist becomes a murderer and kills Zapata.

The Daily Worker, *a Communist paper, did not attack the film as being Rightist, but as being Trotskyist!*
My true feeling personally is that in one guise or another, all revolution is permanent and always will be permanent. I think there always has to be

some struggle within a society to keep it moving forward, and attack the tendency in people to become crooked, to become bastards. One of the very effective moments in the picture is when he discovers his brother is corrupt; but an even more effective moment is when he discovers that he has become just like the man that circled his name at the beginning, that *he* did the same goddamn thing. When the peasants come to see him, he does exactly the same that the man did to him at the beginning. So, there you are! The fact that it troubles him, that he has a conscience about it, seems to me to mean that he's not that kind of person—that at bottom he realises the danger and seeks a way to overcome it.

At the time *Viva Zapata!* was made, the communists in this country condemned it because, they said, I'd taken a revolutionary hero and made a wavering intellectual of him. All right. Time passed. Twenty years later the New Left, which is the students, the non-communist Left, the Left I've always felt an allegiance towards, and especially an organisation like the Young Lords (the Puerto Rican revolutionary group I became acquainted with when I was working on Budd Schulberg's Puerto Rican picture) loved *Viva Zapata!*. They used to ask me for a print and look at it again and again, just like they did *The Battle of Algiers,* because both made them understand what their problem was going to be. The scenes of the revolution and of the unity of the people around Zapata, how the people gathered around a cause, was something they felt was going on with *them*. It became a film they showed like an educational picture on the technique and the nature of a revolution. The change in what the Left *is* reversed the attitude towards the picture.

Wasn't Zapata *also a revenge for the fact that you couldn't do* Sea of Grass *as you wanted to, and were making an epic?*
Absolutely right. I knew a lot more about *Sea of Grass* than shows in that picture. But since then, I learned that I had to exert my power and be very tough. I just went my own way. I had a wonderful wife, who, during the shooting, used to get telegrams in the morning from Zanuck scolding me and saying, 'Why are you going so slow?' and 'You're costing me a fortune.' She never showed them to me, but she would keep them, and at the end of the picture she gave me about ten telegrams!

What's missing is any reference to American land seizure.
Zapata was in an isolated province, though. Where American imperialism
was felt very strongly was in Pancho Villa's struggle; he was close to the
US border. It was also felt very strongly on the east coast where there was
oil. But much less in Zapata's land, which was arid and stony and had no
assets that anybody wanted. Zapata's struggle had a certain purity, because
it was based in poverty. When he got to Mexico City, we might have shown
American influence there. But he didn't stay there long; he left very abruptly.

Howard Hawks said that out of a disgusting bandit you made a Santa Claus;
and Samuel Fuller said that out of an idealist you made a murderer!
Jesus Christ! Well, Fuller is some authority on idealism, and Hawks is an
authority on bandits! There's one scene in *Zapata* that I didn't like, though:
the wedding-night scene. They look too glamorous; they look like Hollywood stars. I also didn't like the way he said, 'I can't read' and all that. It
didn't seem 'native' to me, it didn't seem out of that book of photographs,
Brando looked too gorgeous, I should have covered his top, his body
looked too well fed, too classically healthy, too athletic in an American
way; he didn't look *stringy*, like a Mexican horse, he looked like a fine
American thoroughbred. And *she* looked like an American beauty queen,
sort of all made up.

Do you think there was something 'Russian' about Zapata *in the sense that you*
had the sweep, the movement of the people?
Yes, there was, in that sense. There was even a mystique about the people,
in that they were aware, they responded, they were looking for leaders,
looking for leadership; they were a force that had to be dealt with. One
of my favourite scenes is of the women making tortillas and hitting the
stones, and also the scene when they bring the body back and throw him
on the well-top, on the brick platform; and the women are in the shadows,
and they don't move. I like the way I had the women in the corners, out
of the sun, watching the action—sort of like the way I use blacks later in
other pictures, you know: watching it, judging it.

Zapata *is the first film where you do not have a professional screenwriter.*
Right. I began to go to authors like Steinbeck, Budd Schulberg, Inge—who
were not screenwriters—and I'd say to them, 'Let's do a picture about

this.' What I needed most was not the technique of how to construct a screenplay, I needed that help too, but what I needed most was someone who saw in Zapata what I saw in Zapata, or someone who saw in *On the Waterfront* what I saw in *On the Waterfront.*

Steinbeck always loved the Mexican people; he was brought up very close to them. He had written *The Pearl* and made many trips to Mexico before *Zapata.* And after all, what greater authority on puritanism could I get than William Inge? I mean, he's a victim of puritanism, he knows it like someone whom it has hurt.

With Zanuck you now had a different relationship from the one you'd had on the previous films?

Yes. In the first place, I still don't know why he did *Zapata.* I guess because I'd made money for the company, and he was looking for something exciting and unusual; maybe he liked some things about it, I don't know. It seemed very foreign to him, at that time. I don't think *Grapes of Wrath* was; *Grapes of Wrath* was about people he knew. But *Zapata* just bewildered him. His contribution to *Zapata,* the one I remember most, was the white horse. That was his idea. I don't know where he got it, from an old Western I suppose. And at the time I regretted agreeing to it, though I don't regret it now. I think the white horse works beautifully at the end, where they bring Zapata his old horse as a present. Then, when Brando says to the horse, 'You got old,' I think it's a beautiful moment in the picture. But, as always with Zanuck, he was absolutely straight with us; anything we needed, we got.

The thing he opposed most was Marlon Brando. Brando had not made *On the Waterfront* yet, remember. He'd made *A Streetcar Named Desire,* where everybody laughed at his mumbling. He was sort of a joke, an industry joke, because of his terrible speech. I did a test with him and Julie Harris, because I wanted Julie Harris, at first, to play the part Jean Peters played; Zanuck saw the test, and he wired me to say how worried he was. He said: 'I don't understand a goddamn thing the sonofabitch says. Can't you stop him from mumbling?' He said: 'He's too young for it.' He wanted to get—I dunno, some sort of Mexican type. He said: 'This is just an Illinois boy, what the hell are you trying to make a Mexican out of him for?' Well, I couldn't explain it, but after a while he just accepted it and half gave up, and sort of trusted me that it would turn out all right. When the picture was finished, he rather liked it; he wasn't nuts about it, but he rather liked it. But when it started to do no business, he turned against it, and so did Fox. They did very little to promote it; they tried to forget it.

I can understand its lack of success. You're telling the story of a failure. Furthermore, you're telling the story of the expropriation of land by a Mexican failure. There's no love interest that ends the way they want. It goes against so many in the audience's desire to be deluded. I didn't realise it when I was making it. When I saw it afterwards, I thought, how can they like it? But in Turkey or Greece, where they have that problem of land, they scream their approval, they yell at the picture!

It was your second film with McDonald as a cameraman.
I was more satisfied with his work here, and he was a great help to me. He was rugged, in the first place; he would go anywhere and do anything. He likes to work in heat. He didn't do anything to spoil the sand, the dirt, and the desert, the cactus plants; it all came over very well, and I think he did an excellent job.

For the locations, I went down there to look for them long before. I always do that very carefully because I think it is a critical choice that you make; it can be a disaster, or it can make the picture. I rode all along the US-Mexican border, along the back roads until we came on this town that was originally a Mexican town. It still looked like one. We built a few more little things, just to make a complete square, and that was it. The interiors were real interiors, not sets. We came back and shot a very minor portion on the Fox ranch near Malibu.

Had you seen Eisenstein's Que Viva Mexico!?
Yes, but it didn't have much influence on me. It was a very formal, sort of stationary, passive, a set style. I read the script, but I didn't get much out of it. It was a poem, really. I don't think it was a good poem, in words.

Viva Zapata was a terrific experience for me. It changed a lot in my life and films. When I got through, I felt I had a much broader scope... I was influenced by Eisenstein and Dovzhenko, but now it was a digested influence, I never thought about them while shooting. I used the long shots that I had discovered in Ford, but creatively, whereas I had used them mechanically in *Panic in the Streets*, because with *Zapata,* it was a subject matter I liked.

Man on a Tightrope *was, I think, the only film you made that was about a country you don't really know. Otherwise there is always a kind of physical experience of the places you speak about.*
I tried to correct that by going there; I lived very close to the circus, I lived in a trailer, I played with them. I like circus people. I don't think it's a successful picture. The one part I think is good is the way I showed the circus and the people in it. What interested me in it is that it's truly democratic and cosmopolitan — there's no race, religion, creed — people are judged by their ability to do a job. I saw there, in a microcosm, a society that had its own dignity within the world chaos.

What I thought was poor was the love story, and the discussions between the Commissar and the honest man were schematic. I had no chance to change them. Sherwood, the scriptwriter, said to Zanuck: 'I don't want anything changed,' and left. Sherwood had prestige and power, and he had his rights. I did my best with that. Many scenes were embarrassing. They were just statements of politics, rather flat New Deal statements which, by 1952, eight years after Roosevelt, and in the context of a little circus, seemed absurd. I do believe that if I had had a young writer and worked three months more on it, I could have made a helluva good picture. It could have been exciting, colourful, touching, sad, every goddamn thing a picture should be.

Didn't Zanuck cut twenty minutes of Man on a Tightrope?
That's what finished me with Hollywood, really. I came back from five months in Germany — I hadn't seen my wife and children, I hadn't been home — so when I got to New York I called Zanuck up and said: 'Look, while the editor is finishing the first cut of this thing, I'd like to spend a few weeks in New York with my family, and then I'll come out and work with the cutter.' We had been working in Germany on it, so the cutter and I understood each other. In California I had had a nice office in a big building — I was a big shot when I had left. I didn't feel the picture was going to be too good, but I thought that if we worked on it we could make it good. I went to the doorman on my first morning back at the studio and said, 'Where's my office now?' and he said, 'It's down in the Old Writers' Building.' The Old Writers' Building was a building where they put the beginning writers and so on. I got the idea. I said, the picture's a flop in their eyes, or they would have given me my old office . . . I went down to

the office, and on the desk was a letter from Zanuck saying: 'I have cut twenty minutes out of this picture. I think you'll like it. Anyway, keep your mind open till we see it together.' I saw it with him, and I said: 'I don't like it at all, I'd like the footage back.' He said: 'No, it's terrible, what I cut, it's better this way.' I don't claim that if those twenty minutes had been in, it would have been much better, but I do think that I should have cut it with the cutter first, before showing it to him . . . I made a mistake in putting it in his hands. He's a man who prides himself on his cutting ability. That may be good in melodrama; in the pictures he's done, he may have done wonderful cutting, but I don't think this picture was well put together.

I said to myself: 'Well, I'm never going to do that again. Even if I don't make pictures, I'm going to insist on cutting rights.' I had cutting rights for *On the Waterfront*. After it was a big success, I was a producer on *East of Eden*. I had absolute rights on all my pictures.

Working with Schulberg: *On the Waterfront* (1954), *A Face in the Crowd* (1957)

MICHEL CIMENT/1974

Much before On the Waterfront *you were thinking of doing a film about the docks.*

Yes, that was in 1951, before *Zapata.* I spoke to Arthur Miller. There was a struggle within the Longshoremen's Union at that time, and Art knew a lot about longshoremen. He worked in the Brooklyn Navy Yard as a steam-fitter, a plumber's assistant or something of that kind during the war, before he could make his living as a playwright. He knew the waterfront, and I think the idea of a film was his. I was very enthusiastic about it. He began to work on a script; it was called *The Hook.* I don't remember much about the script, but we got quite a way into that thing; the script was completed, and we arranged the financing from Columbia Pictures. Then I got a phone call from Art saying that he had decided he didn't want to do it. I still don't know why he did that. Anyway he called it off, and I was annoyed with him because I'd spent a lot of time on it. It was an extremely abrupt and embarrassing decision.

From what you remember, was it very different in point of view from what was going to be On the Waterfront? *Was it also an individual story?*

No, it was much less an individual story. I have the script somewhere, but I haven't read it since. It was very different in feeling. I think Art saw the Un-American Activities Committee coming, and there was something that

From *Kazan on Kazan*, Viking, 1974. © 1974 by Michel Ciment. Reprinted by permission of *Sight and Sound* and the British Film Institute.

had suddenly developed in his personal life that made him not want to have that film done. Things were much touchier then, people were threatened and on trial and being forced to take stands.

The Hook is a section of the waterfront, 'Red Hook' it's called, but it's also the longshoreman's hook which you hold with the handle, like the communist sickle. You hook the baggage with it. It's seen in *On the Waterfront*—all longshoremen use it. That script was never in good shape; I don't think it was ever really ready to do. What we did with *On the Waterfront* was rewrite and rewrite it. Finally with Spiegel's help and persistence and Budd's hard work, we got a very good script out of it.

On the Waterfront *was the first film you made in New York.*
All the next pictures were made from New York. *Face in the Crowd* was made in a New York studio and on location in Arkansas; *Baby Doll* was made in a New York studio, from a New York office, and on location in Mississippi. I was determined, after my last experience at Fox, to make pictures in the East. I put together the first good crew in New York—Sidney Lumet used it later. Before, they were doing only TV shows in New York.

Part of this decision—a considerable part—was due to my revulsion at the Hollywood environment. This is simple-minded but . . . there you go from your house to the studio in a car and you see nothing. In the studio you're in a non-environment, in your house you're in a swimming pool. You never talk to anybody except the crew and your agent, and your friends, who are like you. None of the buildings have any identity; they're all imitations of other buildings. It's all like living in Disneyland. Even the people's tans seem false. I love the West, I love the northern half of California, from Santa Barbara up—I think it's one of the most beautiful states in the Union. But from Los Angeles down to San Diego, that belt there, it's what I like least in American life. It's also very reactionary, hateful, dangerous. That's where Nixon comes from; that's where he chose to live. For good reasons.

But in New York City, if I walk from my house, on the street, down to my office, I see twenty things every day that remind me of the fate of the world, of the nature of the conflicts in the city, of the problems of ecology—everything is all around me, and it's stimulating to me. I can grow in it. I'm in touch with it; things strike me and pinch me and turn me and affect me. In Hollywood nothing happens. I didn't want to be like the others there, more and more attenuated, more and more abstracted, less and less 'in things.'

On the Waterfront is a good example of this contact with reality because it is about living issues. And furthermore, it's about an issue that was being decided as we made the picture. Watching me shooting, there used to be all the gangsters that we described in the picture! And they'd come up — once a guy grabbed me and was going to beat me up. A longshoreman beat *him* up. I always had a bodyguard a few feet behind me, a former detective on the Hoboken force, he was always close to me. I worked in among activities on the dock. They were loading ships while I was directing. It was my ideal of how I'd like to make pictures.

There is a difference between the film and the book that Schulberg published after the release. In the book, Terry is killed at the end and the priest has been moved from his parish: it is much more pessimistic.

Schulberg was responding, when he wrote the book, many months later, to some criticism that was made of the ending. However, the priest was exiled, after we had finished the film. Budd knew that; Budd stayed close to that priest. So he wrote that in. I didn't read Budd's book. But 'Terry' was never found dead; he was still working, I believe.

What we intended to show at the end was that the workers there had found, or thought they'd found, a new potential leader. He had almost been killed, remember? And very often, in the labor movement, a new movement starts with the death of a person, through the memory of a martyr. The boss in the doorway, to me, seems rather futile, when he shouts. The workers gather around Terry, as if they were going to continue their struggle. But after all they have to work for a living, they're not going into some intellectual state of withdrawal from it. It was as close as I could get to what actually happened on the waterfront.

There's no background to the gangsters' action — we only see a man's back.

Budd and I wished we had been able to go deeper into the social structure which supports the gangsters. On the other hand, if we had gone more into that, we would have lost some of the unity of the film. It was a tough problem. We would have been diffuse, at that point. I think we probably could have done it with one other glimpse, one other piece of action, if we'd found it.

The film related, in a sense, to the gangster films that could be said to sum up real American life on the screen.
That's absolutely true. The first breakthrough into working-class life came through gangster films. They were the first view from underneath.

Face in the Crowd *and* Waterfront *had a journalistic impact.*
Budd has worked a lot as a journalist, but he also works when he writes a script by immersing himself in the environment, doing research and taking notes. I work more in terms of dramatic symbols than Budd does. The love scenes are the best thing in the film. The scene on the pigeon's coop with Eva Marie Saint is beautiful, and the scene at the bar table with her, where Terry says: 'Don't say that.' Eva is wonderful in those scenes, and so is Marlon.

Brando was as close to a genius as I've ever met among actors. He was on a level apart. There was something miraculous about him, in that I would explain to him what I had in mind, and he would listen, but his listening was so total that it was an amazing experience to talk to him: he would not answer right away, but go away and then do something that often surprised me. You had a feeling of 'God, that's better than what I told him!' You had a feeling 'Oh, I'm so grateful to him for doing that!' He was, like, giving you a gift. It was essentially what you'd asked him, but in feeling so *true,* so re-experienced through his own artistic mechanism. It's almost like directing a genius animal. You put things in him, and then you wait, you have to wait, as if it's going to hibernate or something; and then it comes out later. I don't know, I'm describing it externally. But he has everything. He has terrific feeling and violence, he has great intelligence, he's extremely intuitive. He is bisexual in the way an artist should be: he sees things both as a man and as a woman. He's strong in his sympathies to people, to all small people on the set. He's a very honest man, in that he speaks plainly to you. He's also a very devious man, in that he conceals his processes and reactions; they're none of your business. He even surprises the other actors. Sometimes you don't even know that he's acting: he does something and you say: 'Oh yes, he is! He *is* doing it!' He's very, very underground—you don't know *how* he gets to what he gets. Part of it is intuition, part of it is real intelligence, part of it is ability to be empathic—that he connects with the people. If the role is within his range, which is large, nobody can compare with him.

The first play he was in was something I produced—Harold Clurman directed it. He only had a three- or four-minute scene but he was marvellous. I called up Tennessee Williams, who had given me *Streetcar Named Desire,* and I said to him: 'I think I know the actor who should play Stanley Kowalski. He's young for it, but I'd like to send him up.' I said to myself, Tennessee won't like him, because he's too young, he looks like a gentle boy, although he's got strong shoulders. I got hold of Brando, and I said: 'Here's twenty dollars to pay your bus fare to Boston, and from Boston to Cape Cod. Go up there.' He took the money, said 'Thank you,' and left. I called Tennessee Williams the next day and said: 'Well, what did you think of him?' and he said: 'Who?' Brando had never shown up! I called him the next day and said: 'Did you like him?' and Williams said: 'Who? Nobody's come up here at all.' The third day he called me and said: 'Boy, that's it! I love him. That's the part.' I said: 'What happened?' He said: 'Well, twenty dollars is a lot of money for him. He hitch-hiked up here so he could keep the twenty dollars!' He was living that way, living around—so I'd heard—in different girls' apartments, rent-free. After that, for about three or four years, ours was a terribly close relationship. I was like his father. He used to come up here and play with my son Chris when he was a little boy. Then, when I testified, he got cool to me, but he was ambivalent. On the one hand he was grateful to me, he loved me. He told me, when he didn't do *The Arrangement,* 'You're the only director I've ever worked with'—you know, he gave me all that; and I told him, 'You're the best actor I ever worked with, too,' and he embraced me, and then he kissed me! And we parted. Still, he had this feeling of anger at me—the way a son does. A son has finally to kill his father, doesn't he? I was close to Jimmy Baldwin once too, he was like my son, I looked after him, and he watched me, and I was friendly with him. Then, all of a sudden . . . I had given him an idea for a play about Malcolm X, worked on it with him, really gave him some good ideas—he called up one day and said, 'I can't do it with you.' I said, 'What's the matter?' He said: 'I want to see if I can do something on my own. You're like my father, I don't want to do it.' So that was the end of that. But it's funny, people's relationships to me: some handle it, some don't, sometimes I can handle it, sometimes I can't . . .

Waterfront has some of the best scenes in this first part of your career; on the roof, or the scene between Steiger and Brando in the car; but the end of the film is over-directed.

Perhaps. Possibly I over-exploited the end. My first wife used to say that when I felt uncertain about a scene, I would make it more forceful. That's been true. 'I'm uncertain, therefore you *must* believe this.' I would contest with you the idea of the scene, which is right for me; but I do agree with you that I shot it too insistently. Now I would make the longshoremen going back to work more scraggly. It looked like an army, but I would make it less cohesive. I think the music hurt that picture, Bernstein's a brilliant guy, but—you remember, the film opens with a kind of drum-beat which puts it right away on a level of melodrama, rather than just showing the murder, the body falling, just showing it—it's strong enough by itself.

Also the secondary characters were more social masks than people, and they were presented for vividness, rather than the camera just passing by them as part of life on the docks.

The photography was superb. I can't say too much good about Boris Kaufman. I think he's a real artist. He looks frail, but he was very, very strong on that picture. The picture was made in hardship. It was close to zero often, and not only that, but the wind was coming in off the Hudson River, and sometimes I had to go into the hotel myself and take Brando by the arm and pull him out. A lot of the actors just huddled around bar-rels in which fires were burning at all times—they're shown in the picture, by the way. The New York skyline looked like the real thing, never pic-turesque in the wrong way; always grimy, it always had fabric to it.

In *On the Waterfront* we had a beginning crew, a crew that had not worked together. They were not coherent, and they were not very friendly towards Boris; I was protecting him all the time. They disliked him—he was a foreigner, he seemed to fumble; he didn't express himself in a forth-right manner but, like an artist, in subtle things. This annoyed the fellows who had come out of television and commercials, mostly. I thought, well, Kaufman is the best cameraman I've ever got, so I'm going to stay with him. I did *Baby Doll* with him. In that film, I thought, the photography was even better.

Spiegel was a great constructionist, at that time.
I thought so, yes. He helped with the script a lot. He taught me a lesson—never to be satisfied with the script that you have. He said a wonderful thing that I never forgot: 'Let's open it up again.' By which he meant: 'Let's open our minds again to a basically different construction, let's keep

our minds open.' In time I augmented this: 'If you feel something is wrong, admit it yourself.'

Spiegel worked on the script month after month. He drove Schulberg crazy. Schulberg got up one night, in the middle of the night—he was living in Pennsylvania then; and his second wife saw him in the bathroom at 3 a.m., shaving, and she said: 'What are you doing shaving at three in the morning?' He said: 'I'm going to New York to kill Spiegel.' He was shaving himself, and he got dressed, and he went to New York; he wanted to kill Spiegel, because Spiegel kept saying: 'It's very good now, I think we've got it. Let's start casting; all right.' And then the next day he'd say: 'Let's talk about this again, let's open it up again.' Schulberg thought Spiegel changed his mind because he'd had other people reading the script and making suggestions—probably Spiegel had. He annoyed me too, except that later I felt: well, he's right. I think he contributed an enormous amount to that film. There's an interesting gossip story about Zanuck and *On the Waterfront* that I ought to tell you, too.

Schulberg and I worked with Zanuck for a while on *On the Waterfront*. Fox was going to do it, and we worked four or five months on it. We went out to California to show Zanuck the result of our work. I'd become disillusioned with Zanuck, I wanted to get out of there anyway; but I owed him a picture by contract. Zanuck said: 'I don't want to do this picture. Who the hell gives a shit about labor unions?' After that meeting, I got into his Cadillac limousine with my agent, and my agent said: 'What are you going to do next?' which meant he'd given up. I said: 'I'm going to do this picture, in 16mm, if necessary. I'm going to make it like a home movie, but I'm going to do it.' I was mad at my agent, I was mad at Hollywood, I was mad at everybody in those days. Spiegel was at a low point in his career at that time. In fact, his difficulties were so bad that he was forced to do a picture, and I think ours was the only picture he could get. But he turned out tremendous as far as helping us went.

The scene with the pigeons is the first lyrical love scene you have in your films. I think the reason I had so much feeling then was that I was being so criticised by old friends; and my wife was so true and loving, all through that experience . . . I think people grow through pain and difficulties. I'm talking about artists; I'm not talking about architects or people who design and build cars, or farmers.

I guess the success of *Waterfront* was one of the happiest moments in my life. After *Man on a Tightrope* closed—it had one of the lowest grosses in Hollywood history—I was *persona non grata* among the intellectuals, *persona non grata* everywhere. I was nothing. The sense of triumph I had when we got the Academy Award for a New York picture made inexpensively by a lot of people like Spiegel, who was a clown, and I, who was *persona non grata,* and Budd, who wasn't anything much then either—the fact that we beat them all—was a great pleasure to me!

Terry Malloy felt as I did. He felt ashamed and proud of himself at the same time. He wavered between the two, and he also felt hurt by the fact that people—his own friends—were rejecting him. He also felt that it was a necessary act. He felt like a fool, but proud of himself because he found out that he was better than the other people around him. That kind of ambivalence. It wasn't as deep as what comes later, where everything is ambivalent. Terry's considered a hoodlum—that has a personal element, because I was considered a rough boy. I wasn't thought much of when I was young either. I always thought my father preferred my younger brother to me; he always called my younger brother 'sweet Abie,' and I felt he disapproved of me and was disappointed in me all my life because I wouldn't go into the rug business. This is partly imaginary, because he probably liked me. I dunno, I can't tell now; it's too late to find out.

The character of the priest is too dominant—and the ending looks almost like a crucifixion, like a Christian ending. The social criticism is undermined by this symbolism.

I can see your point and, though I don't agree, I'm not going to contest it. I did another thing that people took as symbolic. I guess it was. You know, when the bald-headed longshoreman gets killed down in the hold, they put him on a rack; and the priest stands there, and some people have said his soul is rising to heaven. But that's the way you get out of the hold of a boat; there's no other way. There's a narrow little iron staircase that you climb up but you can't climb up with a dead body. But they said no, it's the priest taking his soul up to heaven. The fact is, I'm not in the least religious.

Three years later, you made your second film with Budd Schulberg.

We approached *A Face in the Crowd* like *On the Waterfront,* like people who are determined to know a subject thoroughly. We wanted to work together again because we had a good friendship, worked well together, and felt very quick to understand each other, 'in tune', very *simpático*. We were looking around for a subject, and Budd suggested I read a short story of his. It was much more satirical than the movie finally was. We decided to do it, and he got a house in Connecticut, about a mile and a half down the road, and moved in with his family for the whole summer. Then we began to do research, the way you would for a book on economics or history or an exposé of the automobile industry. We went to advertising agencies and to the place where the story takes place: Piggott, Arkansas. We agreed on a basic outline, which was not hard, because we see life and things the same way.

Then we separated. I did *Cat on a Hot Tin Roof* on the stage, and he wrote a first draft based on our plans. Then we began to plan the production together. I suggested some rewriting to strengthen the script. It was an ideal relationship, and I urged him to be around every day we were shooting. Then I edited it and, at the end of the cutting, he was back again and we discussed it. It was a totally collaborative effort, even down to the book, for which I wrote the preface. Theoretically, I think one man should make a picture. But in the rare case where an author and a director have had the same kinds of experience, have the same kind of taste, the same historical and social point of view, and are as compatible as Budd and I are, it works out perfectly.

You made most of A Face in the Crowd *on location.*
We became acquainted with a community of strangers—it was not like a work experience; it was a life experience, a thing that affects you very deeply. We became part of that Arkansas community, settling down in new homes there. It was a terrific experience, right from the beginning, the people we met, the insights we got, the privilege we had of being inside a society that otherwise we would never have touched. We met the Governor of Arkansas, we met the mayor of this town, we met everybody in this town. Everywhere I walked, in Piggott, people were following me. It was like we had the whole town under the reverse of martial law! As though we had liberated the whole town. Like the American troops coming into a small village south of Paris. People ran up to us and spoke to us. . . .

We cast many people from Nashville; Lonesome Rhodes's friend who twitches his toes, he's from the Grand Ole Opry, a regular comedian there. We went around a lot of clubs, picking up entertainers. I had heard Andy

Griffith on a record, then I saw him on TV. In most ways he did very well in the part. What he did especially well was what I saw in him first. He was the real native American country boy and that comes over in the picture. I had him drunk all through the last big scene because it was the only way he could be violent—in life he wants to be friends with everybody.

You went to Madison Avenue?
They let us into meetings though they knew we were going to write on it. We saw the product discussions; we saw the charts. Everything that's in that picture, we have an example for. We watched many sessions on the selling of Lipton's tea, the discussions of the word 'brisk' and how to picturize it. The key word is 'brisk'—Lipton's tea is brisk. That's not a word that affects me very strongly, but apparently they had success with the word. The discussions were really ludicrous; you could hardly keep a straight face at them. But as well as the ridiculous side, you could feel the intense, neurotic pressure they all worked under. We also went to Washington—we saw Lyndon Johnson, by the way, we talked to him for half an hour and asked him some questions pertaining to the last quarter of the story, the part that has to do with politics. He was impressed, I think, with the fact that Hollywood people were talking to him. The film, though, was organized out of my little office in New York. The crew worked out of there. We went on location from New York to Arkansas. And then we hired a big studio in the Bronx, the old Gold Medal Studio where Griffith and Ince made a lot of pictures in the old days.

It is the only film where you deal directly with politics, from Piggott, Arkansas, to Washington, D.C. Your other films are infused with politics.
One of the points we wanted to make with the picture was the fantastic upward mobility in this country, the speed with which a man goes up and goes down. That we both knew well, because we'd both been up and down a few times. It's best illustrated in the film when he goes down in the elevator. We were thinking of suicide at one time, but we abandoned it. Budd had been impressed with a picture his father had made with a German actor about a king or a prime minister left all alone in his castle and who at the end was screaming for everybody to come back.

We were talking about the danger of power in the television medium; you can look at an audience and smile at them and win them with your smile, not with your thoughts, with your personality, not with your deeds. We weren't dealing with power abstractly, with the fact that power corrupts people, but with the fact that power is attainable in a new way that makes it especially dangerous.

Was Lonesome scheming from the beginning, or just naïve?
Neither. I don't think he was scheming. He always enjoyed playing with people and seducing them. And he was always related to people in a double way, or a tricky way. He lived by his wits. He was scheming in that sense. But he was also fired with a truthfulness which was the ambiguity of his character and which we perhaps didn't get enough of in the production. Even in his worst moments, he should have been saying things that nobody else saw or said. He should have had some more brilliance or honest perceptions—even at the end.

There was something about him that was down-to-earth truthful. He saw the truth and said it right away. And there was the real source of his power. The real source of his power was not his trickiness but his knack of seeing something that everybody feels but doesn't dare say, and he dares say it; or something everybody's afraid of, and he takes a stand against it, and they think they need him. We thought of a man who had great attraction, great potential, and great danger. We made fun of him a little bit too much, and, except at the beginning, didn't show his strength or his appeal to human beings.

Our basic interest in this picture was Lonesome Rhodes as a legend. It was to make a legendary figure of him, and to warn the public: look out for television. Remember, this was Eisenhower's time, and Eisenhower won the elections because everybody looked at him and said: 'There's Grandpa!' We're trying to say: never mind what he looks like, never mind what he reminds you of, listen to what he's saying! I was trying (and I didn't quite succeed) to make Lonesome Rhodes walk a tightrope, so you'd feel: 'Jesus Christ, *I would* give in to that man!' And at the same time, 'If I gave in to that man, it would be a disaster.' I think I let the audience off too easily, in a position where they could patronize him, where they could look down on him, and say: 'Oh, those jackasses! How could they be taken in by that man!' But they shouldn't feel that. They should say: 'I could be taken in.' It left them in a safe position. I think that's the single failure of the film.

We were also saying, however, that television is a good thing. Abraham Lincoln said: 'Tell the people the truth, and they will decide what to do.' Well, we said that television is good for that—it's a better way. Television deludes some people, exposes others. What interested us in the character of Marcia was that after she learned and knew for sure that Lonesome was a no-good, she still couldn't resist him. That's very much part of the legend of Hollywood; it's full of attractive, cruel, sadistic but sexy bastards. It's Pygmalion in reverse. I guess, since she made him, she had to stay with him.

This film *was* in advance of its time. It foretells Nixon. I don't think it was about McCarthy particularly. I think it would have been better if we had had a political figure in the Senator who could conceivably have won an election. Our senator, you feel, is such an ass, that you never think he might. I think we made fools of the side we didn't like. Marshall Neilan, the former director, played the part, and he couldn't remember a word— he was terrified. He was so grateful; he'd been out of films for so many years and that made him nervous. It was sad and very touching.

It is your most misanthropic film.
Possibly. I was conscious of it. But I really thought that's the way that world was—the advertising world. Here and there, there are decent people, but they're all under such pressure, they all live in such fear of losing their jobs, that it tends to become that way. The journalist played by Walter Matthau was not dealt with mercifully. I've never been very favourably inclined towards 'intellectuals.' I mean—I like *intellect*. But the intellectuals around New York who sit and complain about why they're not doing things, and a lot of the intellectuals I know from the progressive movements at various times—I dunno, maybe some of that got in there. Budd thinks the character *is* sympathetic. But I don't think he has much gumption, or strength.

The hysteria is more carefully controlled than in On the Waterfront.
I think it's done better, and there's a lot of humour in it. I've never done anything as funny as this. The majorettes . . . Lee Remick was marvellous. She went there three weeks ahead, she lived with a family in the town, and she trained with the local high school's majorettes.

You are less satisfied with the second part of A Face in the Crowd?
I learned a lesson about style in that film. Thornton Wilder used to tell
me: 'The hidden cause, the concealed cause, of most of the serious trouble
with good scripts is the mixture of styles.' It's the most difficult thing to
catch, and you can delude yourself. He told me that again and again, and
he dealt in mixtures of styles. *The Skin of Our Teeth* could have gone off a
lot because he mixed styles, but he did it successfully. I don't know how —
by making it a little grotesque, I guess.

The first part of *A Face in the Crowd* is more of a satire, and the second
part tends to really involve you with Lonesome's fate and with his feelings.
I think the first part works perfectly, and the second part doesn't quite.
Maybe the change should have been in the first part, despite the fact that
it worked. If I had made him more humanly attractive, it might have been
less funny, but it would have made the two parts coherent. I think this is a
good example of that mixture of styles which I think is a critical point in
films. When you mix styles, you're in a lot of trouble. In the beginning of
a film, you are saying to an audience: 'I want you to listen to this story
and take it this way.' Afterwards you can't break it, you can't say: 'I want
you to laugh at Lonesome Rhodes.' If it's a satire, you can't be terrorized
emotionally later.

Why do you think entertainers seek power?
In the first place, they deal with power. Their power is with an audience.
When they step in front of the audience at the Grand Ole Opry, there are
five thousand people sitting there who start to run up and want to touch
them and follow them in the streets. They're offered money and that's
power, isn't it? And they feel it and enjoy it. They have this magical thing,
confidence, or beauty, or talent, that people are attracted to. Billy Graham
and Huey Long were models for the character. And Arthur Godfrey, definitely. But Huey Long did a lot of good in Louisiana. He was basically a
tyrant, but he got many, many reforms; and he was genuinely interested,
at the beginning, in the problems of the poor. Lonesome Rhodes should
have been more like him, more genuinely interested in the poor.

Why wasn't the film successful? How were the reviews?
They were pretty good. I don't know why it didn't go. We said: 'Oh, they're
not ready for it,' and in a way they weren't. We said: 'Oh, they don't want

us to criticize America,' and in a way they didn't. And we said: 'Oh, they think we are communists, and putting America down, trying to destroy America,' and we were attacked some for that. But I think a picture that tries to do something as difficult as this picture has to be perfect, and I don't think we were, not quite. There was a great gaiety, making up those ads, the Vitajex sequence . . . I was both repulsed and attracted by them. TV is always on the verge of being ludicrous; it's always on the precipice — and you say, 'I can't believe they mean that! Are they kidding?' What I like in the film is the energy and invention and bounce which are very American. It's really got something marvelous about it, this constantly flashing, changing rhythm. In many ways, it's more American than any picture I ever did. It represents the business life, and the urban life, and the way things are on television, the rhythm of the way this country moves. It has a theme that even today is completely relevant. Finally what I think is that it was ahead of its time.

Dialogue on Film: Elia Kazan

THE AMERICAN FILM INSTITUTE/1976

MARLON BRANDO, IN HIS more laconic days, once summed up the only unanimous view of Elia Kazan: "He's wonderful with actors." On nearly every other aspect of a long career as a stage director, film director, and novelist, Kazan has always drawn a stormy array of conflicting comment.

But in his direction of actors—particularly the new and promising—Kazan holds a unique place. Playwrights have praised him. Tennessee Williams has spoken of Kazan's "phenomenal rapport with actors." And demanding critics like Harold Clurman have praised him: "He is one of the best directors for actors—both on stage and in films." Kazan has been associated with many of the more extraordinary actors of the last few decades: Brando, Rod Steiger, James Dean, Kim Hunter, Warren Beatty, Lee J. Cobb, Julie Harris, Karl Malden, Lee Remick, Montgomery Clift, Eva Marie Saint. And even when the films have shown the wear of time, the performances have not. Brando's overwhelming portrayal of Stanley Kowalski in *A Streetcar Named Desire* (1952) remains one of the achievements of American film.

Kazan started in the theater as an actor. After two years at the Yale University School of Drama, Kazan joined, in the early thirties, the Group Theater in New York and appeared in a number of plays. Clurman recalls that Kazan in 1935 gave "magnificent performances" in a series of three Clifford Odets plays, including *Waiting for Lefty*. He also acted in several films, perhaps most memorably as a gangster in *City for Conquest* (1940).

From *American Film*, March 1976. Reprinted by permission.

Kazan, while at the Group Theater, turned to directing, and in the for-ties mounted such important works of the American stage as Thornton Wilder's *The Skin of Our Teeth* with Tallulah Bankhead, Arthur Miller's *All My Sons* with Ed Begley, and *Death of a Salesman* with Lee J. Cobb. Kazan's production of *Death of a Salesman* has become the measure by which all subsequent productions of that enduring work have been judged.

Kazan's stage work led to his founding—with Cheryl Crawford and Lee Strasberg—of the Actors' Studio in 1948. The studio's approach, sometimes called the Method School of Acting, gained wide attention—and notori-ety—from the fiery performances of celebrated graduates like Brando, Dean, Paul Newman, and Eva Marie Saint.

Kazan came late to filmmaking. His first feature, made in 1945 for Fox, was a benign *A Tree Grows in Brooklyn,* with Dorothy McGuire. But, as a director, Kazan went on to explore strong social themes: Anti-Semitism in *Gentlemen's Agreement* (1947); miscarriage of justice in *Boomerang!* (1947); racial prejudice in *Pinky* (1949); and union corruption in *On the Waterfront* (1954). Kazan's work in the theater with such notable playwrights as Wilder, Williams, Miller, and William Inge gave him an unusual respect for the screenwriter—a respect not always shared by other directors. Budd Schulberg, who wrote *On the Waterfront,* says, "He's been a pioneer, sometimes I think the *only* pioneer, in treating screenplays with the same respect that he would give a work written for the stage."

Kazan has also been something of a pioneer in impassioned, personal work, in controversial work—and controversy has embroiled him in his own life. His candid testimony in the early fifties before the House Un-American Activities Committee is an example. If anything, his work has taken on a more unapologetically personal stamp—particularly his best-selling novels. *America, America,* published in 1961, is a thoroughly personal account of his family's emigration to this country. Kazan, who was born in Istanbul, Turkey, in 1909, emigrated to America in 1913 with his parents, both of Greek descent. His other novels, *The Arrangement* (1967), *The Assassins* (1972) and *The Understudy* (1975) have also shown a strong personal vision.

The results of Kazan's widely ranging work, by his own admission, have been of varying quality. But the works have always been infused with the intensity of an individual response to the experience of living in America. At the time of this seminar, Kazan was about to begin the direction of *The Last Tycoon.*

QUESTION: *Fame sometimes affects the work of directors. Do you think it's affected yours?*

ELIA KAZAN: You'd be amazed how unfamous I feel. I still feel in many ways like a beginner, and part of it is that I've never continued the same thing. I'm writing books, and all my books are put down in America. I've never gotten a really good notice, except once for *The Arrangement*, and a couple medium-sized ones on the other books. I've never really been accepted by the literary fraternity, and that keeps you on your toes. I'm still writing. I've got two more books in first draft. So I've never felt "arrived," if that's the word. I don't feel like an expert or a particularly knowledgeable person. I'm trying hard. I don't think any of my films are completely successful. But taking them all together, I'm proud of them. I think I've done something that is myself. But I'm not finished yet. I feel like a young man. I've got good spirits and good energy. I'm still a person in the middle of life, even though I don't look it at times.

Q: *You have a reputation for discovering stars and for not being afraid to use untrained actors. What do you look for in a performer?*

EK: Very often big stars are barely trained or not very well trained. They also have bad habits: They don't want to look bad, and they protect themselves; or they're not pliable any more. They know what their act is. If I put them in a scene that's a little bit dangerous, their agents come to see me. Besides, they cost a lot of money. I'm now doing a picture that's a circus. It's got everybody in it: Robert DeNiro, Jack Nicholson, Robert Mitchum, Tony Curtis, Jeanne Moreau, Donald Pleasence. Like in a circus, first the lions come on, then the tightrope walkers. I don't mind it though. It's sort of fun.

But if the subject is very real, and you're saying, "This actually happened, not quite as I've shown it perhaps, but real life is reflected here," you'd better get real people all around you. There's a new breed of stars coming up now which is a hell of a lot better for my purposes. To take unknowns is a gamble, and I've taken that gamble. Sometimes it has come through, and in a couple instances it has not. I think the time it hurt me most was in *America, America*. That picture would have been better if I'd run across DeNiro or Al Pacino or Dustin Hoffman. I took a calculated risk and lost. But I am not afraid to use anyone, because I was an actor and this makes me have less respect.

I don't have a mystique about what an actor can contribute. You can have damn good actors, and they can louse you up. But I don't have an awe of them, nor am I afraid of them. Now what I try to do is to get to know them very well. I take them to dinner. I talk to them. I meet their wives. I find out what the hell the human material is that I'm dealing with, so that by the time I take an unknown he's not an unknown to me.

Q : *Where did you find the lead actor, Stathis Giallelis, in* America, America*?*
E K : He was from around Athens, a property man for a small Greek film-maker. He had never acted before. I bundled him on a plane and brought him back to America, with some misgivings. And I still have some. I rehearsed him a lot. I did about three weeks of improvisation before we started, and I gave him voice lessons. The damned voice lessons didn't take. He doesn't speak English any better today than he did during the film. It hurt the film, I think, because I was worried about his being understood. The boy, with the change of administrations in Greece, has gone back to Greece, which is where he belongs.

Q : *Where did you find those evocative faces for the Ellis Island sequence in* America, America*?*
E K : That scene was shot in an abandoned customs warehouse in Athens. We sent trucks up to the border between Greece and Bulgaria. There were camps up there of people who had crossed over from the Communist countries of Bulgaria or Rumania into Greece. By God, their clothing, their looks, above all their faces, were perfect for that part. These people's deprivation, their hardship, and their continuous anxiety worked for me. How do you direct them? Well, you didn't have to much. What counts is what they looked like and how they were dressed and the positions I put them in.

   Sometimes the face of a real person is far more eloquent than any actor can achieve. There's something about almost all actors that is well-fed looking. If you have a scene of either a working-class person or a person deprived by life or a person who is hard up, it's much better sometimes to get a face. You can't beat cops in cop roles. They play cops very well. Fellini says, "I don't give a damn how they talk or whether they talk at all. I'll dub that in later. Give me the face." The face is a piece of statuary, it's a piece of revelation.

Q : *Andy Griffith wasn't exactly an unknown before* A Face in the Crowd, *though he wasn't known as an actor. But his performance is probably the best of his career.*

E K : He was not an actor, but a monologist. He was very eager to be good, and he had none of the defenses that stars usually have. He didn't necessarily want to look a certain way or come on a certain way. There are scenes in that movie that I would say would be difficult for anybody. It's a very hard part to do. I think the film walks a very tight line, and I'm not sure it bridges satire and tragedy altogether successfully. We were satirizing the whole scene of public communication. The film was made in 1956, and I think we anticipated a lot of what happened in Nixon's time and what is happening today. We tried to both satirize it on the one hand, and then get some sort of human portrait of a man on the other. I would say that considering what Andy was he gave an excellent performance.

Q : *Was there any relationship between the McCarthy hearings and this film?*

E K : No. We started out from a short story by Budd Schulberg on the threat of television and the power of television. We were saying beware of it, but also saying that it would be a force for good. I believe that television is a terrific force for good. When you see people in close-up behaving off guard, I think you understand them. That was the case in the McCarthy hearings when McCarthy at one point whispered to Roy Cohn. I don't think anyone who saw it will ever forget that whisper.

Q : *Like Andy Griffith, James Dean came to you as something of an unknown — a temperamental unknown. How did you work with him on* East of Eden?

E K : He did a thing that always attracts me: He wasn't polite to me. He made me feel he wasn't straining to butter me up, that he had a real sense of himself. When I met him he said, "I'll take you for a ride on my motorbike." It was very hard for him to talk, and riding me on the back of his motorbike, which I did like a damn fool around the streets of New York, was his way of communicating with me. He had his own way, and I thought he was perfect for the part. I thought he was an extreme grotesque of a boy, a twisted boy. As I got to know his father, as I got to know about his family, I learned that he had been, in fact, twisted by the denial of love.

I went to Jack Warner and told him that I wanted to use an absolutely unknown boy. Jack was a crapshooter of the first water, and he said, "Go ahead." He wouldn't do that now. Nobody would do that now. I went back to New York and said to Jimmy, "We're going to California. Be at my house at such and such a time." Jimmy shows up with two packages—wrapped in paper. He'd never been on an airplane before. We arrived, and we were heading toward the studio when Jimmy said, "Can we stop here a minute? My father lives in there." We stopped, and he went in and got his father. Out came a man who was as tense as Jimmy was, and they hardly could look at each other. It was the goddamndest affirmation of a hunch that I had ever seen. They could hardly talk; they mumbled at each other. I don't know what the hell Jimmy stopped to see him for, because in a few minutes he said, "Let's go."

I got him fixed in a room, and I took him to the lot to shoot some wardrobe tests. The crew couldn't believe it. They said, "Is that the stand-in?" This was a good sign for me because he looked real. He looked like an actual person. We started working. With his first money, Jimmy bought a palomino horse. When he got into problems with a girlfriend, I moved him into a dressing room at the studio, and I moved in next door. I was anxious that he was going to do something terrible. I didn't think he would complete the picture. He was an extremely sick boy at that time. There's a saying that success is harder to take than failure. It's a rather shaky statement, but let's say there's some truth in it. Success was sure hard for him to take.

Q : *I know you have a high regard for* East of Eden. *Would you call it your best film?*
E K : I don't think I've ever made a film in which I've achieved everything I've wanted perfectly. I don't think any of my films are perfect. The nearest one to it, I think, would be *East of Eden*, though it's not my favorite film.

Q : *Which is?*
E K : *America, America* because I wrote it and it's about my uncle. I have a great fondness for that film. I love the music, and I love the country. But it's far from perfect. It's full of flaws. *East of Eden* achieves its goals almost without fault. I think all the actors are excellent. Another film that I like a lot is *Viva Zapata!*, which is most imperfect. I think some of the sequences are not achieved well at all. There's one sequence in the picture I detest, where he says, "I can't read." Every time I look at it, I turn away. I wish

they'd put a commercial there. But I think other sequences are as good as I've ever done.

Q : *Did you run into any problems dealing with a mythical figure like Zapata?*
E K : I sure did. John Steinbeck and I did the script. We wanted to shoot it, naturally, in Mexico, and we thought, these guys would love it. We're going to make an international film about Zapata, their national hero. But we ran into Gabby Figueroa, who was the head of the syndicate down there, and he asked for certain controls and script changes. When we said no, he said, "We won't let you shoot it here. Don't you understand? Suppose I took a crew, went up to Illinois, and did a picture about Abraham Lincoln with Mexican actors. How would you feel?"

So we shot it right on the border of Mexico. We used to go over to Mexico for lunch, and we had a lot of Mexicans come over and got a Mexican band. We got as close as we could get, but I think I could have done it better in the state of Morales, which is south of Mexico City. When I saw the city down there with its rocks—it's a little bit like Galway in Ireland, with its rock walls—I knew I could have been photographing the poverty rather than talking about the poverty.

Q : *You once said that you regard* Zapata *as your first cinematically structured film. That makes* Streetcar Named Desire *a photographed play.*
E K : Exactly. On *Streetcar* we worked very hard to open it up, and then went back to the play because we'd lost all the compression. In the play, these people were trapped in a room with each other. What I actually did was to make the set smaller. As the story progressed I took out little flats, and the set got smaller and smaller. But the first cinematic picture I ever did was not *Viva Zapata*. I had made up my mind to do a silent picture, and it was called *Panic in the Streets*. There is talk in it, but really the story is all told by pictures. Then I did *Zapata*.

I had learned a lot, as I did from two directors I liked when I first came here; Jean Renoir, whom I think is a god, and Jack Ford. I used to hang around Ford and get his goddamned sour answers, which I adored. I began to say, I must learn from Ford. I must learn to hold the long shot and trust the long shot, not cut into it. A theater-trained person wants to jump in and see the facial expression when the facial expression is sometimes more banal than if left a mystery. The first film I made that I feel is cinematically interesting is *Zapata*.

Q : *As a theater-trained director, what difference do you find in working with actors in film?*

E K : In a film what you're trying to do is to lay down the basic behavior patterns of a person. For example, I'm now doing *The Last Tycoon*. Robert DeNiro is playing Monroe Stahr, an urban Jew, an intellectual, who was born with a rheumatic heart, who dresses up to his role as the head of the studio. Bobby has never played anything but a street-smart kid. Bobby has never played an educated part, an executive who could run a studio. So I've been doing improvisations with him in an office with a secretary and an assistant secretary and four or five people coming in. The phone never stops ringing.

I've impressed on Bobby that what he says is never a comment. Whatever he says is an instruction which someone has to do something about. For several days on the set I've harassed the hell out of DeNiro. I've made him feel that his life is at the mercy of his anteroom, that he's a victim of the phone. I've now got him realizing what it means to be an executive. I've tried to use in the improvisations the actors whom I'm going to use in the movie so he'll begin to get familiar with the world he's going to move in. I've also tried to get DeNiro, one would say, to "think" like an intellectual, to consider things in ambivalence, to see more than one side of something. Also, I've kept him away from the actress who's playing Kathleen, an ethereal or unearthly figure. If he becomes too familiar with her, it'll hurt the scenes when we shoot them. So he's been instructed by me not to chat with her, not to make friends with her, not to go around with her, not to have dinner with her, but to keep her at a distance.

So what am I doing? I'm building up behavior patterns. In a play you have two-and-a-half weeks to prepare. They tell you three-and-a-half—it's a lie. Somewhere in the third week everyone descends on you with the sets and the costumes and his worries. Everyone comes after you saying that this is not working, that is not working. You have to be very strong and very clear about what you want, because one of the first things you have to do is mount the play. I take much longer than most. I don't do it until the end of the second week. A lot of anxious directors do it earlier, and maybe they're right. Garson Kanin has a run-through after two days. I just don't believe in that. No play is perfect, and you're going to make changes in it. You may also go out on the road with it. You're trying out the play, not just the performances.

Sam Spiegel, who's producing *The Last Tycoon,* worked a year and a half
with Harold Pinter on the script. I made up my mind to do it as written.
So here I'm not trying out the play anymore. I'm trying to do what the
French call "realize" the play. It's a very apt word. You do "realize" it. You
do bring it to life.

Q : *DeNiro excepted, what atmosphere do you work for among your actors?*
E K : A continual effort of getting them to know each other. For example,
I take them to dinner. When I see them together, I realize a lot about their
relationship which is basic and not even expressed. I see how they relate,
how they look together. I have kept people apart. In *The Visitors*—don't
repeat this—I stirred up small antagonisms between the actor who played
the husband and others. It's certainly uncomfortable, but I do it. I think it
adds a lot.

Q : *How much room is there for the contribution of the actors?*
E K : Once I give the actors the basic objectives of a scene, I try to leave
room so that anything they have to contribute can be used. In other
words, I say, "Here's the road. Now you can run or do anything down that
road you want, but you've got to stay on that road." Somebody once said
you're much freer when you know your boundaries. There is truth in that.
When I talk to the actors, they begin to give me ideas, and I grab them
because the ideas they give me turn them on. I want the breath of life from
them rather than the mechanical fulfillment of the movement which I
asked for.

Q : *How do you work with actors on a typical scene?*
E K : You know, they say I'm an acting director, which I don't take as a
compliment. I don't really agree, but I do deal with actors a lot. I love
actors. I used to be an actor for eight years, so I do appreciate their job. One
of the most important things in an acting scene, especially a short acting
scene, is not to talk about the scene that precedes but to *play out* the scene
that precedes. You play out what the actors come from, or where they
come from psychologically, so that their ride into a scene is a correct one.

In other words, the actors come in with the experience that they would
come in with in life. And none of us comes into any scene in life naked.
You go home to your wife after you've had a bad day at the office, and it's
a different scene than if you've had an exhilarating day. What precedes a

scene is important. Once you've done that, you divide the scene—or I tend to—into sections, into movements. Stanislavski called them "beats." The point is that there are sections in life. Sometimes even a short scene has a three-act structure. You lay bare to the actor, you make him understand and appreciate, the structure beneath the lines. That's what's often called the subtext, and dealing with the subtext is one of the critical elements in directing actors. In other words, not what is said, but what happens. Particularly with a writer like Harold Pinter, who is so oblique. What he says is often the opposite of what is happening, or only related indirectly to what is happening.

Q: *You've performed in plays and in several films. Does your own acting experience help you to communicate with your actors?*
E K: It definitely does. I put it in a bad way before when I said that I'm not afraid of actors. I'm not afraid to make demands on them. I believe they can give me more. I reach into them for more. And I think it's fascinating to see this on the screen instead of just a face and a piece of behavior. There are directors, very famous ones, who completely disagree: "I don't want you to act. Don't give me any goddamned Actors' Studio stuff." Basically, the people I choose to work with are creative people who are sensitive, who want to be good, who have some aspiration in them. You don't deal with actors as dolls. You deal with them as people who are poets to a certain degree.

Q: *Still, for you the director's role is paramount. Have years of experience as a strong director made your choices easier on a set?*
E K: I find that the more you know, the more difficulty you're in, because you know how many different ways something can be done. The terrible thing about film directing is that you wake up at four in the morning and say, "Damn it, why did I do that scene that way? I could have done it differently." The most important thing is to get alone on the set in the morning, when your brain is still fairly clear, and sit there with coffee or a cigar and just think about what you feel and what you're trying to get over and *how* you can get it over.

Q: *Are you ever in conflict when you both produce and direct the same film?*
E K: Let me give some background first. I'd produced eight films, and there was no conflict because I had my own group of actors, more or less.

They were all my friends, most of them in the Actors' Studio in New York. I had my own staff; they were all close friends of mine. I wouldn't even call them a staff: They were friends of mine with whom I made pictures. I had an ideal situation. This ended for me when I started to write books.

Now I want to make films again, and I want, above all, to make the other half of *America, America* and another film—two films I very much want to make. But it would take me a year to write a script, so I decided to jump in now and do a film. Sam Spiegel I admire. I like him. He's a very bright guy. And Harold Pinter I love. He's one of the nicest men I've met, and one of the most interesting. And when they offered *The Last Tycoon* to me I said, "What the hell, I'll start." Now, is there a conflict? There *are* conflicts now. There are conflicts when you produce and direct because you're watching two things at once: You're watching the budget, and you're watching your own desires. And there are conflicts now: I want one thing, and Spiegel wants another.

There's no way to take the conflicts out of work. As a matter of fact, conflicts are stimulating. Fights are stimulating. Differences of opinion, if they are between people who basically see the same thing, are much more exhilarating than no conflicts. There's an old corny saying in show business: When everything goes well, the production is going to fail. That doesn't mean you've got to stir up fights. But there are producers who do stir up fights, who do set people against each other. I've heard them say, "When you're in trouble, you're going to think faster and better." I don't mind conflict, and I like an argument. I like it in people. Sometimes you learn a lot.

Q: *How do you set your priorities if you are both producer and director?*
E K : They're always the same, and the obstacles are the same. If a producer is there, your obstacle is a good one. You try to convince him that your goals are more important. You have constant arguments. There's nothing wrong with that. We're arguing now about how many suits DeNiro should have. The producer just left, and he said to me, "Does he need fourteen suits? Doesn't he ever repeat?" So I said, "I'll try to cut out a couple." But I think to myself, well, if he needs fourteen suits, he'd better have them. But it's a tiny point. Does he need this set? Do we need all this? So I cut something. He's blocking you in a way, but he's helping also. Don't try to take the conflict out of anything. Whenever there's a group that makes some-

thing, as the Group Theater used to, as soon as the conflicts go out of it, it means indifference. The number one enemy of art is indifference, or not caring a lot. When you say, "What the shit, it's only a picture," don't do it. Go home.

Q: *Do you think that the more personal you get in your films, the more you lose your dramatic objectivity?*
E K: I guess so. I don't give a damn, though.

Q: *For whom do you make your films?*
E K: The unwritten premise of every director, in my opinion, is this: If it moves me, it's going to move a lot of other people. Sometimes a lot of other people; sometimes a few other people. If you finally are saying, whom do you make them for, you make them for yourself. I think that's the same reason painters paint.

Q: *How do you approach a film like* The Last Tycoon? *Do you prepare an elaborate shooting script?*
E K: If you do that, there's no use getting good actors because there's no surprise. If you're going to squeeze them into a straight jacket, I think you should get marionettes. I keep a notebook in which I try to describe every character. I try to get at what the essence of each part is and how that part serves the whole. And as I make these notes, I begin to find the moments that are significant, particularly the climax. I don't want to go into *The Last Tycoon*, but I made a big fat notebook for it because there are so many characters and it's so involved. I've got to be very clear about these characters, otherwise they'll run away with me. When I begin to direct a scene, I know what I want out of the scene, and I know what each character is supposed to contribute.

Q: *Do you work out camera movements with your cameraman?*
E K: I arrange a scene with the camera in mind. I sometimes say to the cameraman in the morning, "Take this wall out; I'm going to shoot this way." I'm not a great guy for moving the camera. I nail it down a lot. I don't like it when it moves too much. I never get on a crane. I don't dolly much. I love a set thing because you're not aware of the camera. As for close-ups, I think they're most useful when you're recording a change, when you want to see the effect of something on a character.

Q : *Do you leave the composition of a closeup to your cameraman?*

E K : Hell, no. I don't leave anything to anybody. I don't mean to be mean about it, but I think everything tells a story. Hitchcock's the best example. The way he does close-ups is fantastic. In *The Last Tycoon*, I've tried to make DeNiro look like a very sensitive person. You've seen what he usually plays. I used a still camera, and I found out that when I got up high, his cheeks sunk in a little bit, and he looked more drawn, more ascetic. That's something good for me to know. So I try in certain scenes to go up a little bit higher.

Q : *Do you keep a journal on your filmmaking?*

E K : Yes, I try to. I keep a diary, and every morning when I go in, I write for ten or fifteen minutes, unless somebody grabs me right away. I write on whatever happened the day before and whatever feelings I have. The first entry in my diary of *The Last Tycoon* is a letter I sent to Sam Spiegel dubious about doing the picture. When I read the script again, I realized there was more in it, that there was a lot I had missed. I'd have to bring that out clearly, and I began to like the script better.

Q : *What made you take the long trip from Broadway to Hollywood back in 1944?*

E K : I was just anxious to make films. For a while I was the fair-haired boy of Broadway, and I got a lot of offers from Warner Bros. and Metro and Fox. I liked the producer at Fox best, and I committed myself. But it was much harder to get into films then than it is now. There is a big road to films now called television. A lot of film directors—Arthur Penn, Marty Ritt, John Frankenheimer—came out of television. Television is sort of a training ground, although it's a monster training ground for a little job. But back then, it was very hard to get into film, so I just grabbed that opportunity because I wanted to make films.

Q : *You already had a strong interest in films?*

E K : The first artist I admired in my life was Sergei Eisenstein. The second man I admired was Alexander Dovzhenko and a picture called *Air City* (*Aerograd*). These men were like idols, and you are affected by your idols, as I was by Renoir's films. So, I became a film director out of admiration, out of wanting to be like that—hero worship. I think it's the most wonderful art in the world.

Q : *You did* Pinky *while at Fox in the late forties, a fairly bold picture on blacks. Do you have any regard for it these days?*

E K : I'm not too proud of that picture. It's the first time "nigger" was said on the screen, but I think it was a conventional picture. I think there were a lot of clichés in it. I took it over from Jack Ford, and I didn't work on the script. Now I think I should tell my *own* story. That's why, instead of getting broader and more catholic, I think I'm getting narrower. But *Baby Doll* is the picture in which I think I did the black characters best. They were old retainers on a broken-down plantation, but they laughed at the whites. The laughter was scornful. Affectionate to a certain extent but scornful. But I don't think I've ever done a black person the way a black person can do a black person. I have great sympathy, but I don't think it's possible for me.

Q : *You say that television is a training ground for directors in films. But there is a big difference between the television I see and your movies. For instance, framing in television is very shallow, but you have action going on three or more different planes.*

E K : That's correct. I believe that's the essence of movie composition. In a movie, a long shot is one of the greatest forms of expression. The other great form is a close-up. A medium shot is valuable but often literal. But a long shot often can achieve poetry. In a close shot, the camera works more like a microscope; it is a penetrating device. But when you have a twenty-five-inch screen and a long shot, it's just a blur back there often; it doesn't mean anything. I think the best-directed shows on television are football and baseball games. In a football game you see a play, you see it in slow motion again, you see the coaches looking worried. When someone makes a great play you see a close-up. It's a fantastic piece of direction.

Q : *How has filmmaking changed for you since those early days at Fox?*

E K : The key word in art — it's an ugly word but it's a necessary word — is power, your own power. Power to say, "I'm going to bend you to my will." However you disguise it, you're gripping someone's throat. You're saying, "My dear, this is the way it's going to be." Whenever anybody blocks that, you have less power. So for me I would say that things have gotten better, and they're going to get better yet.

I had trouble with California financially because *America, America* lost a fortune; *The Arrangement* lost a fortune. I would say most of my films, except *Splendor in the Grass, On the Waterfront,* and *East of Eden,* lost money. The studios finally said, "If you leave him alone, he's liable to lose you a bundle." So power interests me very much. The director with the greatest power in the world is Bergman, because he makes his films with few people, and he makes them with few sets. But read *Bergman on Bergman* and see how even he has to practically crawl to someone in Stockholm and say, "What about this project? I want to make this project. I'll make you two comedies after I do that. Will that make it all right?"

You are dealing with power in filmmaking, even with a low budget. I made *The Visitors* for $165,000. *The Last Tycoon* costs $39,000 a day. Nobody would put up money for *The Visitors.* I finally borrowed the money from a bank, hocked some stuff, made an arrangement with United Artists, and did the film with a crew of four. I did the properties. When there was a pancake-eating scene, my son cooked the pancakes. He kept the books. I made the film this way because I did not want to be terrorized by money. I went to see Godard shoot *A Woman Is a Woman* in a room where there was barely space to walk around in. He made that film for very little. When you reduce your costs, you gain some power.

Q : *What happened to* The Visitors?
E K : You're touching on a very sore spot with me because United Artists killed the picture. They opened it for nine days in New York, and it got a wonderful notice in *The New York Times,* terrible notices everywhere else. But they didn't promote it. They just put it away. I'm now trying to buy the picture because it meant a lot to me. It's imperfect but it has value. I'm still very angry. I think United Artists did an inhuman act.

Q : *The problem with a personal film like* The Visitors, *of course, is getting around the distribution system.*
E K : The hope of directors like me is to start our own distribution outfit. Francis Coppola is trying to do that now on a large scale. I own *Baby Doll* and *A Face in the Crowd,* and I have someone who books these in colleges. The rights to *America, America* will revert to me, and I'll do the same thing. I'm trying to create another source of distribution rather than to the big theaters. The theaters are never going to show *Wild River,* though I think that it's an unusual picture and that the last half of it is wonderful.

Q : *Why won't they show it?*

E K : Because they don't make any money from it. Minimum advertising in *The New York Times, The New York Post,* and *The Village Voice,* gets up into $25,000. Nobody's going to risk $25,000 unless they think it's going to come back. The record shows them that they won't get it back.

Q : *You said* A Face in the Crowd *lost money. What sort of response did it get when it opened?*

E K : I think it received better than average. I think it's a hell of a good film myself, with all its faults. I think it says a lot, anticipates a lot. Nora Sayre said in *The New York Times* last winter that it anticipated a lot of the Watergate hearings. I wish she could have reviewed it at the time. But we didn't do too well with it. A lot of my films didn't. *America, America* started like a house afire in New York City and died everywhere else. Now it's played nine times a year in Paris. In Athens, it's constantly playing. In Germany, it's played all the time. *Wild River* was an absolute financial disaster. I heard last year that when Twentieth Century-Fox cleaned house they burned a lot of negatives, and among them the negative of that picture. Imagine how I feel.

Q : *You wife's movie,* Wanda, *also suffered at the box office. Is Barbara Loden now planning any more films?*

E K : I think that *Wanda* is a marvelous picture. It's completely honest. My wife is now getting ready to make another picture on the same small scale. *Wanda* got excellent notices, but it died everywhere. What does Barbara feel? She feels hurt. She doesn't get any offers. She's been trying to get backing on her new picture for a year and a half. Something's wrong, and I don't know what to do about it.

Q : *Some of your films, of course, have been commercial successes. Have you been able to isolate a common element to explain the success?*

E K : I think so. I think they're films that are recognizable to audiences emphatically. In other words, they say, "There's a piece of me." *Splendor in the Grass* was one of my successful films. It's family life in a small town. Everybody knows people like that, and they respond immediately, simply. But when the message is gritty, when the message is disturbing, I don't know if people want to be disturbed. Then you can have films in which the core is moving to an audience, like *On the Waterfront*. There it was the problem of conscience which Brando had. But it was also very exciting, in terms of physical conflict, in terms of danger.

Somebody said that the three things people respond to are death, money, and sex. I don't know if any of that is true, but I think people certainly respond to things that worry them in their own lives. I think audiences are much smarter in the intuitive sense than filmmakers in the big studios know. I think they're anxious to see their own lives reflected and to work out through the behavior of other people their own problems. I think if you can get that tie, you will have a film that will be popular. I don't use the word "successful." I say "popular." I think people like to be scared—*Jaws*. And I think people like to be reassured. It has something to do with the relationship between an audience and a film.

I don't know why anybody should go see *The Last Tycoon*—but don't quote me. I hope to make it so they will. I hope to make it so they'll see a talented guy under the stress of business and everything else. They'll watch him and say, "Yes, I have talent, I have feeling, and I have known that stress." I'm trying to direct it so it'll relate to the experience of the audience.

Q : *Would you say that a successful film as opposed perhaps to a popular film hinges to a large extent on structure?*
E K : I'm a great believer in structure, though many excellent films are unstructured. I believe in telling a continuous story, in coming to two or three climaxes, each of which changes the relationships in the next section. That doesn't mean that episodic films like *8½* are bad. I thought it was a masterpiece, and it's one of my favorite films. But I personally believe in storytelling and structure and tension.

Q : *You think in movements as opposed to acts?*
E K : No, in inner acts as opposed to movements, inner acts which cause behavior. If you think of people as changing things, as dynamic rather than static, you have to have structure. Godard, for example, shows people in a static state. I don't see life that way.

Q : *Your concern for structure then means a close attention to editing?*
E K : I think editing is part of directing. That's why I don't like it when editors get the same credit that directors do. I think a director should do

absolutely everything. I think the sets are his. The costumes are his. The editing is his. I'm a believer in the dominance of one person who has a vision.

Q :   *Your films often contain recurring devices or symbols—*the jacket in On the Waterfront, *the gift of shoes at the beginning and end of* America, America.
E K :   I'm given to symbols. For example, water is a recurring image in my pictures. I constantly feel something about water. There's always a hydrant spouting water or a lake or the sea. It happens again in *The Last Tycoon.* I am aware of repeated symbols. I don't know if it's good or bad. Sometimes after a film I think, "I wish I hadn't been so obvious."

Q :   *You're filming* The Last Tycoon *here on the coast. As a New Yorker who loves the streets and the pace, do you find yourself less stimulated here? In other words, do you work better in New York?*
E K :   I think the greatest loss you people have out here is that there's fewer stimuli from the place where you work to the place where you live. In New York City, I live on 68th Street, and I write on 54th Street in a little office. There are always five, ten, fifteen things I see on the way there that I can't forget. Recently, I was riding on a train to visit my mother in Rye, New York, and I saw a twelve-year-old girl with a Vivaldi concerto spread out on her lap. She was moving her hands as if she were at the piano. Now where could I possibly see that in Los Angeles?

But here, where I'm supposedly successful, I never see a goddamn thing. I get up in the morning. I ride in the car that the studio provides to Paramount Studios. On the ride down, I'm semiconscious. I don't see anything because I'm thinking about what I'm going to do. I get to the studio, and I'm in an office, which is a protected environment. It's like a hiatus in my life. I'm a fellow who gets a lot from what he sees around him. But I feel terribly isolated here. I feel de-natured here. When I made pictures in New York, I always got something. I used to walk around the streets to get something. I'm not hostile to this neighborhood, but I'm a New Yorker. I always will be. New York is a battleground, a vicious, dangerous, dirty, mixed-up but terrific place, and everything about it I love.

Q :   *What led you to switch from filmmaking to novel-writing?*
E K :   It's very personal. My first wife died. We were very, very close, and I decided I would stop everything and just leave the country for a while.

"Re-find" myself, whatever the hell the word is. I had been making a film every year and a play every year for a long time, and it was hard work. I began to write some notes, and that slowly began to develop into a book called *The Arrangement*.

I found myself saying, "I'm not in sympathy with the work of Tennessee Williams, although I love him and I think he's a wonderful writer. And I'm not in sympathy with the point of view of Arthur Miller, although I love him personally and I like his work. And I'm not in sympathy with Bill Inge. I've got to start viewing things as *I* do, and when I go back to films I want to make films that in some way or another expresses my opinion." The next film I'm going to make, I hope, will be a follow-up on *America, America* which is about what happened to my uncle after he got to this country. I want to make more personal films.

Q: *What do you look for when you consider doing a film?*
EK: I don't move unless I have some empathy with the basic theme. In some way, the channel of the film should also be in my own life. I start with an instinct. With *East of Eden* I said, "I don't know why it is but the last ninety pages of Steinbeck's book turn me on." It's really the story of my father and me, and I didn't realize it for a long time. When Paul Osborn and I began to work on the screenplay, I realized that it's just the way I was. I was always the bad boy, but I thought I was the good boy. In some subtle or not-so-subtle way, every film is autobiographical. A thing in my life is expressed by the essence of the film. Then I know it experientially, not just mentally. I've got to feel that it's in some way about me, some way about my struggles, some way about my pain, my hopes.

Hollywood Under Water

CHARLES SILVER AND
MARY CORLISS/1977

THE MELANCHOLIC TONE OF *The Last Tycoon* may seem
at first glance to grant the film's authorship to F. Scott Fitzgerald
and Harold Pinter. Elia Kazan always saw his screenwriters as vital
collaborators rather than as adversaries; he is most generous in
crediting Pinter with giving shape to the film, and modest in making any claims for auteurship. But Kazan's career-long passions and
preoccupations are still apparent — in the film, guiding Robert
DeNiro to a superb performance as Monroe Stahr, and in this interview, as he expresses his satisfaction with *The Last Tycoon* and his
outrage at the recent wave of "bloodletting" action movies.

He spent much of our hour with him pacing around his
Manhattan office, his restless intelligence leading him through
energetic meditations and remembrances. Though he now considers himself a novelist who occasionally directs movies, it's
hard to think of Kazan confined to a typewriter and a blank page
that never talks back. He would seem to need the industrious
chaos of a movie set as much as ever — and to agree with others
that the movies, in this age of paralysis and turmoil, still need
Kazan. — M.C.

There's the question of authorship on The Last Tycoon. *You came to the project*
fairly late, and you've said that you didn't change any of Harold Pinter's dialogue.

From *Film Comment*, January/February 1977. Reprinted by permission.

Mike Nichols and Harold and Sam Spiegel had done the basic script, which
I haven't changed. I was writing a book, and having trouble with it. When
you get stuck on a book, it's a terrible situation. You've spent months and
months on this, and you realize it may never work. And on that day, Sam
called me and said, "Do you want to read *The Last Tycoon*? Mike and I have
busted up on it." I read it, and I liked it, and I did it. That's all, that's how
that happened. Mike contributed a lot—the idea of opening in an Italian
place with that shooting and all that, that was his idea. Of course, Harold's
very capable, and Spiegel is a hard worker.

I did make some changes: the walking into the soundstage at the end,
which somebody called an evasion. Pauline Kael saw that as a proof that
the film was empty, but I agree with Frank Rich [of the *New York Post*] who
said that it was absolutely apt. Rich says that Stahr was engulfed in his
environment finally, and that's where the moguls die. They don't break
away and jump off a cliff like the old Greeks used to do. They get engulfed
in their environment; they go lower and lower. I mean, Thalberg kept
coming back to the picture business; he didn't escape it. Anyway, I made
some contributions, but it's not like a film that I produced or wrote or
something like that. It's Harold Pinter's script!

Were you pleased that his script adhered so closely to the F. Scott Fitzgerald
novel?
Well, they made that decision, and I thought it was the right decision
because, honestly, I didn't care for Edmund Wilson's notes of what he
thought Fitzgerald meant to do—since I write novels myself, I know that
you make structural plans that you do not follow, because when you get
right down to it you say, "Well, that's just mechanics." Fitzgerald would
not have used the stuff about the airplane blowing up, or the union. He
doesn't give a shit about the union struggles. I think Sam, Harold, and
Mike probably realized that and said, "Let's stick to what he actually
wrote."

Now, he would have rewritten it because he starts the book off with
Cecilia narrating, and he drops that. In the end, he could not have had
Cecilia narrating at all. Cecilia, by the way, is a phony character in the
book because she doesn't have the intelligence or the insights of a nine-
teen-year-old girl. She has Fitzgerald's sensitivity, Fitzgerald's intelligence.
So we had to do something with it. Dear old John Simon [of *New York*],

who's a very bright guy, says we lost that character—but, we didn't lose a
damn thing. We had to do something with her. To me, the way Cecilia is
now, she's a candidate to be a Beverly Hills housewife who marries an
agent, makes him even a bigger agent, and throws big parties that she
plans meticulously. She becomes famous for them. Then fucks the chauffeur. Finally, joins the Roman Catholic Church. I feel compassion for the
girl. I feel she's in a trap. She's in a place where *that's* the only life she'll
have.

*Will Cecilia know that she once had a fine moment in her life when she was in
love with Stahr?*
Well, I think so, don't you? I think her love as depicted in the picture is
extremely idealistic and very winning. Theresa Russell looks like a child,
and she also looks like a dowager at the same time. That's why I cast her.
She never acted before, you know; she trains horses.

Are you pleased with Ingrid Boulting's performance as Kathleen Moore?
It's not a matter of being pleased or not. Yes, I was, because she accom-
plished what I wanted to do. I always thought of Kathleen as an ap-
paritional figure, not a real person—someone to whom he could attach
his romanticism. She's not a human figure. I never meant her to be like
an ordinary girl. She's been whipped, and she's full of a mysterious pain.
He looks at her, and he sees there that same mysterious pain his wife had,
and he puts on her a lot of things that are not true. She's not like what he
makes her. So, when her real person comes out, he doesn't know what the
hell to do. She says, "I don't want to marry you; I don't want to be with
you; I don't want your life." That's the real girl coming out, and he can't
understand that. He doesn't deal with it because he's built her up into this
romantic image. That's what I was trying to get over. That's not likable or
unlikable. It's a person; it's a Fitzgerald person. Make sense or not?

*It does. Fitzgerald also says in the notes that the one attractive quality that she
had was that she did not depend on Stahr, and he seemed to like that, since he
was surrounded by people who really drained him dry every day.*
Don't you find in your experience that there is a certain type of man who
gets more ardent when he is rejected, or when you don't come back as
strong as he comes back? Girls know that, so they play it cool.

So you think that Ingrid Boulting had the right look?
And feel, too. When you look at her, you say she's someone from outer space. Listen, you put an ordinary girl up on top of that figure that's coming down in the flood, and you think, "What the fuck is she doing up there? How did she get on the lot in the first place? If she doesn't like movies, what is she doing on the lot? How did she come in—follow the trucks? Bullshit!" But you put her up there, you say, "Yeah, I guess she *would*. I don't know where the hell she came from, but maybe she just materialized." That's what I was trying to get at.

It's been suggested that she looks like both Zelda and Sheilah Graham. Was there any intent in either case?
Not intent, but I was pleased to notice that. Well, Ingrid's a dancer and does modeling. She dances all the time. In that sense she's like Zelda.

How much casting was done before you came in?
I suggested Robert DeNiro. I felt sure, and I took Sam by the hand, and I took him up to DeNiro who was staying in Francis Coppola's suite in the Sherry-Netherland, and I introduced them. And I said, "Jesus, this is the guy, this is the guy." And, when I think about it, I was right.

How would you compare working with DeNiro to working with Brando when he was DeNiro's age?
Well, you can't compare anybody. Every actor that ever lived is different, and you never work with anybody the same way. Bobby is more meticulous and more hardworking. He's very imaginative. He's very precise. He figures everything out both inside and outside. He has good emotion. He's a character actor: everything he does he calculates. In a good way, but he calculates, just how he sits, what his suits are, what ring is where, the eyeglasses, everything is very exact. He's the only actor I've ever known who called me up on Friday night after we got through shooting and said, "Let's work tomorrow and Sunday together." He's the hardest working actor I ever met and one of the best guys I ever met in show business.

Brando is like something else, you know—mysterious. You don't know where the hell he gets his ideas. He's really very intuitive. He's very emotional, very subterranean; in a sense, he's more brilliant. Brando kept surprising me. Brando does something that is unique of all the actors I've known. You tell him something, and in the middle of your telling it to him he'll walk away and say, "All right, OK." And then he'll do it, and he'll do it better than you said. He'll do something you didn't expect. And what his walking away means is that "I've thought of it, and I've thought of something better than what you said, you bastard." So Brando does more unexpected things, but I wouldn't say he's a better actor than DeNiro— he's a different *kind* of actor.

How much of this performance, without taking anything away from DeNiro, would you say you brought out? How much of it is your idea?
I would tell him a lot of things. But with a good actor, you can tell him a lot and you have to watch what he latches on to and what he does not latch on to. He picked from what I told him, 'cause I can talk about that character a long time. He picked out the right things; he worked hard on them, and I would say he contributed an awful lot. I'm a director who does work with actors. So, I did contribute, but I would say that anything anyone might praise me for, they should first mention Bobby because it's Bobby's performance. He "takes on" a character. You know that old cliché about how an actor becomes the person. He'll stay off the set until you're ready to shoot—I don't know what the hell he does. He gets there early. He works hard by himself. Bobby's wonderful! He's a wonderful fellow. I don't know how that fellow got to be that way. He's a marvelous man.

I had the crazy idea that DeNiro as Stahr looked a little bit like you in your youth.
A lot of people said that. We looked at pictures of Irving Thalberg, but it was a little bit different than that. It was more to make him like a properly brought-up middle-class Jewish intellectual who was in a flamboyant business. He's got that look of a proper boy. Moss Hart used to have that look when he was young, too. I worked with Moss once on a picture, and I got to know him well; Moss and Thalberg were both romantic and good businessmen. I wanted the audience to feel that Stahr could manage the studio well, but, at the same time, he could get lost in a dream that was false with a woman. I also wanted him to appear inept sexually. Pinter has a stage direction which says, "He trembles." Well, when Kathleen takes off her clothes, I couldn't show him trembling, or it would make you laugh, but he does reach for a post. You remember where he sort of reaches back, and he can't find the post, and he looks terrible; he looks frightened to death.

Some people thought he was impotent because of that, but a minute later he isn't.

Did you find Jeanne Moreau exciting or difficult to work with?
Oh, Jesus, she's a complete pro. I mean, she's a director. You have to say three words to her; she's way ahead of you. She's as smart a person as I've ever met. I liked her a lot. It wasn't like working with anyone mysterious. It was more like working with a European star where you have a discussion, and you don't have to help them accomplish it which is the way the English actors are. They go and do it; they do it in their own terms, and that's the end of it. They are different from ours. We have a tradition — especially since I started with Brando and all that bunch — of the director helping a lot and seeing them through a lot and making a lot of suggestions. But with English or continental actors, they're supposed to be trained to achieve the director's goal — that was the case with her.

I had never met Jeanne. So I thought, Jesus Christ, I'm going to show her up as being a faded star — maybe I'll have difficulty with that. Not at all — she got the idea way ahead of me. And when she says "How do I look on the screen?", I think it's a terrific closeup of her, and she's perfectly aware of how bad she looks. She doesn't look well in the picture; she looks like a faded out star. But when she saw it she said, "It's a great picture; you made a great picture." She flattered me more than anyone else; I was real pleased with her praise.

Did you cast Tony Curtis as Rodriguez?
No, that was Spiegel's idea. Dana Andrews was my idea. We all contributed. Spiegel's very good. He's an excellent producer. He cares. He's a desperate carer. By God, he's a hard trier when he wants something. He sweats, waiting for the rushes. He goes to see them, and when they're bad, his face gets white, and when they're good, he just glows. Against the indifference of the people who run the lots today — the lawyers, the agents, the former agents, the businessmen, the budgetmakers — Old Sam's in there. He dies every day. He's adorable. He's the last tycoon — the sonofabitch!

Some people thought the filmclips within the film were unsuccessful or anachronistic — the Casablanca *parody for example.*
I didn't try either to rest on nostalgia or to make this very definitely a certain period. I didn't say that it is 1938. I didn't play on nostalgia: oh, those

were the good old days or how romantic. I didn't because I don't believe that. And I believe the story has something universal. One thing about America is we're both romantic and we're expeditious—we're good business people, and we're also dreamers. So, I thought it had universal meaning—that's why I didn't nail it down or anchor it to a period. I, therefore, felt a certain liberty not to make them a parody of *Casablanca,* which I'm not interested in doing—that would be terrible. But I have elements that remind you of *Casablanca* but also of other things. The flashback I think that's best is the first one that's played in black-and-white and suddenly switches to color, and she says, "I want to do it again. I want to do it again." That, to me, gets the period better than any of the other stuff.

The Hollywood that comes through in the film—does that reflect any of your attitudes toward the period?
The silken murder—the congenial murder. The last reel's my favorite reel in the picture. I love when they fire him, and it's all done so politely, so nicely. Meantime, he's out; they're in; and the deals are being rearranged; and they've had meetings with the lawyers. They always have these pre-meeting meetings. That silken murder—that's part of it. The other thing I think is very telling is the music in what you call the *Casablanca* scene. I think that really heavy portentous music helps that scene a lot.

The scene that's most Hollywood of all—that comes from my memory, that I put in—comes after that scene is over when you have this medium long shot of them all just sitting there in the projection room, and nobody says a damn word, but a few people clear their throats. They're all waiting for Stahr to speak first. They're just sitting there. I remember that so well in Zanuck's projection room, and I extended that. As a matter of fact, now that I see it, I wish I kept it longer; it could have gone on for twenty more seconds. Until he commits himself, they're afraid to. That's the most Hollywood scene of all in the picture.

I imagine that, when you were out there as an actor in 1936 you must have been somewhat estranged from that.
I was a hard-working kid. I was sitting at home trying to write screenplays. I never went out with those people. Another thing that's typical is the loneliness of when he comes home, and the Filipino butler is there, and there's no one at home. There were big shots like that, but when you got to know them, they had no life at all except their work. When you see him

in bed, he's surrounded with scripts—that's another thing that I remember seeing.

Stahr reads the letter from Kathleen saying that she's engaged to be married, but you don't yet know what the letter says, and then you have her voice-over reading as he goes up the stairs. Was that your idea?
No, that was Harold...he's damn good. He's a remarkable intelligence.

Was he on the set at all?
No, he was in England, but I swore to him, I said to him—it wasn't Fitzgerald that I was reverential toward, it was Harold—I said to him that I wouldn't change any of his dialogue. And I didn't change one syllable of it. I found a way to stage it all.

You're a novelist, and yet your fidelity was toward Pinter's screenplay rather than Fitzgerald's novel.
Well, I don't think novelists are immediately screenwriters, or even particularly qualified to be screenwriters. The compression in a screenplay is its own special compression. It's not like the theater, either. Especially with Harold—he suggests so much, and they talk about the pauses, but there are no pauses in that thing. At every pause, something is happening. The inner action is continuous. You're waiting to see when are they going to get down to what the hell is really on their minds. That's not a pause—it's an evasion of confrontation. And then, when the confrontation comes, they can't say it. I think that tells more than anything. Anybody who liked it didn't complain about the pace.

There are a couple of crucial scenes in the novel that are left out of the film. In one scene, Stahr meets the black man on the beach when the grunion are coming in.
We almost put that scene in. We were right on the verge of doing that. I don't know if it was the grunion or what the hell it was. What we did, though, was we put a line in her mouth. He says, "Do you go to pictures?" She says, "Not much." He says, "Well, you should." She says, "Why should I?" He says, "Films give people what they want." And she has an excellent line: "What *you* want." Which is right down to the bone. It isn't what they want—it's been proved it's not—but it's what he wants, his vision. He's giving his vision of the world. That's what we did instead of the grunion.

The other missing scene is the last meeting between Kathleen and Stahr where Stahr decides whether he should go away with her tonight or wait. You never have this conscious decision-making process in the film. I don't know if there is a way of "making pictures" of this.

I think that's strictly Harold's way of looking at life. I'll tell you a story. When I began to work with Harold, I went to England. We worked a little bit, and I said, "Gee, why isn't this confrontation more upfront?" And he said, "I think it's there." And I said, "No, it's like it's all happening underwater." And he said, "Isn't that where things happen?" Now, think about it in your own life. You make a decision to do something important. Are you aware that you're making it at a particular moment? Isn't that often just a convention of drama—that it's upfront? Aren't decisions made and then you hear about them from your inner radio station? I mean, Harold's got a point, hasn't he? It's his view of life; it's his way of seeing things.

You would write it more directly?

My own habit is more direct, to articulate, but in my own personal life, I'm sure I do. Because I'm like most people, I avoid confrontation until it cannot be avoided any longer.

Stahr says, "I don't want to lose you," but he does nothing to prevent that from happening. He doesn't really say, "You're mine, I'm taking you; you're going to worry me back to life."

That's what I would do. I would say, "I don't care about all your problems. We're not only driving up on the road, but we're going to keep going." I think I would do that—I've done that—but I'm not sure that Irving Thalberg would do it. And I'm not sure that the man the script is *really* about, F. Scott Fitzgerald, would do it. I'm not sure that one of his heroes would do it. When you read *Tender Is the Night*, everything is happening without a direct confrontation. It's a special way of dealing with the problems of life. That's the way Harold felt, and I respect it.

Ultimately, it has to be tragic if you don't take action at the moment when it's desperately needed.

Don't you think that at the end of the film he's had a terrific loss? The line where he says, "I was just making pictures"—isn't that full of self-scorn? I think that's the best line in the picture. When you think about it, he doesn't say it in any mean way to himself, but it's full of scorn. "That's what I've done all my life, and I've got such a habit of looking at things as though they were pictures, and in my own life it's become that."

You didn't feel constrained in your directing by the fact that for Pinter things do happen underwater.
People think of me like *On the Waterfront* all the time, but actually if you think about the stuff I've done, a lot of it is very muted. I'm really not a noisy man, although some of my films have been noisy. Even if you look at *On the Waterfront,* what scenes do people remember most from it? What's good about the picture is the tenderness in the middle of the violence.

People send me a lot of scripts, but I will not do a sadistic script. I will not do a script about bloodletting. I will not do a script about hate. I will not add to the violence. I will not say violence is good. I will not say violence is an expression of our time. When you meet the people who make these bloodletting pictures, you find they are people of intelligence and culture—and they make pictures which release the worse things in society. I'll never do that. I think a filmmaker has a certain moral duty. I think that he's got to say, "Look, Mankind is perfectable or is good. Men can be good." Also I just don't like to do it. They're all tricks anyway—it's just mechanics. In *On the Waterfront* we didn't do that. We had a terrible fight which I hid partly behind the wall of that little house. I didn't show it. When you make entertainment out of violence, when you say what fun it is to smash somebody in the nose—take Silver's glasses and throw him on the ground and stamp him out and stick your fist in his mouth and kick him in the balls—well, shit on that!

I think a picture like *The Last Tycoon* is a test of a critic. I don't think *I'm* being tested in it, or Harold's being tested in it, and certainly Fitzgerald's not being tested. But it's a test of a critic's sensitivity; for they basically, I think, have become debased, as the audience has become debased. They think that there's got to be a piece of violence every so often. There's a new technique in pictures which was started by Francis Coppola. The prime example of it is *Marathon Man* where every five minutes on the second there's some bloodletting or somebody's guts are thrown out on the floor. And the picture goes along—nothing's happening, nothing's happening— and the audience says, "Jeez, I wonder who's going to get killed now..." Five minutes! Gow! whew! bang bang! Across the hall, falling out the fucking window, and everything goes along and every thing's smooth — that's the new technique. And the audience! I went to the Loew's State to see this damn *Marathon Man*, and when I went in there was about a five-minute wait before the picture started, and I swear to God it smelled like a zoo at feeding time. The people wanted it. There was a hunger for violence; they have their pent-up violence inside. People are furious. Society's got them nuts!

Has your attitude toward adapting novels changed since you began writing your own novels?
I don't know. What's interesting to me was that to go from novel-writing to filmmaking was not hard at all. But to go from making a film back to novel-writing, that was tough. There's something about the conviviality of a film — we had a damn good unit, all the actors liked each other, we had a great time — it's so easy compared with writing a book. The next thing I'm going to do after this novel is to write the followup to *America, America,* which is my favorite film. When you start getting ambivalent material, it's hard to be perfect. I don't feel life so clearly — I don't even feel it as an unambivalent thing.

Do you admire Fitzgerald as a novelist?
I admire him line by line, little paragraph by paragraph. I think he's brilliant — especially this book. The things he observes and the way he says them; he's great. It's not a finished book. Do I admire his vision as a whole? Well, I'm interested in it, but you know, I don't know truly, if you put the squeeze on any artist in any field, whether he really is very interested in anyone else's work. I do esteem other artists. Jean Renoir is like a god to me. He's the greatest director that ever lived, for my taste. I esteem him, but interest is something else. The more you write your own stuff, the more you're interested in your own vision, and you hold onto that hard. You say, "I don't want to be diverted. I don't want to become someone else's artistic servant. I want to hold onto my own vision."

Interview with Elia Kazan

LLOYD MICHAELS/1981

LLOYD MICHAELS: *I'd like to begin with a few filmography questions. Michel Ciment [in* Kazan on Kazan*] credits you as the director of* People of the Cumberland, *and I've seen that citation many times. When I saw the print at the Museum of Modern Art, though, it lists Ralph Steiner and Eugene Hill as directors. You're listed as the assistant on the credits there.*

ELIA KAZAN: I think that's correct. I think the director was Ralph Steiner. I don't know who the other people were. I've forgotten, I must have known at the time.

LM: *Some of them were pseudonyms.*

EK: Yes, it was a Communist organization.

LM: *I haven't been able to view a short film that he lists called* Cafe Universal.

EK: That's nothing.

LM: *It's like* Pie in the Sky?

EK: No, it's less than that. You know how the French are. They're bugs for thoroughness. It was something done at the 1932 Group Theatre summer camp. It was really like home movies, strictly home movies. They're not my films. They were directed by Ralph Steiner... if you'd call it direction.

LM: *Under radio performances, Ciment lists "The Philip Morris Hour," "Kate Smith," and "The Group Theatre," but in the text somewhere you mentioned that you worked on "The Shadow."*

Interview conducted 20 November 1981. Printed by permission of Lloyd Michaels.

E K : I did, and I also worked on something called "Crime Doctor," but I don't understand why anybody has the least interest in them. "Crime Doctor," in particular, I did quite a lot. As a matter of fact, I was paying my family expenses—we had two kids then—largely by appearing on "Crime Doctor." I played gangsters and that kind of thing, tough guys.

L M : *"It's Up To You," does that exist just as a script? I'm not very clear what that was.*
E K : That was a project by the United States Department of Agriculture to tell the country about rationing. It wasn't entirely successful, but it played downtown on Fourteenth Street. In it, I did a slight . . . six or seven-minute hunk . . . where an actress representing something or other, a housewife, I suppose, talked to herself as she appeared on the screen. It was very cute, but it doesn't deserve any big mention or anything. Anyway, that's what it was . . . a show.

L M : *More recently, I read somewhere that in 1970, you directed a segment of a French film called* Love At Twenty?
E K : No, incorrect.

L M : *Finally, when do you expect your autobiography will be done, or what stage is it at?*
E K : I guess I've got 200 pages of notes now on various periods and aspects—but mostly to remember symbolic bits, anecdotes, strips of dialogue, and so forth. As you get older, those things fade from your memory. I've got an awful lot of material, but I've also got an organization which I'm not entirely happy with. But those things change as you work along.

L M : *Will that be your next written project?*
E K : Yes, it will.

L M : *Now, I have some questions that fall under the category of biography (for* Elia Kazan: A Guide to References and Resources). *You'll remember that I begin organizing your life by describing three important influences on your development: your Greek nationality and consequent outsider status, the Group Theatre, and the HUAC testimony. Would you agree that those were the three most important?*
E K : The HUAC thing had almost no influence on me at all. It made a lot of noise outside among the intellectuals and the left intellectual group, but

it hasn't affected my life, changed my activities, or lost me friends or anything. It's a big lot of stuff...

L M : *That's not what you said in older interviews. You talk about how it deeply*
troubled you personally and how you resented...
E K : I was troubled at the time that I did it, but, since then, it hasn't had
any influence on me. At the time that I did it, it wasn't an easy decision to
come to, but since then it's had no influence at all as far as I know. My
Greekness also had no influence on me for a long time, but now, during
the last twenty years, I'd say it's affected me a lot, and I'm very interested
in it. The Group Theatre did influence me a great deal. But, more impor-
tantly, I'm very close to my family. I'm a very tight family man as I suppose
many Greeks are, and my wives have influenced me a lot. And my mother
influenced me a lot. A lot of things have influenced me. I think your three
points are wrong.

L M : *I don't have a sense in what I've read of your mother's influence. Could*
you touch on that for a minute.
E K : Well, she was supportive, just wanting me to find my own way in the
world, helping me through college. We were quite poor at that time because of the Depression. I was a waiter and dishwasher for six years. She
used to send me my laundry and things like that. They seem trivial, those
little arrivals every week, but something from her always made the difference to me.

L M : *How old were you when she died?*
E K : She died in 1975. Five years ago, I was 67.

L M : *I'm very interested in finding out what you've been doing the last three or*
four years. That's the hardest thing to find out.
E K : I've been writing. I've written two novels, and Barbara was sick.
Barbara had cancer for 2–1/2 years, and during that time, I would stay
around the house, stay close to her. And I wrote two novels. One of which
is now being edited, and the other will have to be re-written quite a lot,
although basically it's all there. I also worked on the autobiography. Whenever I remember something, I put it down.

L M : *Do you still keep to your writing schedule?*

E K : I work every day. I think all professionals do. You're not a professional writer if you don't work every day, I think. Most of them that I have known work every day.

L M : *There are three tidbits of information that I picked up, and I just wanted to ask you what happened to these projects. First, the film you were going to do with Schulberg about Puerto Ricans.*

E K : That one never got backing.

L M : *The sequel to* America, America?

E K : That's now in the form of a novel. It's being edited.

L M : *Directing Burton in* King Lear, *which I read about in the* Times . . .

E K : That blew-up because of a contractual difference between Burton and the producer. I wasn't involved in that difference, so I wasn't a party to it. They just didn't get along contractually. They had a falling out.

L M : *Do you have any plans to make a film again?*

E K : Yes, I do.

L M : *Can you tell me anything about it?*

E K : No. Just that I do have plans. I have several plans. I hope to make more films.

L M : *Do you see any return to the theater?*

E K : Well, I occasionally have ideas about that, too. When you leave something, it doesn't mean that you've lost interest in it. I'm interested in it.

L M : *At the time you left, you seemed very bitter about the theater, and you were quoted as saying that the theater was dead, that movies were where the action is, and so forth.*

E K : I do feel that movies are where the action is, but I never felt that the theater was dead. I felt that the Broadway theater that I was a part of—and that doesn't mean it was good—was over. There weren't as many good plays. I think most talented people, including the talented writers, went into films. Anyway, *my* theatre, so to say, didn't exist in an interesting way anymore.

L M : *Do you still think that's true?*
E K : Well, I think if I were in the theater I would now try to do some different kind of production or different kind of play. I wouldn't do the same thing. I'm not in touch with playwrights anymore except as friends. They're all my friends . . . Miller is my friend, William [Inge] is my friend, Bob Anderson is my friend. They're all my friends. I have a lot of friends, and I hang around the group once in a while. I mean, the group goes back to the studio once and a while, so I see the playwrights.

L M : *What exactly happened at the end of your affiliation with Lincoln Center? Did you resign? Did you resign under pressure?*
E K : I don't want to discuss that because that's a whole chapter in my book. Go to [Robert] Whitehead, he'll tell you. He has a very good memory, and he's very involved in it. As for my own view of that, I don't want to speak about it now.

L M : *Since I went about your biography by trying to think of aspects of your life that were most influential, who do you think were the people in your life who were the most influential? I assume your mother, your father, and you mentioned your wives.*
E K : My wives, the women, my friends. They were all influential. My friend, John Steinbeck, was fairly influential, but the women in my life affected me the most, encouraged me when I needed it.

L M : *Do you think there was any advantage to beginning your career the way you did and at the time that you did in the '30s as opposed to what it's like trying to do the same kind of thing today? You speak of yourself as "a child of the '30s." Do you think that that was ultimately an advantage?*
E K : I neither think of it as an advantage or a disadvantage except that I'm very marked by it. I mean, I was there at the Depression and saw the chaos and so on. It just happened. I was there, and I went through it.

L M : *Some people have commented that your work has grown more pessimistic as you've grown older. They liken you to [John] Ford in that respect. Do you think*

that's true? Your most recent interviews are from the period when you made The
Visitors, *and you were pretty angry.*
E K :   I was angry because we couldn't get adequate money to make the
film.

L M :   *Well, I meant more in a larger political context. Do you think that's
changed?*
E K :   Do I seem like a pessimistic person to you? I don't feel pessimistic
at all, but sometimes there are strains of doubt. No, I'm very, very pro-
American. I think anyone who was born on the other side and comes over
here appreciates the country more than you guys who were born here.
And I'm very pro, so to say, the arts life, the artistic arts. I love the country.
I love my homes. I love my children. They love me. I like my girlfriend. I
liked both of my wives. I don't know what I've got to be pessimistic about.
I've just been an awfully lucky person.

L M :   *But I think you've run into bad luck in the last few years, particularly with
both* The Visitors *and* The Last Tycoon. *Those are films I like very much, but
they really didn't do very well.*
E K :   They did badly, but they're liked in France. They're shown all the
time over there. I'm esteemed in France. You can't be liked everywhere. I
don't want everybody to like me. *The Visitors* was a disturbing film, I
thought. *The Last Tycoon*...well, why *should* everyone like it? You can't
go on trying to please everyone, can you?

L M :   *With* The Visitors, *I think that if it was made a few years later, it might
have succeeded much more than it did. I think it was ahead of its time. And I
think* The Last Tycoon *suffered in part because it came on the heels of* The
Great Gatsby, *and it was perceived almost in the same way.*
E K :   I suppose there's something in that. A lot of people have said that
The Visitors was ahead of its time, especially a lot of the critics in France.
They all feel that. But, you know, that's life. You simply have to occasionally take a licking. I'm in good health, and I live well. I'll tell you the only
person I feel sorry for is my son [Chris Kazan]. My son was quite discouraged about writing for films. But he's now written a really excellent piece,
a TV play. He's back on his feet again, but he was discouraged. He was put
off by it and began to write novels. But I was writing novels all the time.

I'm rather unswerveable, a resilient person. It's very hard to hold me down about anything. I don't think much of the people that didn't like *The Visitors*. It was booed opening night. There were people who booed, and people who applauded. When I stood outside and watched the people come out, I said I don't care if I please these people or not; it's their problem, you know. You get tough after a while, you get strong. I don't know if you want to call it better or tough or not. It didn't have any devastating effect on me. Just like the criticism about HUAC and all that has had no effect on me at all—hasn't for twenty-five years. I don't give a fuck, what do I care... what am I going to do, worry because this person or that person doesn't agree with me? The funny thing is in Paris all the lefties like me, they all agree.

LM: *Why do you think they like you as much as they do?*
EK: They look at me humanly and not schematically. Also, they distinguish between the American Communist party of that time and their own Communist party, which had great differences with Stalinism. The American Communist party was Stalinistic. I consider Lillian Hellman a Stalinist. I don't want to be part of that. I despise her.

LM: *Most of the French who write about you are leftists themselves and usually, in the most recent stuff that I've read, they'll preface discussing you with some political apology and then go on. I mean, there's often that caveat at the beginning.*
EK: They bow to their readers and all that kind of stuff. I don't respect it particularly. I have a right to my opinion, and I've always done what I felt best whether it was popular or not. I've always been sort of controversial. I mean, in my personal life too. Even where I've lived. I could have settled into Hollywood in 1946 and had a home in Bel Air like a lot of those fellows, but I didn't.

LM: *I think of you as the first of the New York filmmakers, people who consciously moved away from Hollywood, and I have a couple of questions about that. First of all, what do you feel is the difference in your work as a result of that decision?*
EK: Just now, I walked from Forty-Fifth Street and Fifth Avenue. I couldn't get a cab to this place at Sixty-Eighth Street, and on the way up I saw four

our five images, people, things that were stimulating to me. In California, you get in your car out of your sheltered home and you drive to work, which is another rarified atmosphere, and don't see anything. There's nothing actually stimulating. That's number one. Number two is the people here are in trouble. They're lively. They're surrounded with people fighting, criminals, psychotics, anxious people, ambitious people, artists coming up. The whole atmosphere is charged with energy and work. I don't see how anyone lives anywhere else in the world but New York City. I mean, it's such a marvelous environment, so stimulating, so much fun. I won't go on with that because that's going to be in my book too.

L M : *So you agree with the perspective of Woody Allen's two New York films.*
E K : Yes, even more than that, I think. They're nice. I like his films. I think they're on the cute side, but they're all right. There's no pain in them exactly. And this city is full of pain, and the people are in trouble— it's scary.

L M : *There was a man on the corner of your block eating ice cream out a garbage can.*
E K : There was a robbery next door two days ago. I had to put bars in these windows. People are getting desperate, you know, but I'd rather be in the middle of it than not. And I'm not pessimistic. I've been through it. I've been through Reagan. A good man will come along.

L M : *You don't talk very much about your contemporaries among American directors in Hollywood with the exception of John Ford.*
E K : Ford was not my contemporary. He was already a master when I got out there. I did go to his house and talk to him quite a bit. I got some good lessons from him, and I admire him too. But my contemporaries are more like—you probably won't believe this—[Sidney] Lumet and Arthur Penn. Talk to Penn if you want to find out. I think I've influenced some of these people. And talk to Scorsese. I think he'll tell you. I think I'm one of them in spirit—rather than with, say [Billy] Wilder.

L M : *I'd like to do my next book on the New York filmmakers.*
E K : They're the best. By far the best . . . way out ahead of anybody in California. I think they're very good, very lively. If not New York, then

Coppola, who lives in Northern California. I had to take my girlfriend's son to a science fiction film the other day. It was a terrible piece of garbage called *The Time Bandits*, really gruesome, awful, bad for the kid, bad for people. It really should be banned. Not for any sex reason or violence, it was just the attitude was so shitty. The people who make those films are interested in stunts. The picture if full of stunts, like in Spielberg's picture . . . a rock rolling after a fellow. That's strictly out of comic strips, and it's entertaining for children. They're professional films that are made by children for children, and none of them are related to theme or intention or, excuse the expression, message or anything.

LM: *I was going to ask you whether you're comfortable with having your own style called "social realist." Would you describe yourself as a social realist?*
EK: That's the kind of inquiry and interest that critics have, I don't care. You can call me anything you want, and you will, of course.

LM: *I ask because the parts of your films that I like the most are the lyrical parts. Like in* Wild River, *for example.*
EK: That's one of my favorite films, but it's absolutely ignored. I heard a few months ago that Fox burned the negative of it.

LM: *I taught a course in film adaptation last term, and I used* The Last Tycoon, *which none of my students had seen. I was afraid that they wouldn't like it, that it would seem too slow, but it turned out that they liked it very, very much. They read the novel, and they thought it was an excellent film.*
EK: It has its faults . . . it has one bad fault, not in the direction, but I don't want to go into that. I think it's well acted and rather well directed, but not brilliant. But in the writing there's one problem, which is the way Harold writes. He wrote some wonderful scenes, but it has that fault—but I think it has merit too. You know, after a while, you just go your own way. I mean, I am not hard up, I'm not rich but I'm comfortably well off. I'm full of activities. It doesn't bother me more than a day if some one pans something. What am I going to do? I can't do anything about it anyway.

LM: *Doesn't it hurt your possibilities of making more movies?*
EK: Very much so. You asked me what happened with the Puerto Rican picture. Well, I've had some flops, so it's, "Oh, we don't need another flop."

L M : *That bothers me if it doesn't bother you.*

E K : It does bother me, but you can't do anything about it. You're in that kind of market. All you can do is fight, and do, and do some more. I wrote five scripts with Schulberg, and I still haven't given up on that film — maybe it'll come out yet.

L M : *I wanted to ask you a little bit about your reading and also about your novel writing. First of all, do you read much? Do you read much literature in between your own work?*

E K : I'm reading *Rabbit Is Rich* right now. Updike is a marvelous writer, an excellent writer, and craftsman, and terribly observant. My god, he's seen and knows a little bit about everything. He's really bright, and peppy, I enjoy it. Yes, I read quite a lot. I always read a little every day in the late afternoon or when I go to bed. But it's hard to read novels when you're writing a novel.

L M : *Of all the American writers, your work reminds me the most of Dreiser.*

E K : That's true, I agree. I've often thought that too. I admire Dreiser. I think he's a strong man. He wasn't sentimental, wasn't mushy. I like him very much. My last book was a Dreiserian book, I think.

L M : Acts Of Love. *One of the things that I admire about your career as a novelist is the sense in which you've gone about learning your craft — and just working at it.*

E K : I started very late. I started at 55. That's pretty late. You're ready to die then, but it's had a tremendous effect on my life because it's made me feel young, and interested, a student again — a writing student, always learning something. I feel that I am learning my craft all over again.

L M : *I wanted to ask you about the isolation of writing, whether you've adapted to that as opposed to the collaborative side of the other kinds of work you've always done.*

E K : I'm 72. I prefer to be alone. Even back then, when I wasn't actually on the set, I tried to get a part of every day alone because a lot of people were always "at" you and so on, and it can eat up your life. So I like to be alone. I don't mind it at all. Now, every day until about 2:00 . . . after Irene comes in the morning, I stay upstairs. That's my secretary. I stay upstairs in my room and work, write, or whatever I do until I get tired.

L M :   *When do you go to Connecticut?*

E K :   I go all the time. Tomorrow I'm going out to see Schulberg about something we might do together. Then on Sunday, I'll go to Connecticut and stay there. My papers are at Wesleyan University, and I haven't opened them yet. Everything is up there. It's an extraordinary collection. Later in your life, when I've opened it up, come and see it. It's really extraordinary.

L M :   *I already tried!*

E K :   There's no way anybody will get to see it yet. They treat me very well. I've got a whole room to myself, and Bill Manchester is down the hall. It's really wonderful. But I don't mind being alone, to answer your question. I like it.

L M :   *You don't have any desire to be back in the public eye?*

E K :   I used to have my name in the paper for one reason or another every day, and I used to long to never see it again, never to see my picture in the paper, never see my name in the paper, all that kind of false media fame and pumped up horseshit, praise and all that. Not that you believe it, anyway. It's a crummy thing, and I have no need for it. I don't miss it at all.

L M :   *You talked about a weakness in* The Last Tycoon. *I'm dying to know what it is, but I'll try to resist.*

E K :   It's the love story, but I don't want to go into detail because I'd have to quote the dialogue that happened between me and Harold [Pinter], whom I like a lot. He's a marvelous man.

L M :   *I don't like the actress.*

E K :   It's just the love story, but I don't want to go into that.

L M :   *I'm still stuck for an ending in the biographical essay.*

E K :   Just say how good-looking I am, and how well-dressed I am.

L M :   *I'll remember that, and how friendly you've been. I was worried about that.*

E K :   Why wouldn't I be friendly to you? I wouldn't have met you if I didn't like what you'd written [an essay on *The Last Tycoon*]. It was a lot of work and good thought, or I wouldn't have met with you.

L M : *You've mentioned some of the directors that you most admired in contem-*
porary American cinema. How about the new German and Australian films?
E K : I see them all. They're very good. The Australian filmmakers are
going to be terrific, and they're already very good. The German films, I
guess, are interesting. I don't like their spirit, but they're interesting.
There's one great film, *The Marriage of Maria Braun*. It's terrific. And I happen to know a lot of the Italian filmmakers personally, so I'm fond of
them, and I also like their movies. I think there's a Greek filmmaker that's
wonderful, [Theo] Angelopoulos. And Satyajit Ray is a good friend of mine.

L M : *I've taught several of his films.*
E K : He's a nice man. I think there's a sort of club of filmmakers around
the world who understand each other, and they're sort of spiritual and
deep. They're decent and deep. They're not snobbish. They're fine people.

L M : *Most of the ones you've mentioned are what I would call humanist directors.*
E K : They are.

L M : *I admire Hertzog a lot, but, I guess, you don't.*
E K : I do admire him, but his spirit puts me off. I just don't agree with
that. I think he's shouting out how tough he is or some fucking thing like
that. A filmmaker I do admire a lot, who's very strong and good, is [Fran-
cesco] Rosi. He's also a very good friend of mine. He's a wonderful filmmaker,
and he has a new film coming out called *Three Sons . . .* or *Three Brothers*. Go
see it, it's really a first-class film, and he's made lots of good films. He made
very political films for a long time. He's a leftist, a strong leftist, and I consider myself a leftist. I think our system is bad. Until everyone can speak in
the world, and everyone has a home, and we obtain peace, then I think, in
one way or another, that we're still plundering too much of the wealth of
the world. He's that way too. He's anti-Communist, but he's extremely left
in his feeling and thinking. See this film and you'll see he's a humanist.

L M : *I'd like to get back to the way the Europeans appreciate your work — revere*
your work, still discuss it, and so forth and the way, in which, I think it's fair to
say, you're a neglected director among Americans. Do you have any sense of why
that is?

E K : I think a lot of it has to do with the intellectuals turning against me because of my testimony. They're also afraid of each other's opinions. There isn't anyone bold enough to say, "Well, I like him despite that." But they're all, when you get them alone, not only respectful but far more than that. It's just the way they behave as a group. They'll get over that. They're bound to because I'm a guy you've got to like. You have to. And finally, because I'm honorable. If they did what they think was right, I did what I think was right. I didn't do it for money. I've never done anything for money. And there were a lot of lies about me at that time that I'll refute in the autobiography, but it doesn't bother me. I don't like the social scene. I don't like to sit in a bar and talk about art with these people. It's not my concern. Or talk about films. I never go to a nightclub. I've never been to a disco in my life. I don't go anywhere. I'm perfectly happy to live where I live. I love my place in the country. I don't know what the hell more I could want. So I don't give a fuck what they say. When they need me, the same people that are critical of me embrace me. Well, maybe they're right. Maybe I'm not as good as the French say. The French think I'm one of the really, really good ones, and so do the Italians. Okay. But maybe the Americans have a point.

L M : *I also think that it hurt you to be so successful so early in America. You reached a peak so early.*
E K : Steinbeck used to say that. Steinbeck's last books were not as good as his earlier books, but I think my films got better. And I think there's another odd thing, I think I only made really good films *after* my testimony. So all the predictions about my having corrupted myself and that I would never be able to be an artist again turned out to be wrong.

L M : *At the risk of angering you at the end of this friendly conversation, I didn't like* The Arrangement *at all as a film. I enjoyed reading the book, but I felt that there was something self-destructive going on in the film. The book was such a success for you, maybe an unexpected success, and a financial success, but, in a strange way, I felt uncomfortable in that film for you, even aside from my critical problems with the film.*
E K : I don't think the film was totally successful, but I think it has some brilliant little pieces. I think the funeral in the midst of the thruway and the scene in the hospital between the father and the son are wonderful

scenes—and the mother sitting there through all that, outside. I think they're marvelous scenes, but I do think I made mistakes in the film, and I don't disagree with you necessarily. But it doesn't matter to me. You have a right to your opinions. It doesn't make me angry because I don't require of my friends that they like everything I do. I'd be dead by now if I did. Right?

Elia Kazan: Method and Madness

BRIAN CASE/1988

"I GOTTA URINATE." ELIA Kazan told the chambermaid who was making the bed. "I'm coming past." She appeared prettily confused. The 78-year-old director doesn't mince words. Short, upright, bow-legged and flat-bellied—"I'm still fucking"—he brings the chair up close until your knees touch. His vivid, cunning cobra face is disconcertingly alert, and the eyes crouch and leap, stirring memories of the Svengali years with Brando, Dean, Clift and De Niro. We could be rehearsing the taxi cab scene. "It's very hard to get me to talk about anything," he says. "I'm here for the book so you've got a good start." His autobiography, *A Life,* took him three and a half years to write, and it is the most troublingly candid book since Art Pepper's *Straight Life*. He is beyond caring about popularity. His enemies keep him young.

Born of Greek parents in Turkey, Kazan adapted to the New World by dissembling. That Anatolian smile hid treachery, fear and hostility and was mistaken by privileged WASP America for concordance and compliant use-fulness, earning him the nickname "Gadge" or "Gadget." He joined the Stanislavskian Group Theatre in 1932, which was founded by Lee Strasberg and Harold Clurman as "an ideologically cemented collective" and acted in plays like Clifford Odets's *Waiting For Lefty*. He once scored the Press epi-thet, "The Proletariat Thunderbolt." These were years of idealism for many Americans who turned to communism in reaction against the Depression and America's neutrality in the Spanish Civil War. A flavour of that milieu

From *Time Out,* 4 May 1988.

comes through in the subsequently blacklisted writer Albert Maltz's letter from Hollywood. "The medium is wonderful we all agree. But I don't think it will be properly used in America until it is state-owned and its function is not profit making. Another reason for waving the red flag." As a rising theatre director, Kazan premiered Tennessee Williams's *A Streetcar Named Desire* and Arthur Miller's *All My Sons* and *Death of a Salesman*, resigning from the Communist Party when he was criticised for elitism. Hollywood beckoned.

Instinct Enthroned

Kazan is identified in the public mind with the rise of the Method on the screen which surfaced with a wallop in the early '50s. *Viva Zapata!, A Streetcar Named Desire, On the Waterfront* and *East of Eden* hit a chord that rocked the spinnet. The physicality of the new young actors was as legible as a headline, the body vivid, the instinct enthroned, and the diction lousy. "How can I lose?" Dean told the press. "In one hand I got Marlon Brando yelling fuck you all, in the other Monty Clift asking please help me."

"There's a case if ever there was one of arrested development," said Kazan. "Self-pitying, sulky and over-respectful to me, whatever he thought in private. The fucking kid became a legend overnight, but all I could think was he'd never grown up. I don't like what he represented. I'm a parent. I have five children. I don't like that shit about parents are always wrong and children are always right. That's crap to me. They're equally right and equally wrong. He went on and on about it, and so did Nick Ray, whom I liked a lot. I wouldn't go for it. Would you be one of the vice presidents of the National Jimmy Dean Club? No. That's all I said. No. I liked some of the rock 'n' roll era kids more. I liked Jim Morrison. He was deeper than these adolescents. His song about his father, "The End," is very much like the story I tell about my father in the book."

In the book, he traces Dean from first audition through the move to Hollywood, carrying his belongings in two paper parcels, to the difficulties on the set as the ego grew. The director took an adjoining trailer, listened to him boffing and arguing with Pier Angeli, and rejoiced when she dumped him for Eddie Fisher. "Now I had Jimmy as I wanted him, alone and miserable." He got him drunk to play the difficult scene on the roof with Julie Harris. It wasn't all Method.

"Yeah. The Jack Daniels School of Acting! I had to get Andy Griffith drunk too for *A Face in the Crowd*. Neither of them were trained actors. They didn't know what the hell to do. It worked all right. I did whatever was necessary to get a good performance *including* so-called Method acting. I made them run around the set, I scolded them, I inspired jealousy in their girlfriends. You know the boxer Tami Mauriello? I hit him in the face to get a reaction on *Waterfront*! The director *is a desperate beast*! Believe me, that is why Strasberg failed as a director. He's a teacher. That's a worthwhile occupation. I guess. But to be a director is something special. You have to get what you want while that day's shooting goes on!"

Over the years his appetite for the unbending Strasberg's teachings has diminished. He avoided reviewing the recent memoirs. He writes of Actors' Studio disciples moving in a miasma of self-devotion, sleepwalking about the stage, sniffing for sense memories. It is a tradition, he feels, that has left American theatre ill-equipped to deal with classical drama, and, by contrast, recalls Olivier preparing his blazing performance in Wyler's *Carrie* by perfecting bits of business. Great performances share immediacy to an immoderate degree—Garbo in *Camille,* Walter Huston in *The Treasure of the Sierra Madre,* Takashi Shimura in *Living*—and transcend systems. Brando, however, of the mumblers, he loved.

Brando and Welles

"I used to see Brando eating, just *eating* all the time, obsessively. And Welles. I used to watch him pig. They both drank. You felt, please, cut it out!

"There was a profound sense of disappointment and discouragement and self-betrayal in both people, and they didn't know where the hell they got their pleasures. Maybe they stopped fucking, or their children didn't like them or something essential in their lives changed. Now Welles is idolised, and correctly, he made a coupla awfully good films, but I'm not sure he thought so himself. Maybe he wanted more out of life than he got. Brando said a real man would have a more worthwhile profession than making faces and so forth. This is what he *told* people—what he *thought* I don't know. He enjoyed it when he was going good, I know that. When he was in a film or a play, after the first hesitation, when he realised what the part was and was given the great respect all other actors gave him at all times, then I think he felt very happy working. I don't know what the hell happened. A guy goes into his house, the door closes, you don't know what happens in there, what's eating him, you don't know anything. I was never an intimate of his although you could say we were best friends. I see him in other people's pictures, and I think he could've been better if I'd directed him. Yeah, I do. I didn't think Bertolucci controlled him enough in *Last Tango in Paris*. Brando needed very straight treatment and a good, firm, friendly hand on him. He didn't need a helluva lot."

Sam Spiegel had resisted Kazan's choice of De Niro for *The Last Tycoon*, disliking the actor's "petty larceny smile." "Maybe it's true. Bobby is a New York street kid, and it was a tough job making him look like an intellectual Jew. Well, those intellectual Jews in California weren't so high class either. They weren't really scholars." He sat back and thought for a while. "Bobby got thin very well," he said.

The director was tiring fast on the subject of actors. Brando apart, he always preferred working with actresses. Except for the nympho junkie Tallulah Bankhead. She gave him hell on the stage production of Thornton Wilder's *Skin of Our Teeth,* and he reserves his special venom for her in the memoirs. When producer Walter Wanger died, Tallulah's comment was: "He had a good cock but he didn't know how to use it." "I imagine," writes Kazan, "she thought that suitable for his tombstone."

"I got fucking tired of her. She divided the company at a critical time, and I had problems more important than the goddamn ego of Miss Bankhead. She particularly liked telling stories about little darkie girls, the children of slaves on her daddy's plantation. Cute stories. I got tired of that too."

Patronising stories?

"You got it right now. Deeply. Profoundly. With affection but patronising. She regarded them as comic figures. She was the daughter of the senator from Alabama. And she was always coming on so you'd have to figure what condition is she in today?"

And busty starlet Terri Moore's alligator love-calls on the phone to Howard Hughes?

Kazan rocked with laughter. "Struck you, did it?" He threw back his head and let rip with a high plangent barking. "Howard Hughes came back with the same goddamn thing. He was brilliant but childish."

Hollywood Babylon

A Life covers Hollywood Babylon, the town where "everybody is a genius until they do something." It puts you in the private screening rooms with the moguls, passing the starlets around. Kazan's own compulsive adultery

he attributes to a testicle shrivelled by measles, the urge to get back at
WASPS by laying their wives, and a need for chaos in his life. He fucked a
lot, and numbers Marilyn Monroe among his scores before turning into
her confidant. "That was her word, 'prepared.' She'd sit in a chair, and
when she got up there'd be a little mark on the back of her dress. 'It was
embarrassing,' she said, so she went to a doctor, and he said, 'You have too
much of that particular thing,' so he gave her a shot, 'and now I'm not
ready all the time.'" Washed-up ex-child star Natalie Wood fell to Warren
Beatty on *Splendour in the Grass* to the anguish of husband Robert Wagner.
Tony Curtis, habitually playing away, came up to Kazan on *The Last
Tycoon*—and can't you just see that Sidney Falco grin?—and said, "Any
man who would fuck his wife is an animal." The comments on Hollywood
are wicked. Mervyn LeRoy, on optioning a novel: "It's got everything.
Surprise, great characters, an important theme, fine writing! But I think I
can lick it." John Ford: "Don't look at the fucking script. That will confuse
you." And a peep behind the scenes at Kirk Douglas, bawling out an inex-
perienced youngster until a veteran cameraman intercedes. " 'Kirk—I
remember you when you came up. You were a nice kid. Now you've become a complete prick.' 'You're wrong,' Kirk said. 'I was always a prick.
Now I've got money I can afford to let it show.'" Typically, Kazan adds a
rider. "Give him A for telling the truth."

In person, the veteran is a disconcerting mixture of stone wall and sudden approbation. "I hope you'll take this exactly the way I'm saying it now,"
he replied in answer to a question about him, Nick Ray and CinemaScope.
"I never talked to anybody about anything to do with film technique. I'm
not a guy who thinks about it. I did the best I could. It doesn't interest me.
Martin Scorsese talks about that all the time, and he's very technically
adept. What interests me is *what* is being said and less how to say it. The
point for me, just personal, is what is the director trying to tell me? What
I feel today is there's a big lack in films and that's thematic. No theme. You
go through a whole damn picture and at the end you say what the fuck
am I supposed to take home from this? But the technique's great, all that
kinda stuff. But I *set out* to write a film about the TVA for *Wild River* and I
set out to write a film about the problems of the waterfront. Well, maybe
there's been enough of that…" He gathered his thoughts. "Listen. Renoir
and Ford did something that I think was more artistic. Somehow films
have to deal with a realism that is so particularly chosen and carefully
manipulated that it gives a sense of poetry. It's like when you're in love for

the first time and all the events and appurtenances are absolutely real, but the elation is so strong that the event is a poetic event."

Wild River, I suggested, had sabotaged itself by using documentary footage of a man who had just lost his family in the flood at the start. How could actors beat that? "I'm going to say something to shock you," he replied. "You're right! Nothing seemed quite as real after that, but I didn't know what else to do because I couldn't get any footage of the flood."

Hate Mail

"Kazan? Wasn't he the one who...?" someone had said as he walked through the lobby, sweater tied over his shoulders. He must've heard a lot of that in the 35 years since he turned friendly witness to HUAC and named names. Hate mail, anonymous phone calls, friends cutting him dead. He is still in the sin-bin as far as the left is concerned. The first reaction to Senator McCarthy's Hollywood hearings in 1947 was shock. Sam Goldwyn laid a Goldwynism. "If Roosevelt was alive today he'd turn in his grave." Harry Cohn, misunderstanding the nature of the witchhunt, tried to trade a gay. Summoned before the House Un-American Activities Committee for performing at a benefit for a communist magazine, Zero Mostel testified that all he had done "was an imitation of a butterfly at rest." Nobody laughed. It was a tough room to play. He was blacklisted for 14 years, his life ruined. The jailing of the Unfriendly Ten straightened everybody up. Most studio heads were of Eastern European Jewish origin and remembered the pogroms and the cossacks. "At least here in the New World it was possible to offer the Cossacks a bowl of chicken soup," wrote Lillian Hellman in *Scoundrel Time.* "And the Cossacks in Washington were now riding so fast and hard that the soup had to have double strength and be served up by running millionaires." In a stormy meeting, Cecil B DeMille tried to force the Screen Directors Guild to take the loyalty oath over Joseph Mankiewicz's resistance. Kazan kept away. "Joe Mankiewicz had called me a jungle fighter," he writes in the autobiog. "Jungle fighter my dimpled Greek ass! My way of survival had been to avoid a conflict and come back when the smoke had cleared." Kazan, with his high visibility as a director of social conscience movies and plays, was high on the hit list. Subpoenaed to testify, he went further than recantation. He named names. Why would anyone resort to the Fifth Amendment unless they were communists? The government was right to investigate the Communist Party. It was an organised worldwide conspiracy. Why sacrifice a great movie career for a political cause he no longer believed in? Kazan's Fifth came after. He refused to discuss his motives. Not until *A Life* did he publicly examine his conscience, and the chapter is painfully ambivalent. "The 'horrible immoral thing' I would do, I did out of my true self. It was correct, but was it right?" Mailer views the entire autobiography as the work of "a man who is trying to find a coherent philosophy that will be tough enough to contain all that is ugly in his person and experience."

"Sure. I avoided talking about the McCarthy era for many years because I wanted to put it in the context of my whole life. When you see it like that, it has a different meaning. It's as if some people who interview me over here are afraid to impinge on something I'm embarrassed about. I'm not. It doesn't bother me two cents. I never told a lie. As far as you English were concerned, you had four or five faggots and communists at college who betrayed your whole country so why be superior to us?"

He toughed it out, joining with Budd Schulberg, who had also named names, to make *On The Waterfront* in which the longshoreman hero defies his corrupt union and informs to the commission. "I was ratting on myself all these years, and I didn't know it," cries Brando's Terry Malloy. "I'm glad what I done." Arthur Miller, who had been working with Kazan on a waterfront story before HUAC, broke with him and wrote his own anatomy of conscience and betrayal in *A View from the Bridge*. Kazan's movie won seven Oscars, and his face as he collected the trophies bore the livid grin of vengeance.

"I got value out of it. I'm tougher than most people, I think. I was an outsider kid, and I had to be tough to survive. Jimmy Baldwin said I was a nigger so I accept that as a compliment." He laughed abruptly. "*You* bastards liked my films least of all. It's a howl. Lindsay Anderson said that *On the Waterfront* was fascist in its ending." He tried to gather saliva in his mouth, his cheeks working convulsively, the Levantine eyes glittering in ancient fury. "Spugh! Spugh! I can't even spit or piss about him!" The ritual was disturbing, the cursing comprehensive. Anderson's 1955 article in *Sight and Sound,* besides forking over Kazan's testimony, had also found the movie hysterical, full of "horrid vulgarity" and lacking in decorum.

"I don't think people will be calling you 'Gadget' any more after this," I remarked, tapping the autobiography.

He exploded with laughter. "Wouldn't that be a blessing! Fuck 'em! I told my truth. I am contented. Put that in your article."

I'm Not Afraid of Anything

ALVIN P. SANOFF/1988

'I'm not afraid of anything'

Like all guys in the art field, I've been continuously interested in myself. I kept notes on everything. At age 78, I thought I'd better lay everything out before I went down.

There's no use doing an autobiography if you leave stuff out. I read John Huston's autobiography—a guy I liked—and there was very little of him in it. Why do all that work and not say anything? So I said what I thought of everything and everybody. I'm glad I did. I feel unburdened. I'm relieved at not having secret thoughts I'm trying to keep from others, my wife included. I let her know everything, including how bad I was when it came to women. I don't know any other biography that is as candid as mine, not any in the world.

It was a hard journey getting to this point. For a lot of my youth, I didn't like myself. I had never felt comfortable with my fame. I thought, "I'm not as good as other film makers; I'm certainly not as good as other writers." But now I think that I don't have to compare myself with anybody. I'm not afraid of anything and don't feel hostile to a soul in the world, which is new for me. I am what I am.

If I had my life to live over, I wouldn't do anything differently. I did exactly what I wanted. It doesn't bother me that I testified before the

From *U.S. News and World Report,* 6 June 1988. © 6 June 1988 by U.S. News & World Report. Reprinted by permission.

House Un-American Activities Committee in the '50s and provided them with names. New York intellectuals who had not been in the Communist Party, who only had been to a meeting or two, had no goddamn business making judgments of the actions of people who had been in the party, as I had. How can you say anything unless you've been there? The people who owe an explanation are those who, year after year, held the Soviets blameless for all their crimes.

I never talked about my testimony with Arthur Miller, who took a different posture before the committee. I directed a play of his, but even then we never talked about it. In the book, I flattered the hell out of Miller. I said he's a brave, courageous man. I have nothing against him, but I don't like him as I once did. He used to be like a brother. I have a lot of friends now who are close to me, but he's not one of them. He's vain and pompous sometimes. It's not a severe fault. All teachers are that way—and he's a teacher. He's always trying to straighten people out and tell them what they should think.

The Gallant Profession

I started out as an actor, and I think actors are the most gallant people in the world. If a play gets terrible notices, the actor has to play it again, knowing the audience thinks the play is stupid and his role horrendous. If he makes a movie and performs terribly, it's still going to show all over the country and maybe all over the world.

Of those I have worked with, the actor I like best is Marlon Brando. He's full of both anger and love—and the two fight. He is filled with very conflicting, ambivalent emotions. Many very good actors don't like acting. Brando is one, and I think John Wayne was another. There are many actresses who are also terrific, including Geraldine Page, Lee Remick, Julie Harris, Kim Hunter and Jessica Tandy. Women, in fact, are better actors than men. Women are always in a sense—I don't mean in a bad sense—acting. A woman who is going out asks herself, "Who am I going out with? And how do I dress to go out with that person?" Life is full of drama for them. Men aren't like that. They go out wearing the same damn suit and have a drink or two while they worry about business. That's a terrible generalization, but something like that happens. Acting fulfills women in some way that it doesn't a man.

A "godlike" Role

I always wanted to be a director, even when I was in Yale drama school. A director's role is really godlike. You make people behave a certain way and then confront them with the consequences. "You feel this; therefore, you do that," "You're hiding this feeling, but you shouldn't," "You love her, but she won't have you." You're arranging lives. And when you get through with one project, you go on to the next. That saves you because you're always finding something new to do.

I have a reputation as a very strong director, but I hardly raise my voice. There's nothing to raise your voice about. We're partners in an enterprise. You just talk to the actors and hope for agreement. I never bullied people the way a lot of old-time film directors did. John Ford and Howard Hawks had a slightly bullying way. Ford would ask an actor what he or she thought about a scene and then do the opposite. He once slugged somebody, but nobody had the nerve to slug him back. They could have killed him. He was just a rickety old Irishman.

When the old-time director came on the set, he represented a force that nobody dared contradict. That wouldn't work as well today. In part, thanks to the Actors Studio, actors have an idea of what they want to do and are able to defend themselves. Also, actors have become successful. Nobody tells Stallone what to do. You can't when a man gets $11 million for making one film.

In the end, the best art, even in a form that's collaborative, requires one guy with an insistent vision. It may be the director, or it can be the writer or producer. But if a work doesn't follow one person's vision, it'll be wishy-washy mush. There'll be a softness in its core. Some guy has got to stand up and say, "This is the way this is going to be," and make it like that.

INDEX